THE ZONE CONTINUUM™

LEGACY

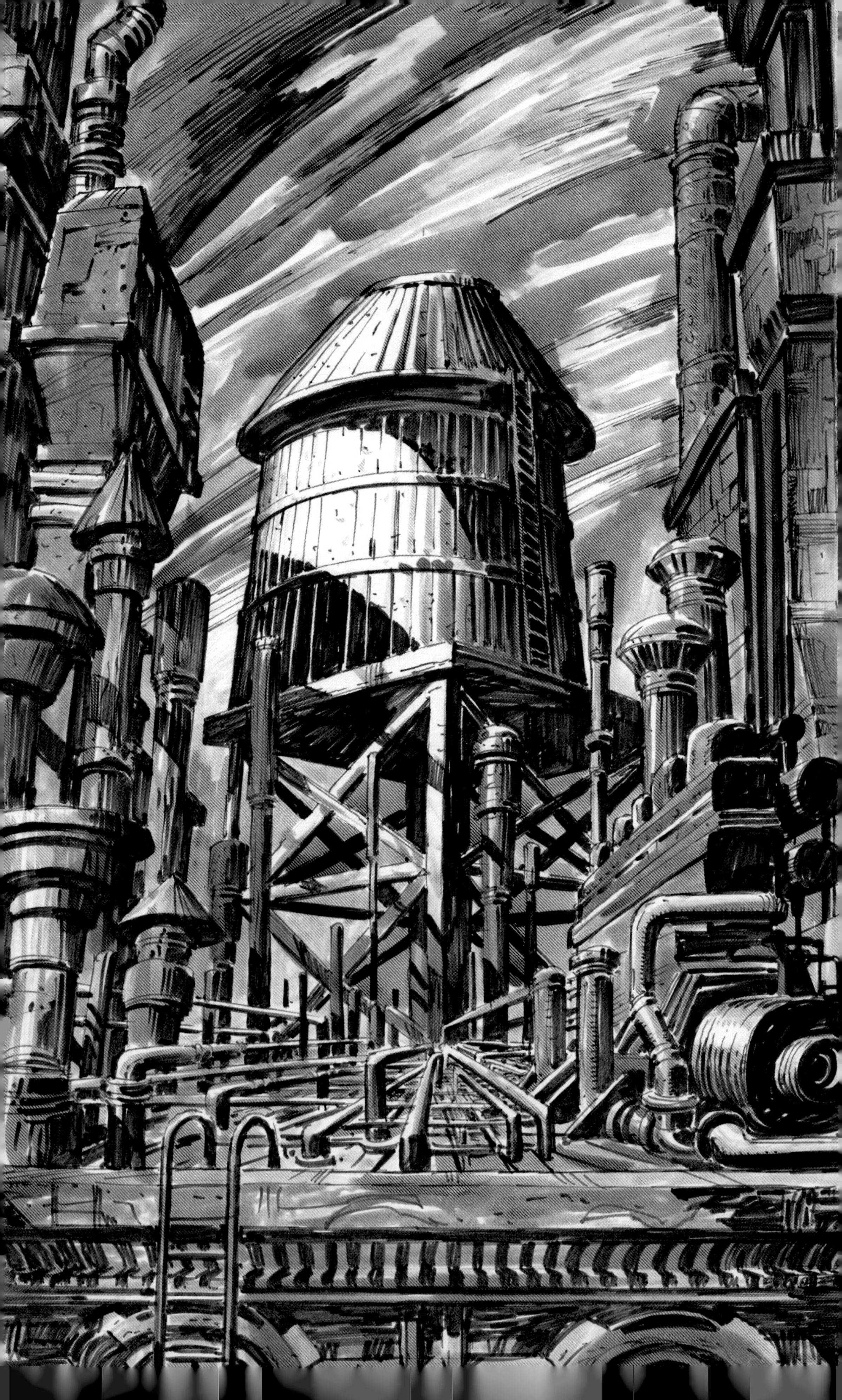

THE ZONE CONTINUUM™ LEGACY

SCRIPT AND ART

BRUCE ZICK

WRITING AND TECHNICAL ASSISTS
LARRY PRATT

LETTERING
**GALEN SHOWMAN
KEN HOLEWCZYNSKI
BRENT CARPENTER**

DARK HORSE BOOKS

president & publisher
MIKE RICHARDSON

collection designer
SARAH TERRY

editor
RANDY STRADLEY

digital art technician
CONLEY SMITH

assistant editors
KEVIN BURKHALTER and
FREDDYE MILLER

Neil Hankerson Executive Vice President • Tom Weddle Chief Financial Officer • Randy Stradley Vice President of Publishing • Michael Martens Vice President of Book Trade Sales • Matt Parkinson Vice President of Marketing • David Scroggy Vice President of Product Development • Dale LaFountain Vice President of Information Technology • Cara Niece Vice President of Production and Scheduling • Nick McWhorter Vice President of Media Licensing • Ken Lizzi General Counsel • Dave Marshall Editor in Chief • Davey Estrada Editorial Director • Scott Allie Executive Senior Editor • Chris Warner Senior Books Editor • Cary Grazzini Director of Specialty Projects • Lia Ribacchi Art Director • Vanessa Todd Director of Print Purchasing • Matt Dryer Director of Digital Art and Prepress • Mark Bernardi Director of Digital Publishing • Sarah Robertson Director of Product Sales • Michael Gombos Director of International Publishing and Licensing

THE ZONE CONTINUUM: LEGACY

This volume collects *The Zone Continuum* Vol. 1, #1–#2, and Vol. 2, #1–#2, originally published by Caliber Press.

Published by Dark Horse Books
A division of Dark Horse Comics, Inc.
10956 SE Main Street, Milwaukie, OR 97222

DarkHorse.com

To find a comics shop in your area, call the Comic Shop Locator Service toll-free at 1-888-266-4226.
International Licensing: (503) 905-2377

First edition: November 2016   ISBN 978-1-50670-076-2

10 9 8 7 6 5 4 3 2 1
Printed in China

INTRODUCTION: THEN AND NOW

There are two Zone Continuums. The first was Then, in 1992; the second is Now, in 2016.

In March of 2016, Dark Horse published the *Zone Continuum* graphic novel of all-new stories in color: *The Zone Continuum* of Now.

The graphic novel you hold in your hand is *The Zone Continuum* of Then, 1992. This is the original four-book series in glorious black and white like you've never seen it before, until Now. Then, the paper was simple newsprint with grayish blacks and off whites; Now, it's beautiful glossy paper with deep, rich blacks and bright whites. Now, twenty-four years later, we can finally see those stories of Then the way I always wanted them to be seen. I just had to wait. And thanks to the good folks at Dark Horse Comics, the wait is over.

Back Then, I wanted *The Zone Continuum* to deal with issues of social isolation and global pollution. In 1992 the state of the environment was worrisome, but still far away from the point of no return. Now, in 2016, the issues of global change have gotten so much worse—with some saying it's hopeless. And while technology and social media have created wonderful new opportunities, they have also created more social isolation. I'd like to think the messages of this story have become more urgent—that this truly is the time to tell the story of *The Zone Continuum*.

I love *The Zone Continuum* of Now. It's slick, in color, more streamlined; it has a larger cast of characters, a simpler story line, and a greater focus on the love story. But I really dig *The Zone Continuum* of Then. It's more raw, more indulgent, more intricate, more obsessive to fidelity. And it's in glorious black and white.

In 1992, I was trying to figure out a story line that dealt with water towers, rooftops, and people in flying raincoats. I was reading a lot of cyberpunk by William Gibson and getting my mind severely blown away by Frank Miller's groundbreaking *Sin City* series. In some strange way, this all melded into a story about a global continuum of Zones, the consequences of manmade pollution, an ancient race deciding if humanity should live or die, and a tragic romantic drama.

It had to be called *The Zone Continuum*.

Caliber Press was willing to print the series, and so four comics trickled out over a few years, until I had to get back to reality and focus on my real daytime job. So the project went into mothballs.

But I couldn't forget about it. The fan response was really terrific, and the series later was called "a cult classic." Once you get that label, you start to feel like you did something good. You also feel like you just can't give up on it, no matter how long it takes.

Looking back at it now, I can't believe how much work I put into it. And how much coffee I poured into my body. The level of detail amazes me, as I have now developed a more streamlined and graphic style of illustration. I love my newest work, but, man, I really dig the crazy attempt to create a very real, intricate world from the bottom up.

Don't ask me which version I like better. They really are two different *Zone Continuums*. Maybe instead, you can tell me which one you like better. And it's okay if you like Then as much as you like Now.

Bruce Zick
Zone 27, Now

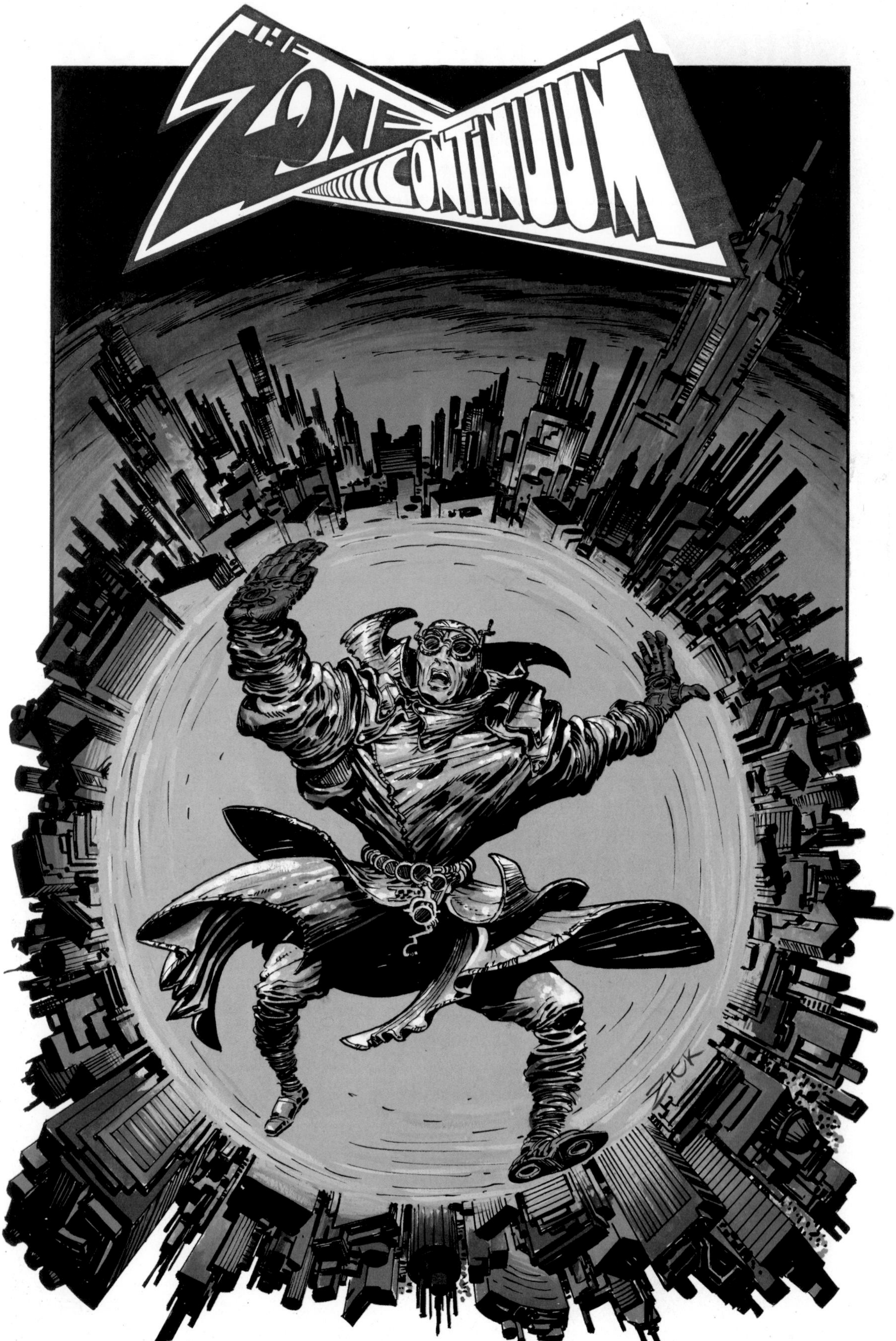
THE ZONE CONTINUUM
ZICK

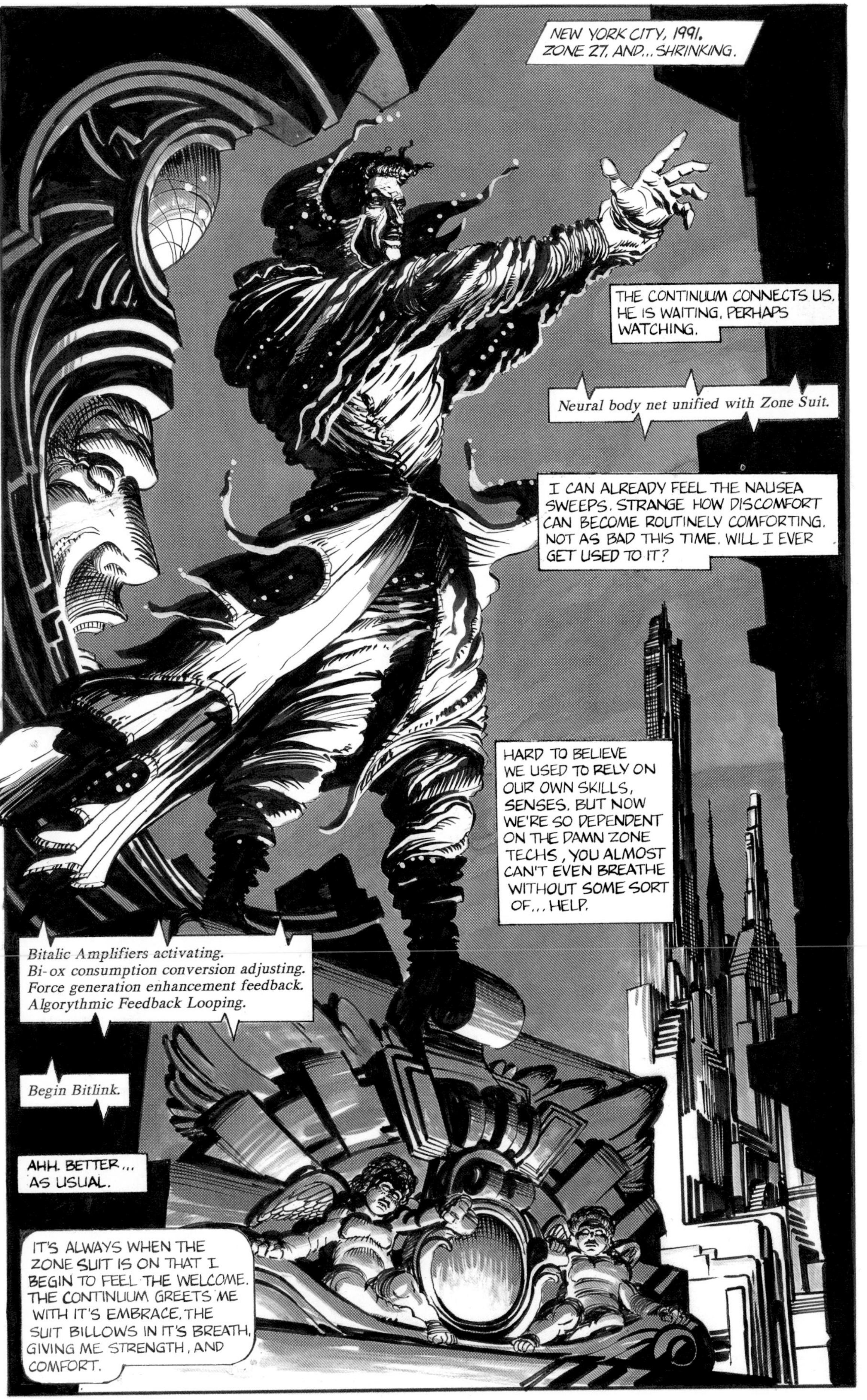
NEW YORK CITY, 1991. ZONE 27, AND... SHRINKING.
THE CONTINUUM CONNECTS US. HE IS WAITING, PERHAPS WATCHING.
Neural body net unified with Zone Suit.
I CAN ALREADY FEEL THE NAUSEA SWEEPS. STRANGE HOW DISCOMFORT CAN BECOME ROUTINELY COMFORTING. NOT AS BAD THIS TIME. WILL I EVER GET USED TO IT?
HARD TO BELIEVE WE USED TO RELY ON OUR OWN SKILLS, SENSES, BUT NOW WE'RE SO DEPENDENT ON THE DAMN ZONE TECHS, YOU ALMOST CAN'T EVEN BREATHE WITHOUT SOME SORT OF... HELP.
Bitalic Amplifiers activating. Bi-ox consumption conversion adjusting. Force generation enhancement feedback. Algorythmic Feedback Looping.
Begin Bitlink.
AHH. BETTER... AS USUAL.
IT'S ALWAYS WHEN THE ZONE SUIT IS ON THAT I BEGIN TO FEEL THE WELCOME. THE CONTINUUM GREETS ME WITH IT'S EMBRACE, THE SUIT BILLOWS IN IT'S BREATH, GIVING ME STRENGTH, AND COMFORT.

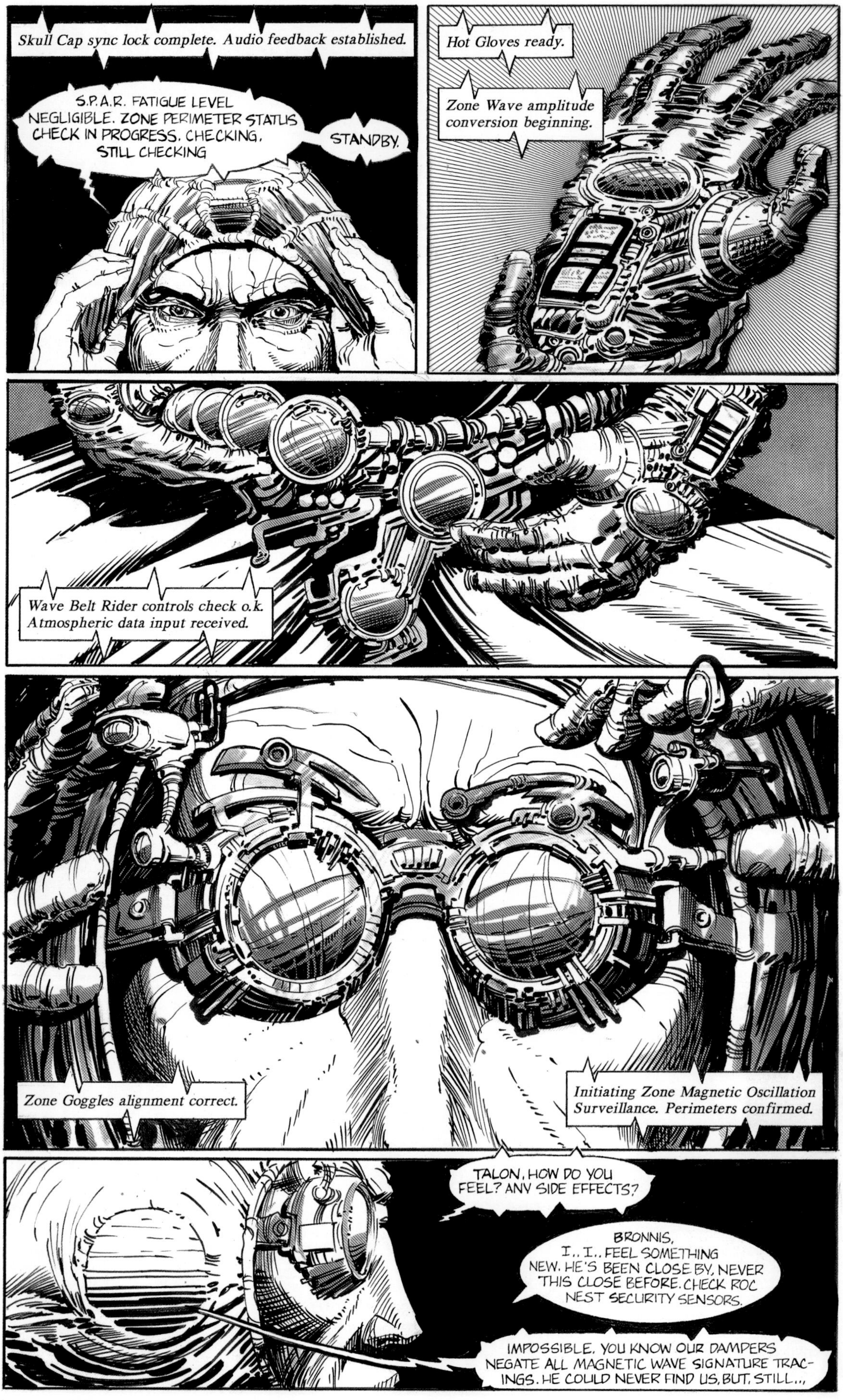
Skull Cap sync lock complete. Audio feedback established.
S.P.A.R. FATIGUE LEVEL NEGLIGIBLE. ZONE PERIMETER STATUS CHECK IN PROGRESS. CHECKING. STILL CHECKING
STANDBY.
Hot Gloves ready.
Zone Wave amplitude conversion beginning.
Wave Belt Rider controls check o.k. Atmospheric data input received.
Zone Goggles alignment correct.
Initiating Zone Magnetic Oscillation Surveillance. Perimeters confirmed.
TALON, HOW DO YOU FEEL? ANY SIDE EFFECTS?
BRONNIS, I.. I.. FEEL SOMETHING NEW. HE'S BEEN CLOSE BY, NEVER THIS CLOSE BEFORE. CHECK ROC NEST SECURITY SENSORS.
IMPOSSIBLE. YOU KNOW OUR DAMPERS NEGATE ALL MAGNETIC WAVE SIGNATURE TRACINGS. HE COULD NEVER FIND US, BUT, STILL...,

....TALON. NEST SECURITY CONFIRMS -- NO VIOLATIONS.

I AM GETTING SOMETHING ELSE. I'VE NEVER SEEN ANYTHING LIKE IT. SOME KIND OF ION-PLASMA FIELD OF STABILIZED PLUTONIUM.

YOU'VE GOT TO BE CAREFUL, AND LOOK FOR... I DON'T KNOW...DAMN...

THE CITY IS BEAUTIFUL TONIGHT. POLLUTION LEVELS DOWN AFTER LAST NIGHT'S RAIN. THE LIGHTS... LIKE DIAMONDS, OR... STARS. USED TO BE, ALL THE NIGHTS LIKE THIS, BUT NOW IT JUST TAKES YOUR BREATH AWAY.

THE GOGGLES' PERIPHERAL INPUT DISPLAY IS AS USUAL... TECHNICAL. NOT QUITE LIKE THE INSTINCTS OF OUR GREATEST WARRIORS. IN SOME OTHER TIME, I WOULD HAVE BEEN AMONG THE FINEST, NOW I'M ONLY A MANIPULATED RECEPTACLE FOR BITLINK DATA. A CYBERNAUT.

Pollution--256 Ozone--Level three
Digital matrix--Condition red
Electro-stasis--Condition red

YOU'RE ON LINE NOW. GOOD LUCK.

I FEEL THE WAVES, THE LIVING FOAM, THE CONTINUUM CLEANSES ME. FEEDS ME. THE VOICES OF THE PARTNERS SING THEIR SWEET MELODY.

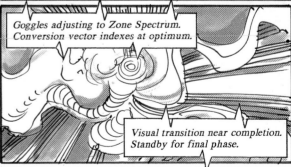

Goggles adjusting to Zone Spectrum. Conversion vector indexes at optimum.

Visual transition near completion. Standby for final phase.

THERE. AGAIN, YET AS ALWAYS, LIKE THE FIRST TIME -- THE VIRTUAL SEA!

IT'S... MAGNIFICENT!!

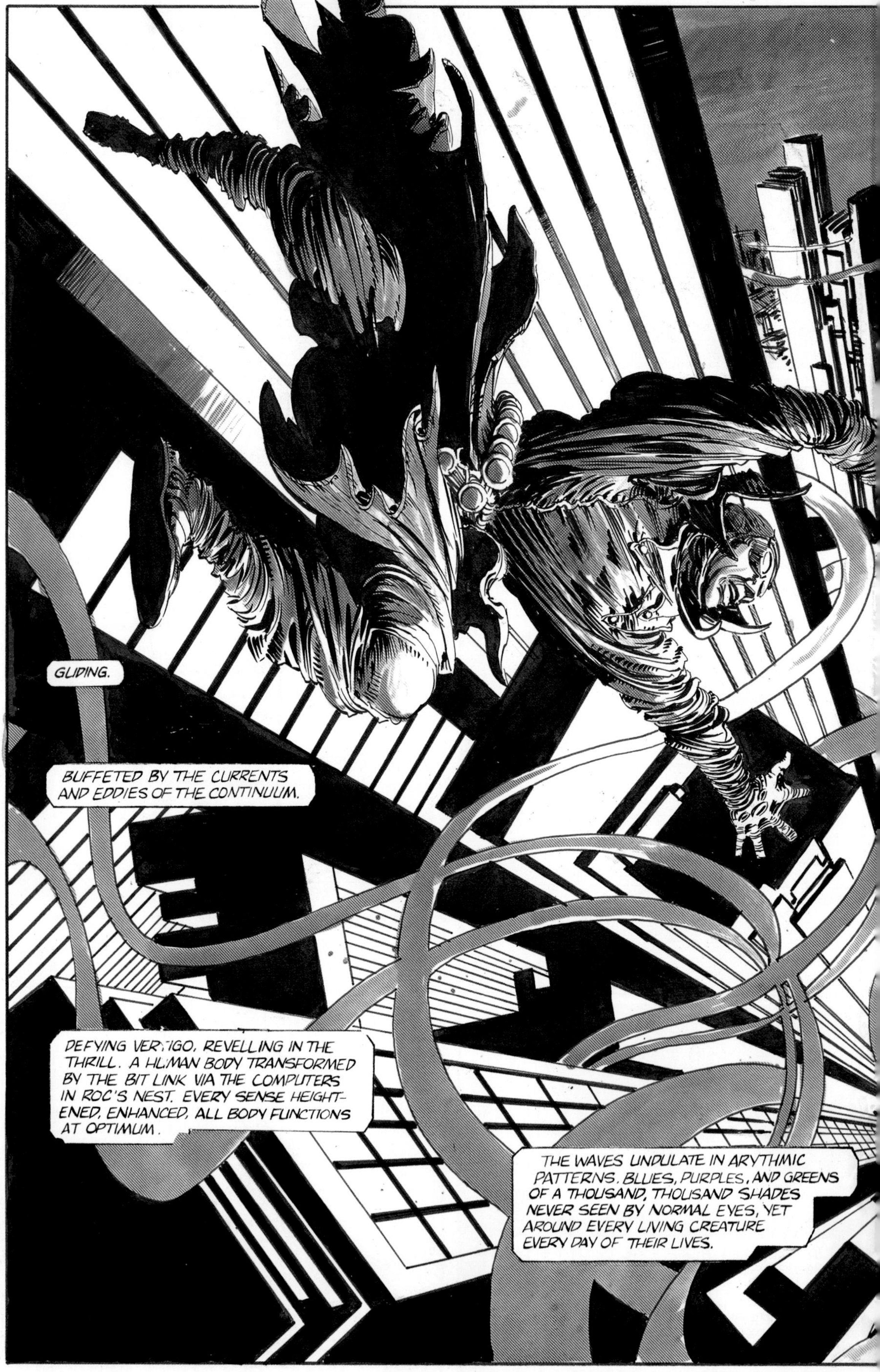
GLIDING.
BUFFETED BY THE CURRENTS AND EDDIES OF THE CONTINUUM.
DEFYING VERTIGO, REVELLING IN THE THRILL. A HUMAN BODY TRANSFORMED BY THE BIT LINK VIA THE COMPUTERS IN ROC'S NEST. EVERY SENSE HEIGHTENED, ENHANCED, ALL BODY FUNCTIONS AT OPTIMUM.
THE WAVES UNDULATE IN ARYTHMIC PATTERNS. BLUES, PURPLES, AND GREENS OF A THOUSAND, THOUSAND SHADES NEVER SEEN BY NORMAL EYES, YET AROUND EVERY LIVING CREATURE EVERY DAY OF THEIR LIVES.

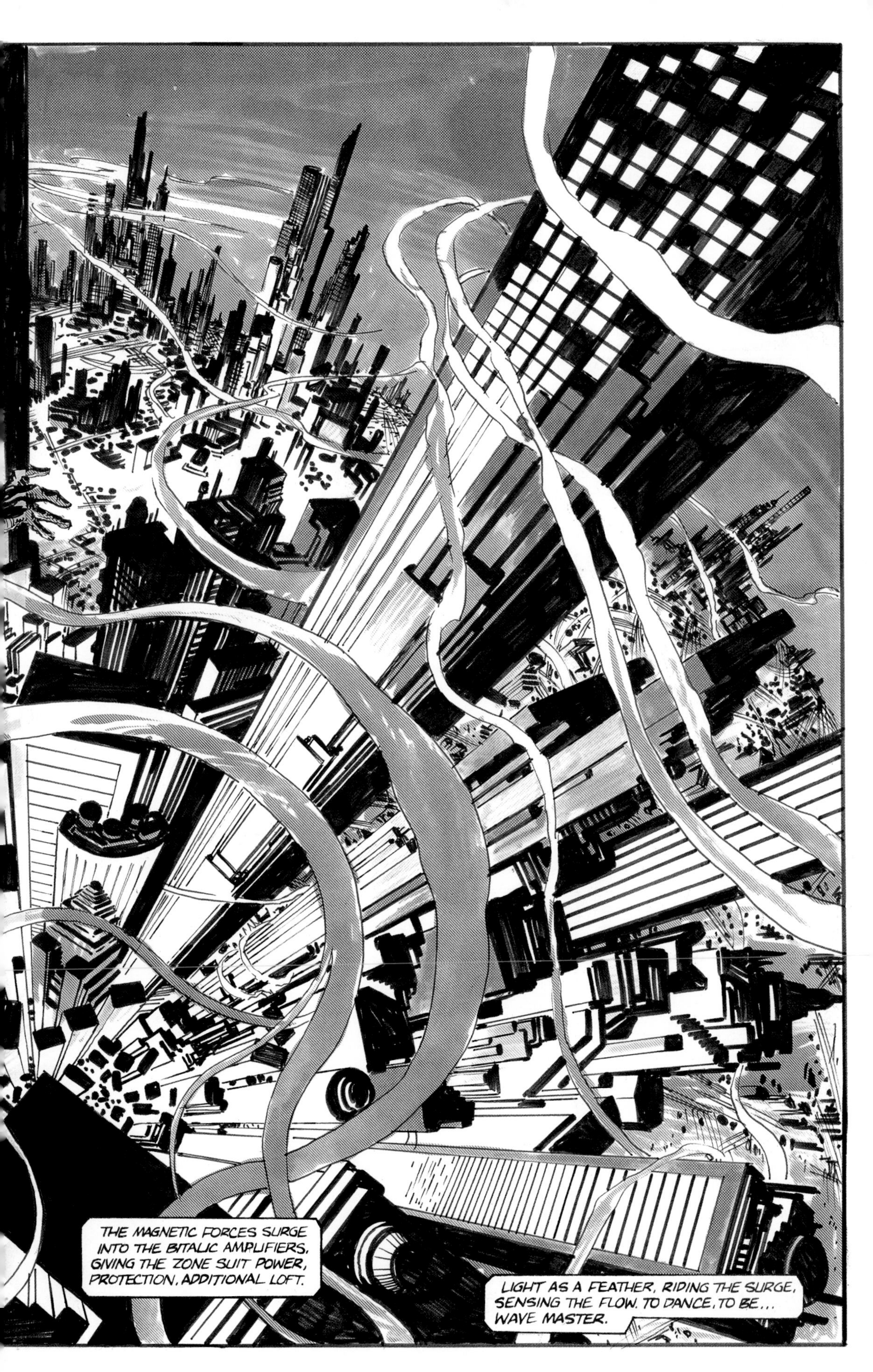
THE MAGNETIC FORCES SURGE INTO THE BITALIC AMPLIFIERS, GIVING THE ZONE SUIT POWER, PROTECTION, ADDITIONAL LOFT.
LIGHT AS A FEATHER, RIDING THE SURGE, SENSING THE FLOW. TO DANCE, TO BE... WAVE MASTER.

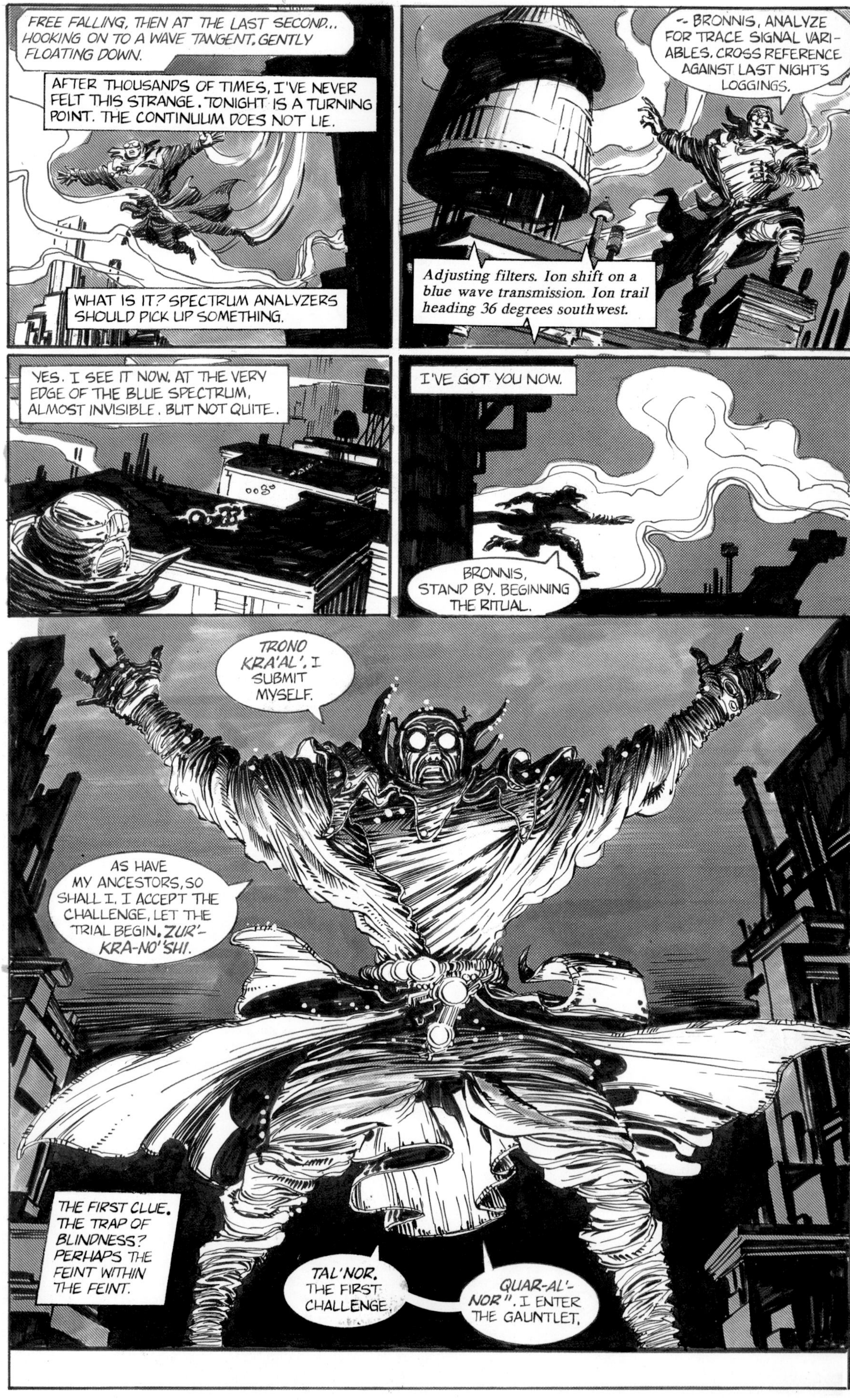
FREE FALLING, THEN AT THE LAST SECOND... HOOKING ON TO A WAVE TANGENT. GENTLY FLOATING DOWN.
AFTER THOUSANDS OF TIMES, I'VE NEVER FELT THIS STRANGE. TONIGHT IS A TURNING POINT. THE CONTINUUM DOES NOT LIE.
WHAT IS IT? SPECTRUM ANALYZERS SHOULD PICK UP SOMETHING.
-- BRONNIS, ANALYZE FOR TRACE SIGNAL VARIABLES. CROSS REFERENCE AGAINST LAST NIGHT'S LOGGINGS.
Adjusting filters. Ion shift on a blue wave transmission. Ion trail heading 36 degrees southwest.
YES. I SEE IT NOW. AT THE VERY EDGE OF THE BLUE SPECTRUM, ALMOST INVISIBLE. BUT NOT QUITE.
I'VE GOT YOU NOW.
BRONNIS, STAND BY. BEGINNING THE RITUAL.
TRONO KRA'AL'. I SUBMIT MYSELF.
AS HAVE MY ANCESTORS, SO SHALL I. I ACCEPT THE CHALLENGE, LET THE TRIAL BEGIN. ZUR'-KRA-NO'SHI.
THE FIRST CLUE. THE TRAP OF BLINDNESS? PERHAPS THE FEINT WITHIN THE FEINT.
TAL'NOR. THE FIRST CHALLENGE.
QUAR-AL'-NOR". I ENTER THE GAUNTLET.

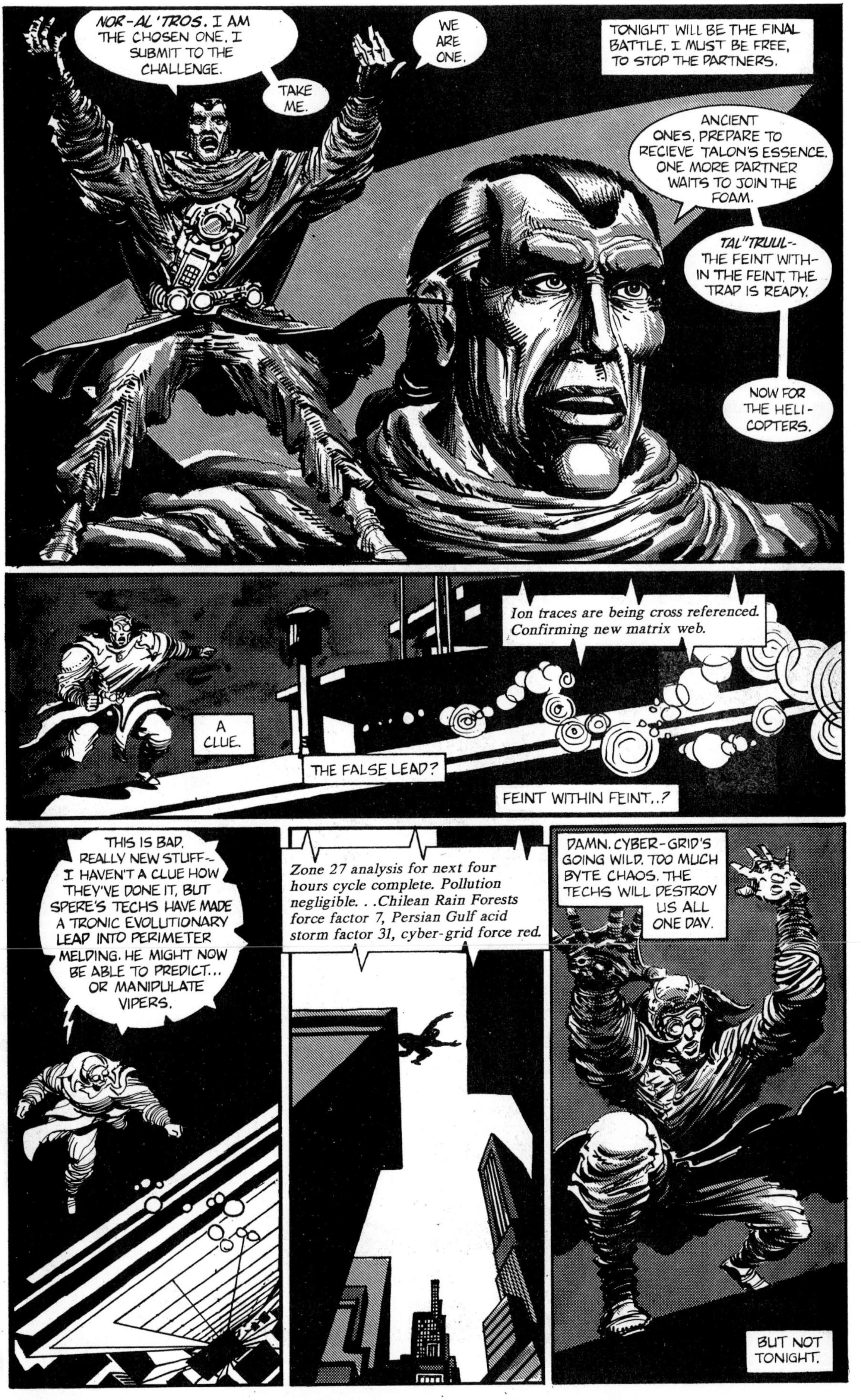
NOR-AL'TROS. I AM THE CHOSEN ONE. I SUBMIT TO THE CHALLENGE.
TAKE ME.
WE ARE ONE.
TONIGHT WILL BE THE FINAL BATTLE. I MUST BE FREE, TO STOP THE PARTNERS.
ANCIENT ONES, PREPARE TO RECIEVE TALON'S ESSENCE. ONE MORE PARTNER WAITS TO JOIN THE FOAM.
TAL"TRUUL- THE FEINT WITHIN THE FEINT. THE TRAP IS READY.
NOW FOR THE HELICOPTERS.
Ion traces are being cross referenced. Confirming new matrix web.
A CLUE.
THE FALSE LEAD?
FEINT WITHIN FEINT..?
THIS IS BAD. REALLY NEW STUFF-- I HAVEN'T A CLUE HOW THEY'VE DONE IT, BUT SPERE'S TECHS HAVE MADE A TRONIC EVOLUTIONARY LEAP INTO PERIMETER MELDING. HE MIGHT NOW BE ABLE TO PREDICT... OR MANIPULATE VIPERS.
Zone 27 analysis for next four hours cycle complete. Pollution negligible. . .Chilean Rain Forests force factor 7, Persian Gulf acid storm factor 31, cyber-grid force red.
DAMN. CYBER-GRID'S GOING WILD. TOO MUCH BYTE CHAOS. THE TECHS WILL DESTROY US ALL ONE DAY.
BUT NOT TONIGHT.

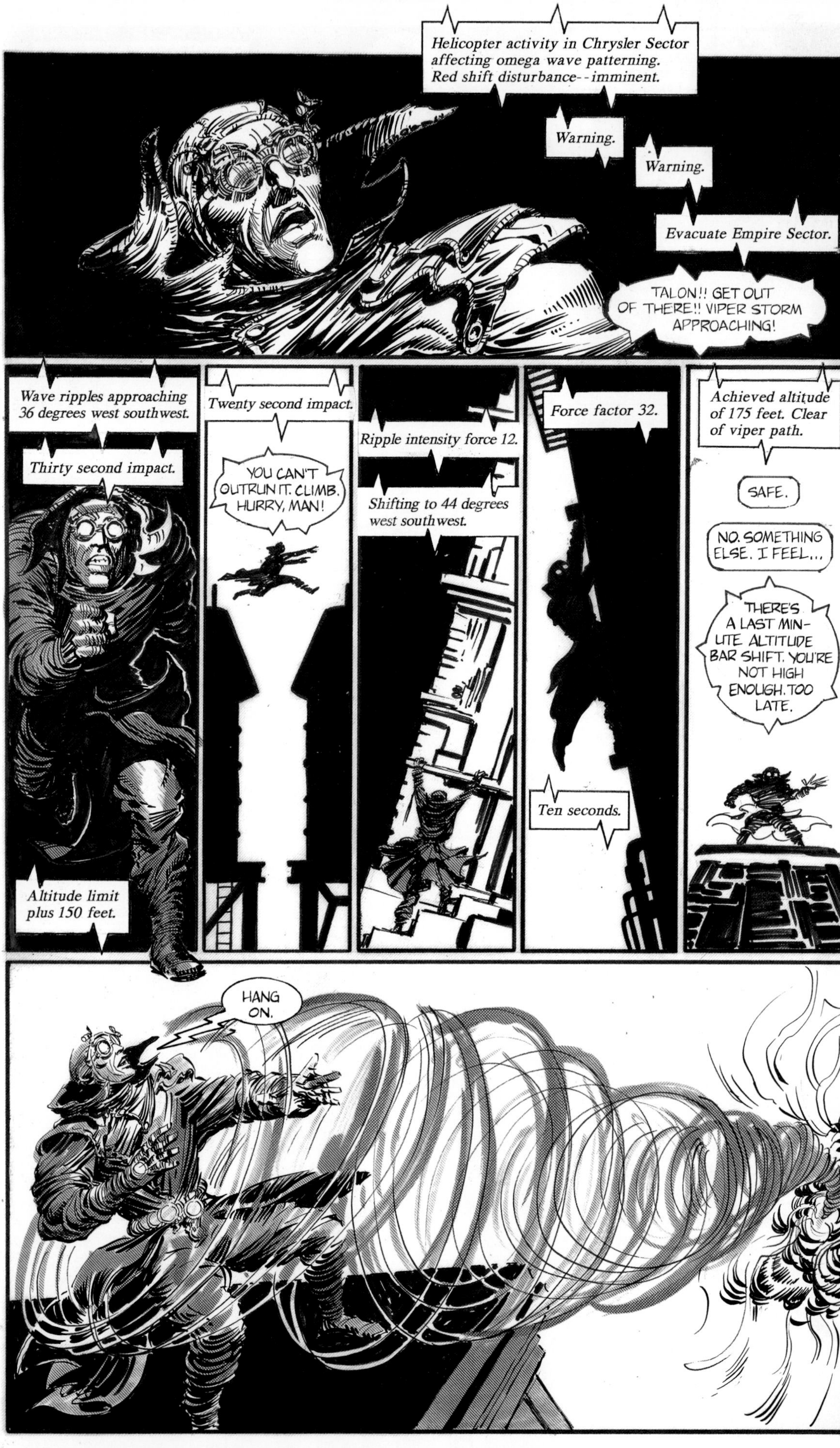
Helicopter activity in Chrysler Sector affecting omega wave patterning. Red shift disturbance--imminent.
Warning.
Warning.
Evacuate Empire Sector.
TALON!! GET OUT OF THERE!! VIPER STORM APPROACHING!
Wave ripples approaching 36 degrees west southwest.
Thirty second impact.
Altitude limit plus 150 feet.
Twenty second impact.
YOU CAN'T OUTRUN IT. CLIMB. HURRY, MAN!
Ripple intensity force 12.
Shifting to 44 degrees west southwest.
Force factor 32.
Ten seconds.
Achieved altitude of 175 feet. Clear of viper path.
SAFE.
NO. SOMETHING ELSE. I FEEL...
THERE'S A LAST MIN-UTE ALTITUDE BAR SHIFT. YOU'RE NOT HIGH ENOUGH. TOO LATE.
HANG ON.

SHOULD HAVE KNOWN... FELT IT COMING.

CAN'T BREATHE.

CHEST ON FIRE.

ONE CHANCE...SHUT DOWN WAVE COLLECTORS.

NEGATE BITALIC AMPS.

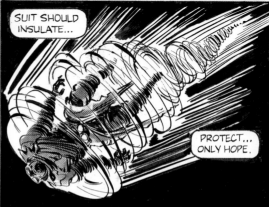

SUIT SHOULD INSULATE...

PROTECT... ONLY HOPE.

Unnnhhhh!!!

EXPRES

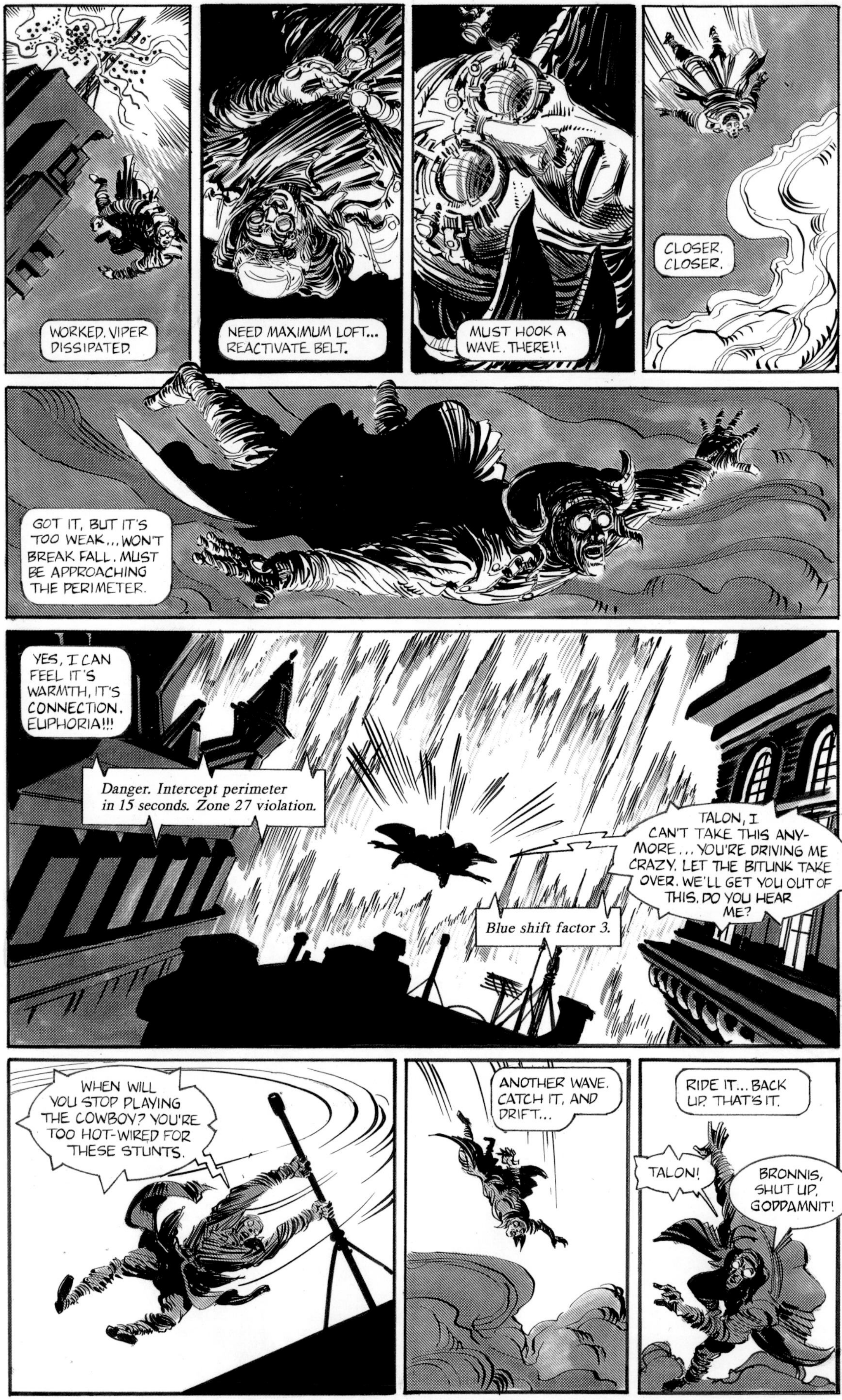
WORKED. VIPER DISSIPATED.
NEED MAXIMUM LOFT... REACTIVATE BELT.
MUST HOOK A WAVE. THERE!!.
CLOSER. CLOSER.
GOT IT, BUT IT'S TOO WEAK... WON'T BREAK FALL. MUST BE APPROACHING THE PERIMETER.
YES, I CAN FEEL IT'S WARMTH, IT'S CONNECTION. EUPHORIA!!!
Danger. Intercept perimeter in 15 seconds. Zone 27 violation.
TALON, I CAN'T TAKE THIS ANY-MORE... YOU'RE DRIVING ME CRAZY. LET THE BITLINK TAKE OVER. WE'LL GET YOU OUT OF THIS. DO YOU HEAR ME?
Blue shift factor 3.
WHEN WILL YOU STOP PLAYING THE COWBOY? YOU'RE TOO HOT-WIRED FOR THESE STUNTS.
ANOTHER WAVE. CATCH IT, AND DRIFT...
RIDE IT... BACK UP. THAT'S IT.
TALON!
BRONNIS, SHUT UP, GODDAMNIT!

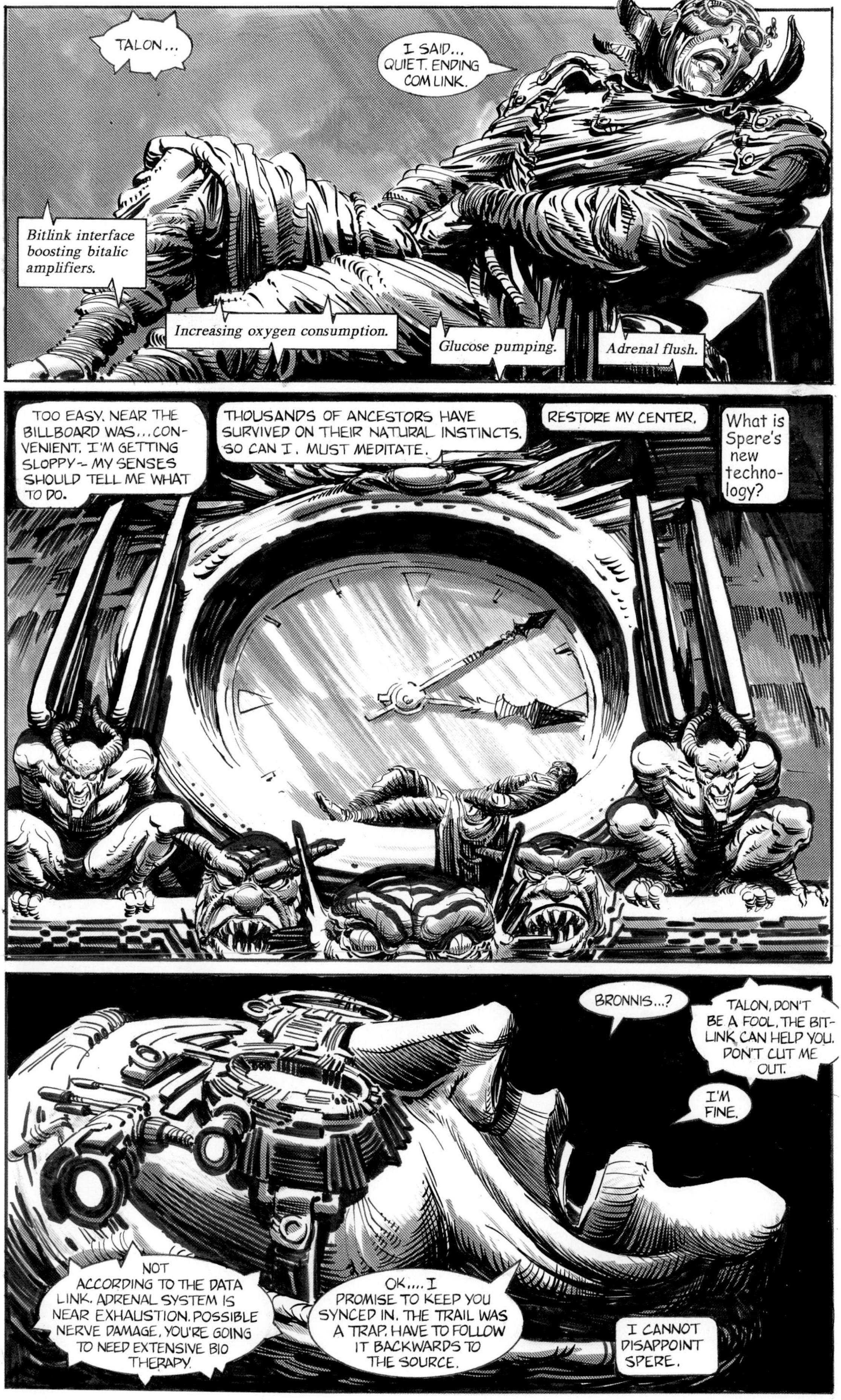
TALON...
I SAID... QUIET. ENDING COM LINK.
Bitlink interface boosting bitalic amplifiers.
Increasing oxygen consumption.
Glucose pumping.
Adrenal flush.
TOO EASY. NEAR THE BILLBOARD WAS... CON-VENIENT. I'M GETTING SLOPPY-- MY SENSES SHOULD TELL ME WHAT TO DO.
THOUSANDS OF ANCESTORS HAVE SURVIVED ON THEIR NATURAL INSTINCTS. SO CAN I. MUST MEDITATE.
RESTORE MY CENTER.
What is Spere's new technology?
BRONNIS...?
TALON, DON'T BE A FOOL. THE BIT-LINK CAN HELP YOU. DON'T CUT ME OUT.
I'M FINE.
NOT ACCORDING TO THE DATA LINK. ADRENAL SYSTEM IS NEAR EXHAUSTION. POSSIBLE NERVE DAMAGE, YOU'RE GOING TO NEED EXTENSIVE BIO THERAPY.
OK.... I PROMISE TO KEEP YOU SYNCED IN. THE TRAIL WAS A TRAP. HAVE TO FOLLOW IT BACKWARDS TO THE SOURCE.
I CANNOT DISAPPOINT SPERE.

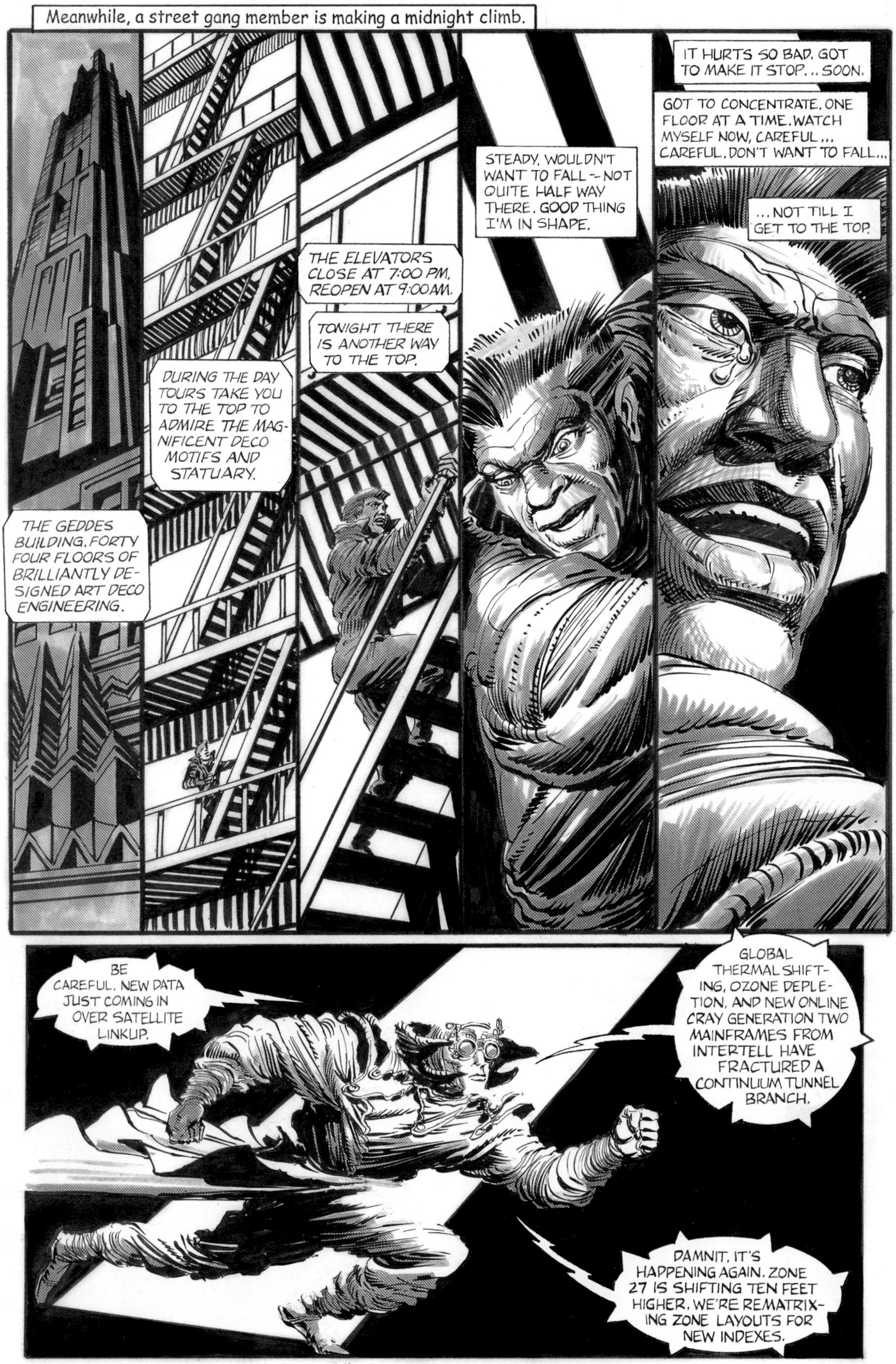
Meanwhile, a street gang member is making a midnight climb.
THE GEDDES BUILDING, FORTY FOUR FLOORS OF BRILLIANTLY DESIGNED ART DECO ENGINEERING.
DURING THE DAY TOURS TAKE YOU TO THE TOP TO ADMIRE THE MAGNIFICENT DECO MOTIFS AND STATUARY.
THE ELEVATORS CLOSE AT 7:00 PM, REOPEN AT 9:00 AM.
TONIGHT THERE IS ANOTHER WAY TO THE TOP.
STEADY, WOULDN'T WANT TO FALL -- NOT QUITE HALF WAY THERE. GOOD THING I'M IN SHAPE.
IT HURTS SO BAD. GOT TO MAKE IT STOP... SOON.
GOT TO CONCENTRATE. ONE FLOOR AT A TIME. WATCH MYSELF NOW, CAREFUL... CAREFUL. DON'T WANT TO FALL...
...NOT TILL I GET TO THE TOP.
BE CAREFUL. NEW DATA JUST COMING IN OVER SATELLITE LINKUP.
GLOBAL THERMAL SHIFTING, OZONE DEPLETION, AND NEW ONLINE CRAY GENERATION TWO MAINFRAMES FROM INTERTELL HAVE FRACTURED A CONTINUUM TUNNEL BRANCH.
DAMNIT, IT'S HAPPENING AGAIN. ZONE 27 IS SHIFTING TEN FEET HIGHER. WE'RE REMATRIXING ZONE LAYOUTS FOR NEW INDEXES.

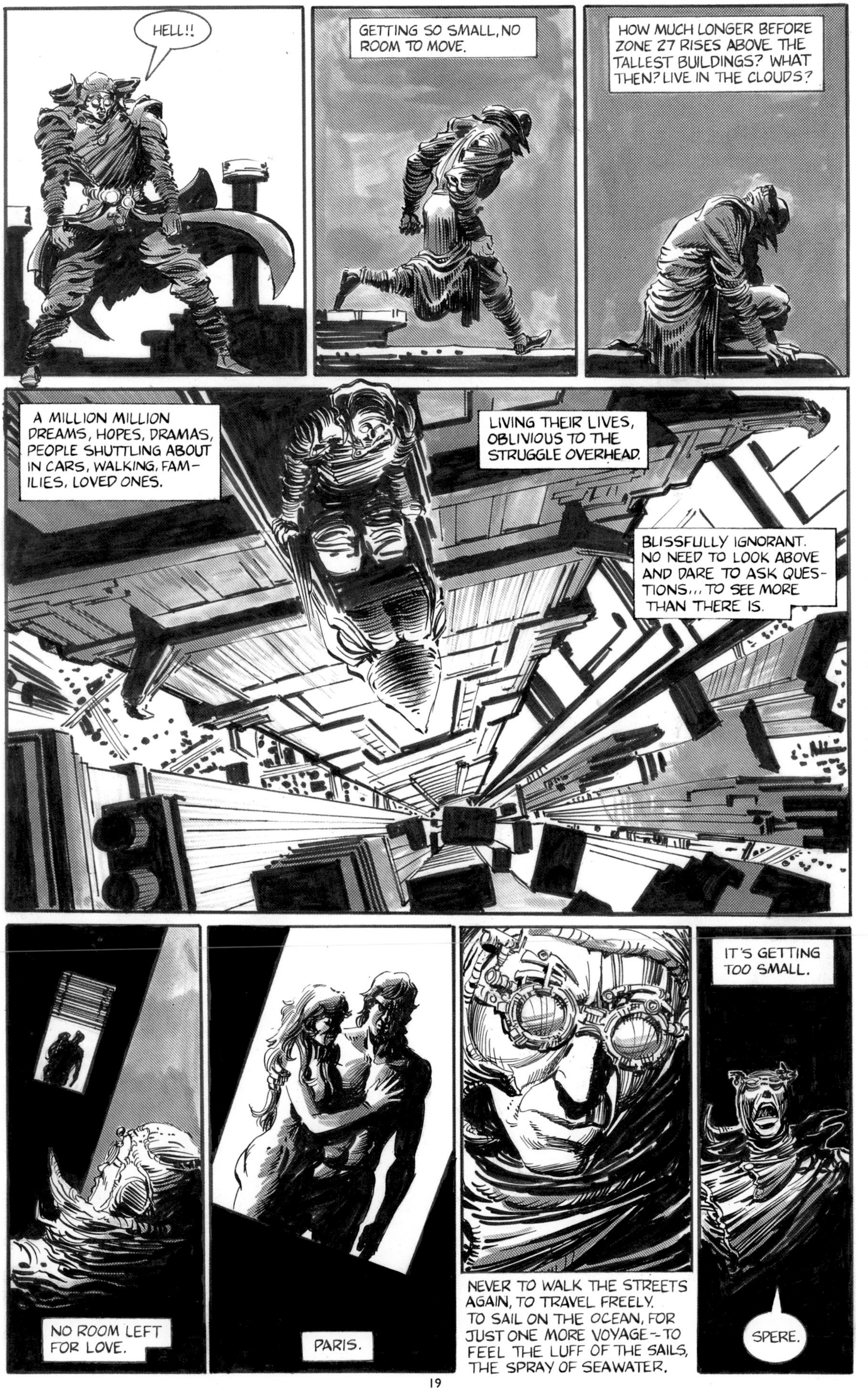
HELL!!
GETTING SO SMALL, NO ROOM TO MOVE.
HOW MUCH LONGER BEFORE ZONE 27 RISES ABOVE THE TALLEST BUILDINGS? WHAT THEN? LIVE IN THE CLOUDS?
A MILLION MILLION DREAMS, HOPES, DRAMAS, PEOPLE SHUTTLING ABOUT IN CARS, WALKING, FAMILIES, LOVED ONES.
LIVING THEIR LIVES, OBLIVIOUS TO THE STRUGGLE OVERHEAD.
BLISSFULLY IGNORANT. NO NEED TO LOOK ABOVE AND DARE TO ASK QUESTIONS... TO SEE MORE THAN THERE IS.
NO ROOM LEFT FOR LOVE.
PARIS.
NEVER TO WALK THE STREETS AGAIN, TO TRAVEL FREELY. TO SAIL ON THE OCEAN, FOR JUST ONE MORE VOYAGE--TO FEEL THE LUFF OF THE SAILS, THE SPRAY OF SEAWATER.
IT'S GETTING TOO SMALL.
SPERE.

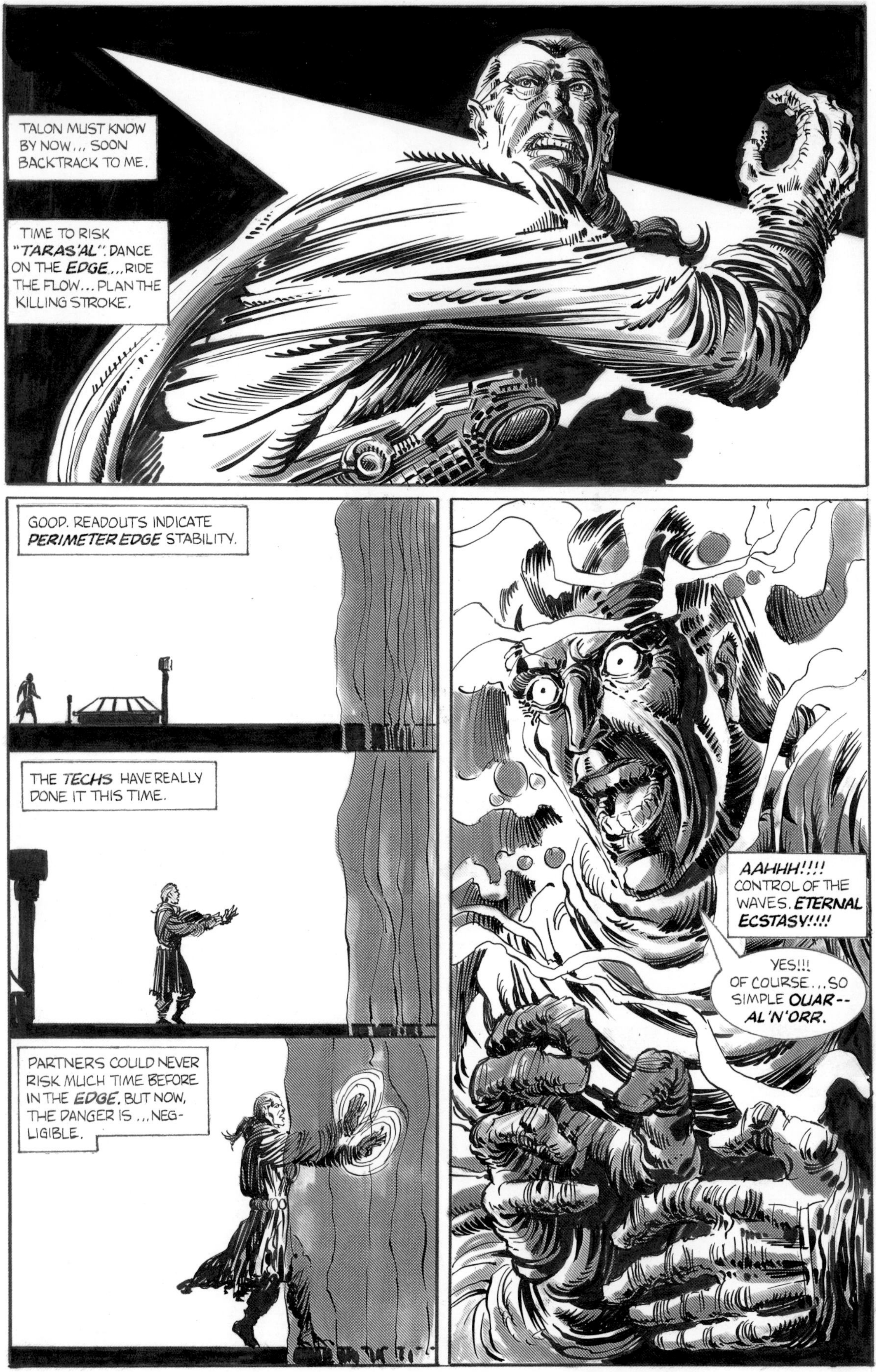
TALON MUST KNOW BY NOW... SOON BACKTRACK TO ME.
TIME TO RISK "TARAS'AL". DANCE ON THE EDGE... RIDE THE FLOW... PLAN THE KILLING STROKE.
GOOD. READOUTS INDICATE PERIMETER EDGE STABILITY.
THE TECHS HAVE REALLY DONE IT THIS TIME.
PARTNERS COULD NEVER RISK MUCH TIME BEFORE IN THE EDGE. BUT NOW, THE DANGER IS ... NEG-LIGIBLE.
AAHHH!!!! CONTROL OF THE WAVES. ETERNAL ECSTASY!!!!
YES!!! OF COURSE... SO SIMPLE OUAR--AL'N'ORR.

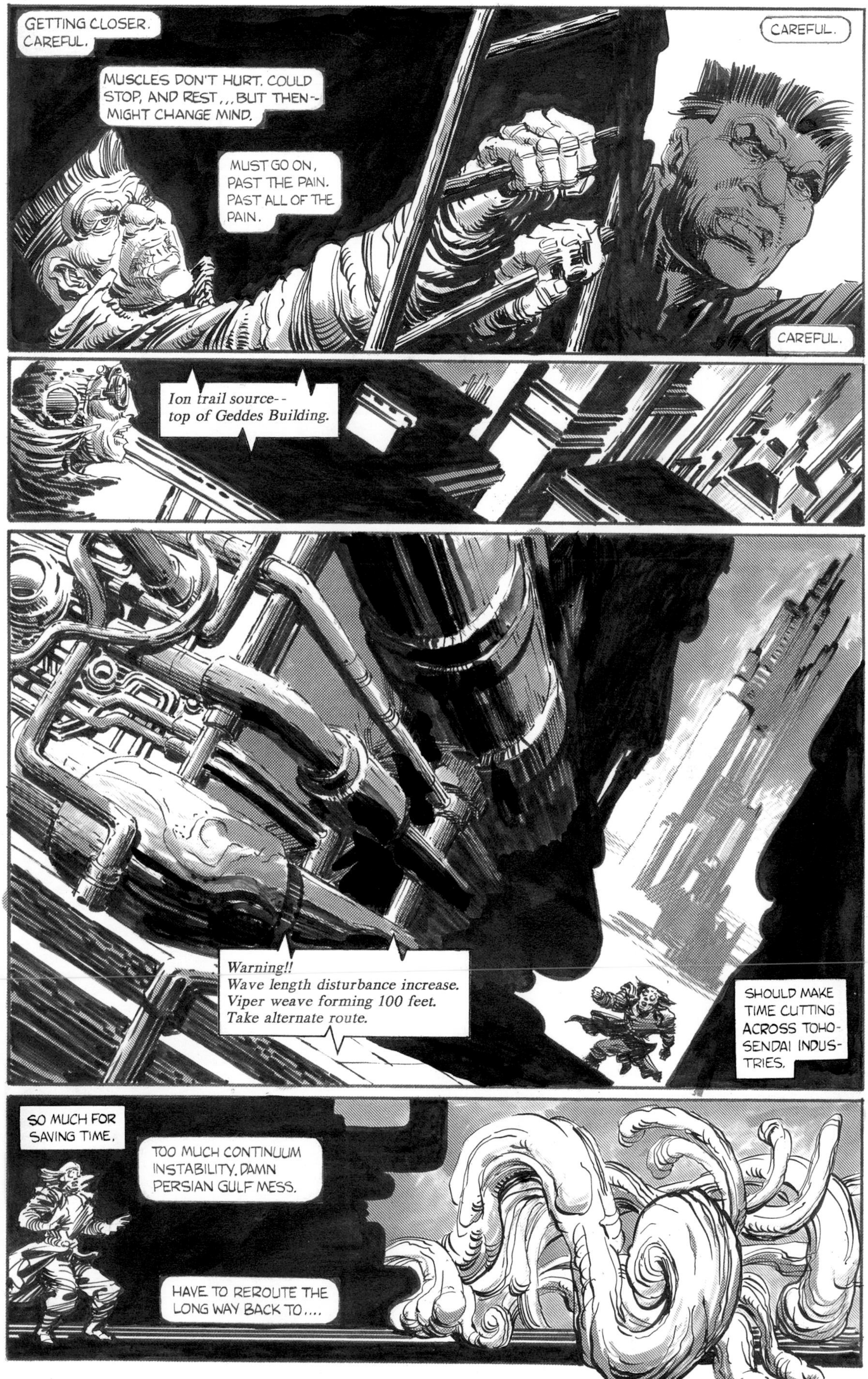
GETTING CLOSER. CAREFUL.
CAREFUL.
MUSCLES DON'T HURT. COULD STOP, AND REST,,,BUT THEN-- MIGHT CHANGE MIND.
MUST GO ON, PAST THE PAIN. PAST ALL OF THE PAIN.
CAREFUL.
Ion trail source-- top of Geddes Building.
Warning!! Wave length disturbance increase. Viper weave forming 100 feet. Take alternate route.
SHOULD MAKE TIME CUTTING ACROSS TOHO-SENDAI INDUSTRIES.
SO MUCH FOR SAVING TIME.
TOO MUCH CONTINUUM INSTABILITY. DAMN PERSIAN GULF MESS.
HAVE TO REROUTE THE LONG WAY BACK TO....

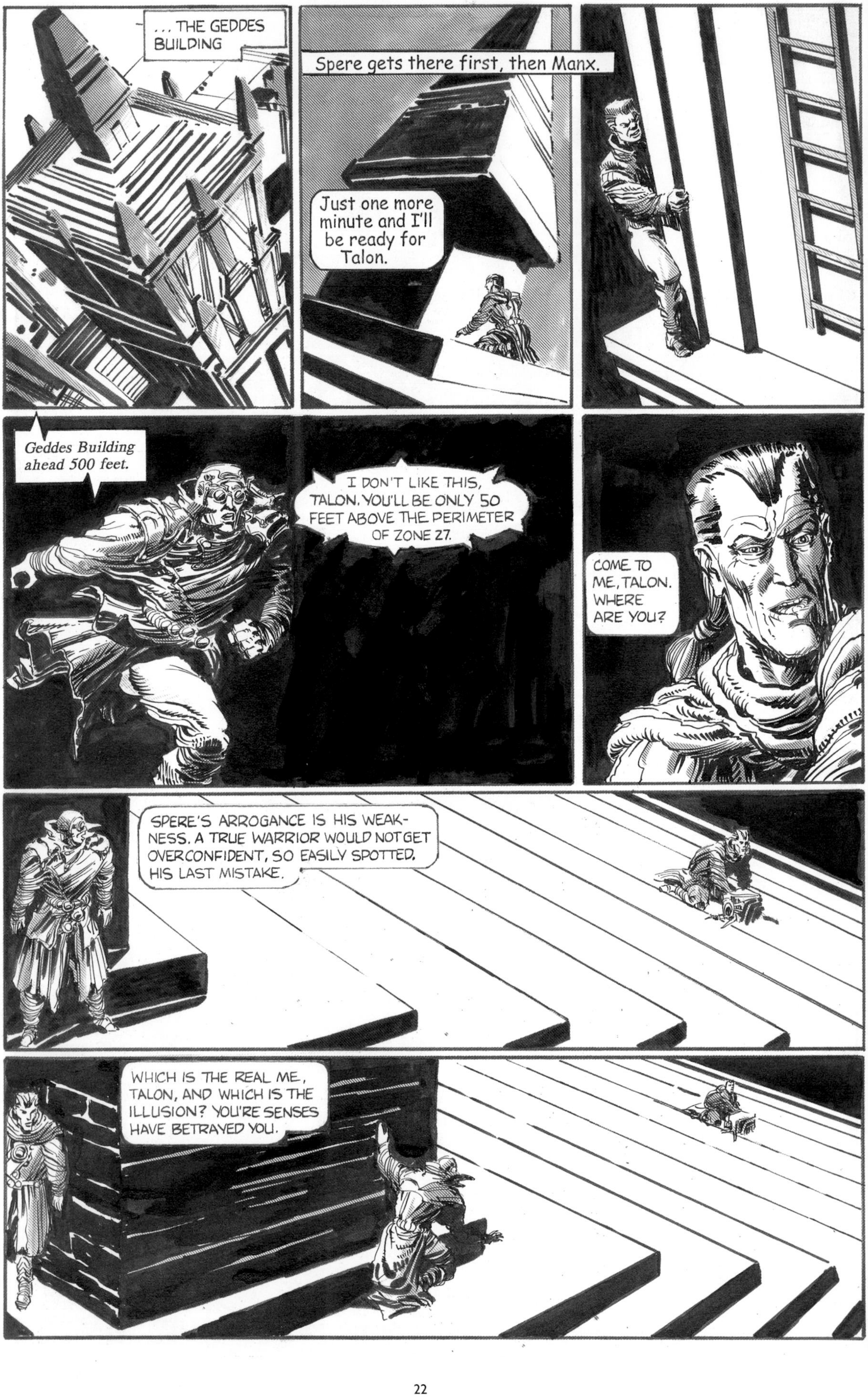

. . . THE GEDDES BUILDING
Spere gets there first, then Manx.
Just one more minute and I'll be ready for Talon.
Geddes Building ahead 500 feet.
I DON'T LIKE THIS, TALON. YOU'LL BE ONLY 50 FEET ABOVE THE PERIMETER OF ZONE 27.
COME TO ME, TALON. WHERE ARE YOU?
SPERE'S ARROGANCE IS HIS WEAKNESS. A TRUE WARRIOR WOULD NOT GET OVERCONFIDENT, SO EASILY SPOTTED. HIS LAST MISTAKE.
WHICH IS THE REAL ME, TALON, AND WHICH IS THE ILLUSION? YOU'RE SENSES HAVE BETRAYED YOU.

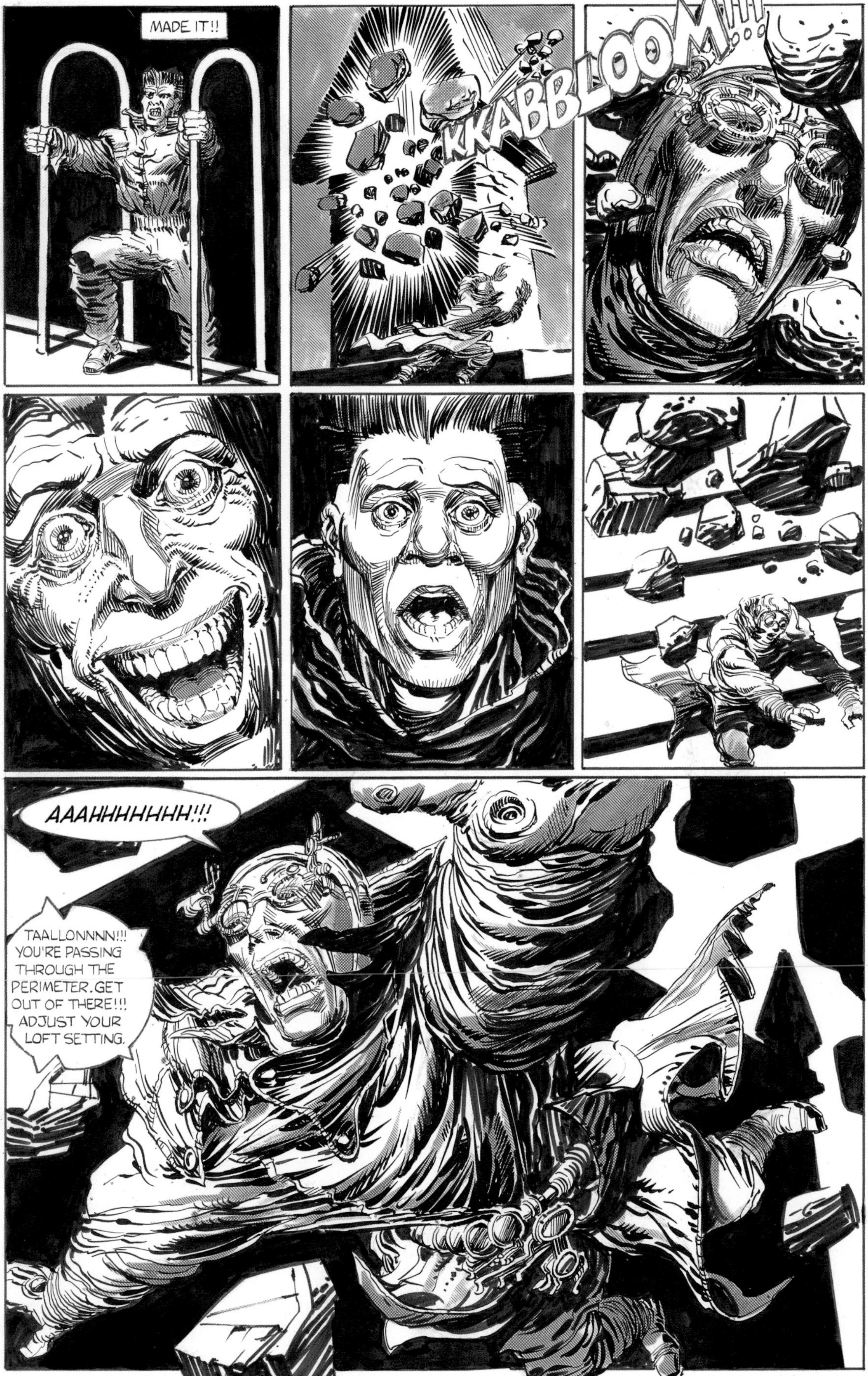
MADE IT!!
KKABBLOOM!!!
AAAHHHHHHH!!!
TAALLONNNN!!! YOU'RE PASSING THROUGH THE PERIMETER. GET OUT OF THERE!!! ADJUST YOUR LOFT SETTING.

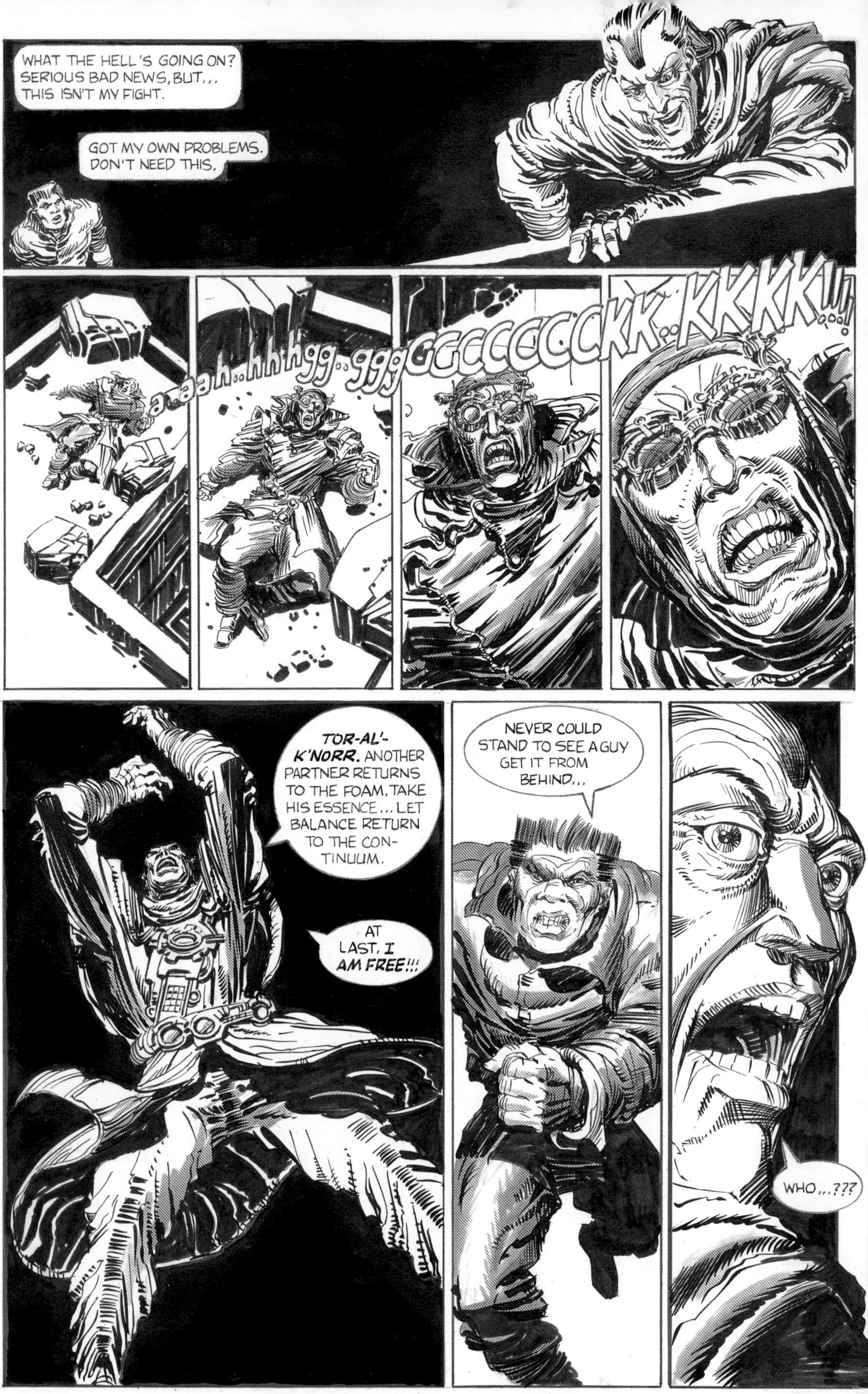
WHAT THE HELL'S GOING ON? SERIOUS BAD NEWS, BUT... THIS ISN'T MY FIGHT.
GOT MY OWN PROBLEMS. DON'T NEED THIS.
a..aah..hhhgg..gggGCCCCCCKK..KKKK!!..!
TOR-AL'-K'NORR. ANOTHER PARTNER RETURNS TO THE FOAM. TAKE HIS ESSENCE... LET BALANCE RETURN TO THE CONTINUUM.
AT LAST, I AM FREE!!!
NEVER COULD STAND TO SEE A GUY GET IT FROM BEHIND...
WHO...???

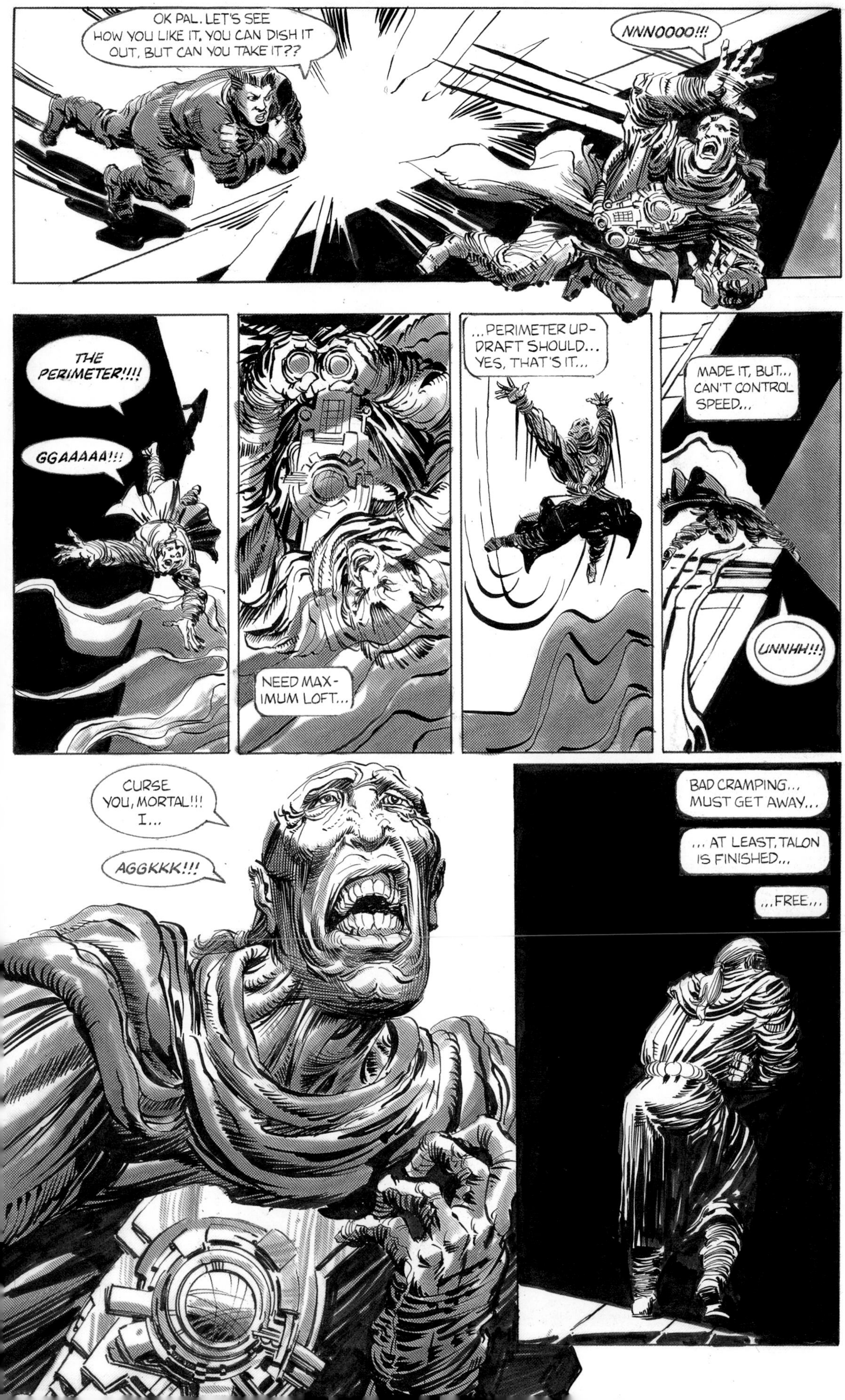
OK PAL. LET'S SEE HOW YOU LIKE IT. YOU CAN DISH IT OUT, BUT CAN YOU TAKE IT??
NNNOOOO!!!
THE PERIMETER!!!!
GGAAAAAA!!!
NEED MAX-IMUM LOFT...
...PERIMETER UP-DRAFT SHOULD... YES, THAT'S IT...
MADE IT, BUT... CAN'T CONTROL SPEED...
UNNHH!!!
CURSE YOU, MORTAL!!! I...
AGGKKK!!!
BAD CRAMPING... MUST GET AWAY...
... AT LEAST, TALON IS FINISHED...
...FREE...

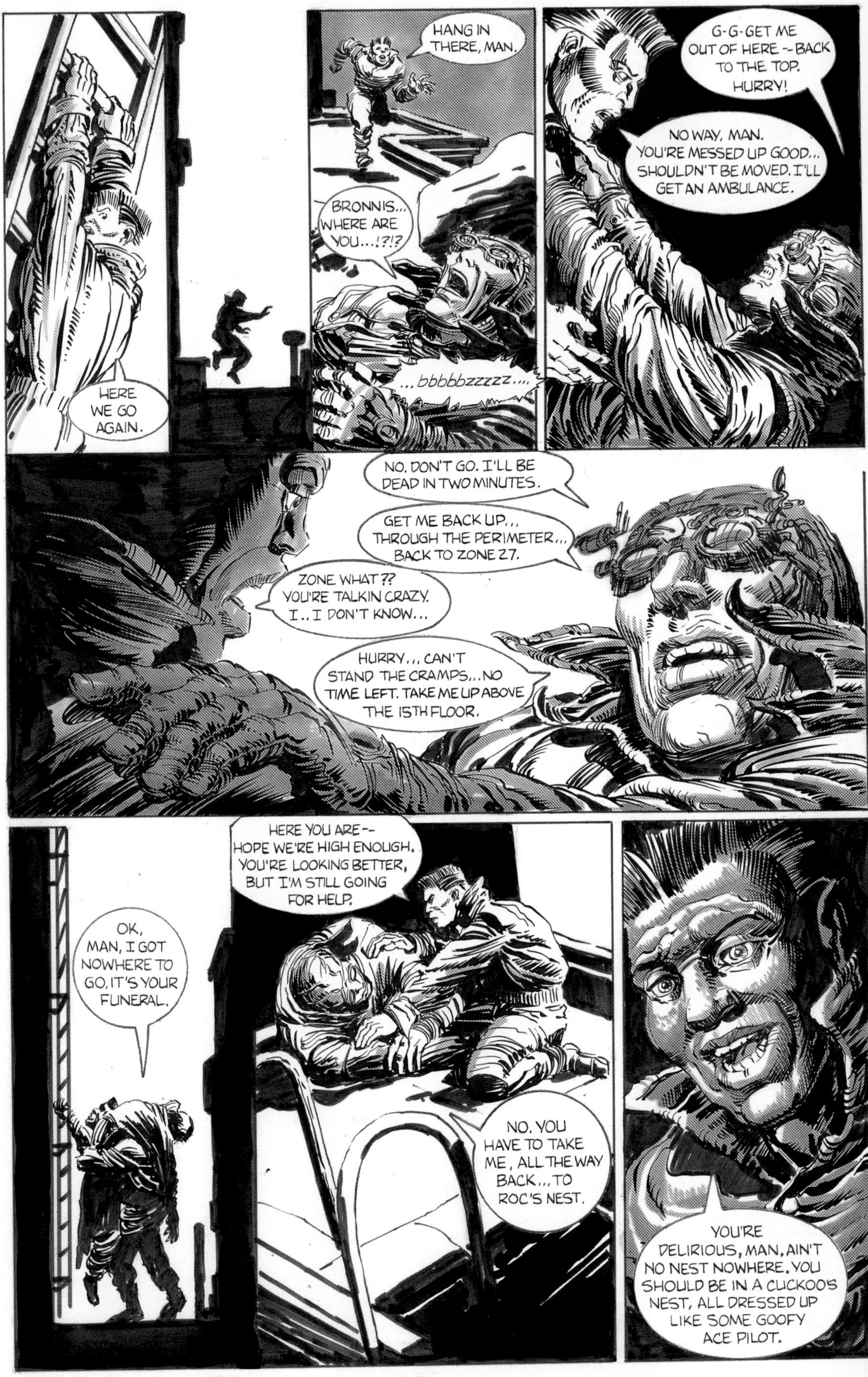

HERE WE GO AGAIN.
HANG IN THERE, MAN.
BRONNIS... WHERE ARE YOU...!?!?
...bbbbbzzzzz....
G-G-GET ME OUT OF HERE --BACK TO THE TOP. HURRY!
NO WAY, MAN. YOU'RE MESSED UP GOOD... SHOULDN'T BE MOVED. I'LL GET AN AMBULANCE.
NO, DON'T GO. I'LL BE DEAD IN TWO MINUTES.
GET ME BACK UP... THROUGH THE PERIMETER... BACK TO ZONE 27.
ZONE WHAT?? YOU'RE TALKIN CRAZY. I.. I DON'T KNOW...
HURRY... CAN'T STAND THE CRAMPS... NO TIME LEFT. TAKE ME UP ABOVE THE 15TH FLOOR.
OK, MAN, I GOT NOWHERE TO GO, IT'S YOUR FUNERAL.
HERE YOU ARE-- HOPE WE'RE HIGH ENOUGH. YOU'RE LOOKING BETTER, BUT I'M STILL GOING FOR HELP.
NO, YOU HAVE TO TAKE ME, ALL THE WAY BACK... TO ROC'S NEST.
YOU'RE DELIRIOUS, MAN. AIN'T NO NEST NOWHERE. YOU SHOULD BE IN A CUCKOO'S NEST, ALL DRESSED UP LIKE SOME GOOFY ACE PILOT.

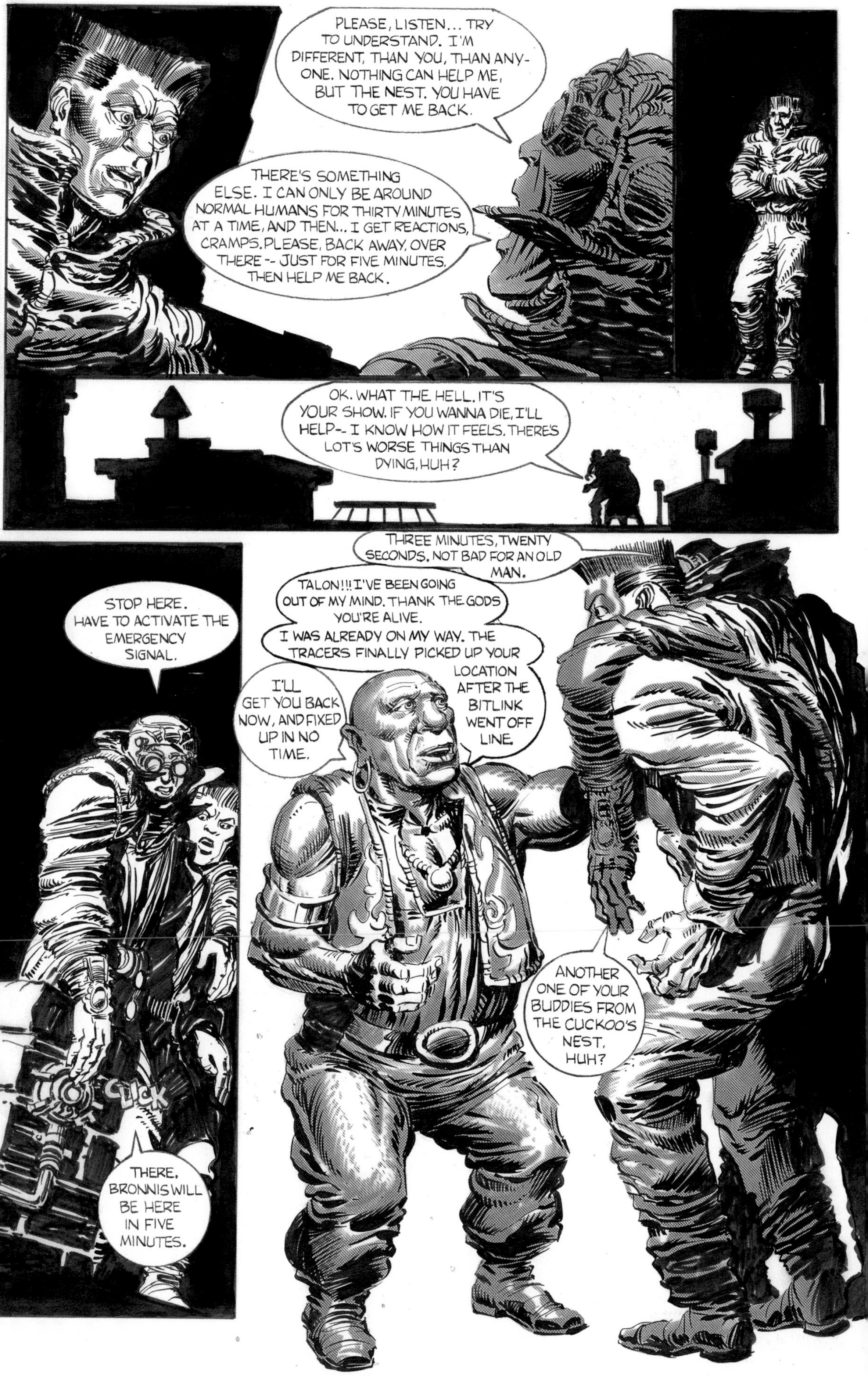
PLEASE, LISTEN... TRY TO UNDERSTAND. I'M DIFFERENT, THAN YOU, THAN ANYONE. NOTHING CAN HELP ME, BUT THE NEST. YOU HAVE TO GET ME BACK.
THERE'S SOMETHING ELSE. I CAN ONLY BE AROUND NORMAL HUMANS FOR THIRTY MINUTES AT A TIME, AND THEN... I GET REACTIONS, CRAMPS. PLEASE, BACK AWAY, OVER THERE -- JUST FOR FIVE MINUTES. THEN HELP ME BACK.
OK. WHAT THE HELL. IT'S YOUR SHOW. IF YOU WANNA DIE, I'LL HELP-- I KNOW HOW IT FEELS. THERE'S LOT'S WORSE THINGS THAN DYING, HUH?
STOP HERE. HAVE TO ACTIVATE THE EMERGENCY SIGNAL.
CLICK
THERE. BRONNIS WILL BE HERE IN FIVE MINUTES.
THREE MINUTES, TWENTY SECONDS. NOT BAD FOR AN OLD MAN.
TALON!!! I'VE BEEN GOING OUT OF MY MIND. THANK THE GODS YOU'RE ALIVE.
I WAS ALREADY ON MY WAY. THE TRACERS FINALLY PICKED UP YOUR LOCATION AFTER THE BITLINK WENT OFF LINE.
I'LL GET YOU BACK NOW, AND FIXED UP IN NO TIME.
ANOTHER ONE OF YOUR BUDDIES FROM THE CUCKOO'S NEST, HUH?

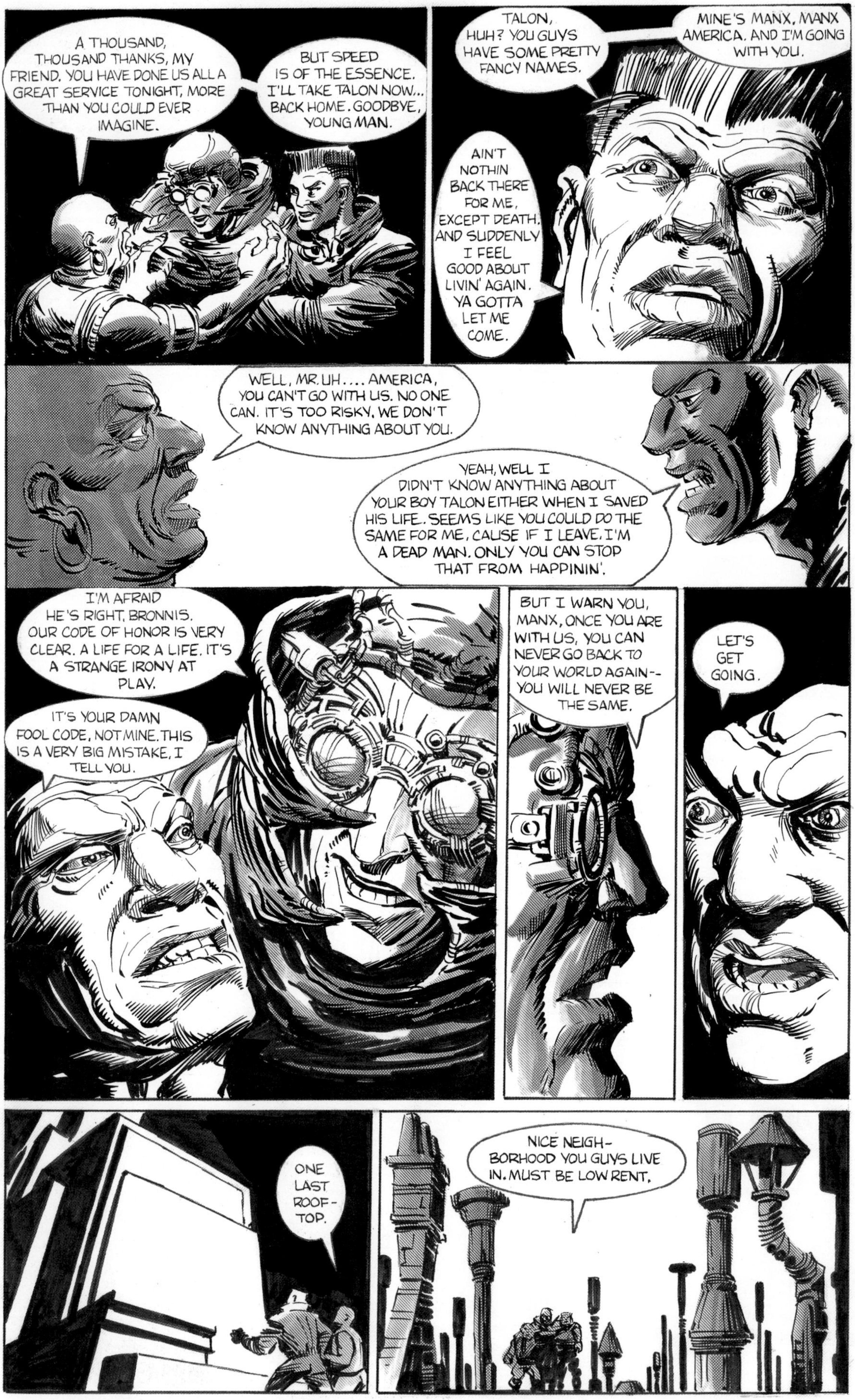
A THOUSAND, THOUSAND THANKS, MY FRIEND. YOU HAVE DONE US ALL A GREAT SERVICE TONIGHT, MORE THAN YOU COULD EVER IMAGINE.
BUT SPEED IS OF THE ESSENCE. I'LL TAKE TALON NOW... BACK HOME. GOODBYE, YOUNG MAN.
TALON, HUH? YOU GUYS HAVE SOME PRETTY FANCY NAMES.
MINE'S MANX, MANX AMERICA. AND I'M GOING WITH YOU.
AIN'T NOTHIN BACK THERE FOR ME, EXCEPT DEATH, AND SUDDENLY I FEEL GOOD ABOUT LIVIN' AGAIN. YA GOTTA LET ME COME.
WELL, MR. UH.... AMERICA, YOU CAN'T GO WITH US. NO ONE CAN. IT'S TOO RISKY, WE DON'T KNOW ANYTHING ABOUT YOU.
YEAH, WELL I DIDN'T KNOW ANYTHING ABOUT YOUR BOY TALON EITHER WHEN I SAVED HIS LIFE. SEEMS LIKE YOU COULD DO THE SAME FOR ME, CAUSE IF I LEAVE, I'M A DEAD MAN. ONLY YOU CAN STOP THAT FROM HAPPININ'.
I'M AFRAID HE'S RIGHT, BRONNIS. OUR CODE OF HONOR IS VERY CLEAR. A LIFE FOR A LIFE. IT'S A STRANGE IRONY AT PLAY.
IT'S YOUR DAMN FOOL CODE, NOT MINE. THIS IS A VERY BIG MISTAKE, I TELL YOU.
BUT I WARN YOU, MANX, ONCE YOU ARE WITH US, YOU CAN NEVER GO BACK TO YOUR WORLD AGAIN-- YOU WILL NEVER BE THE SAME.
LET'S GET GOING.
ONE LAST ROOF-TOP.
NICE NEIGH-BORHOOD YOU GUYS LIVE IN. MUST BE LOW RENT.

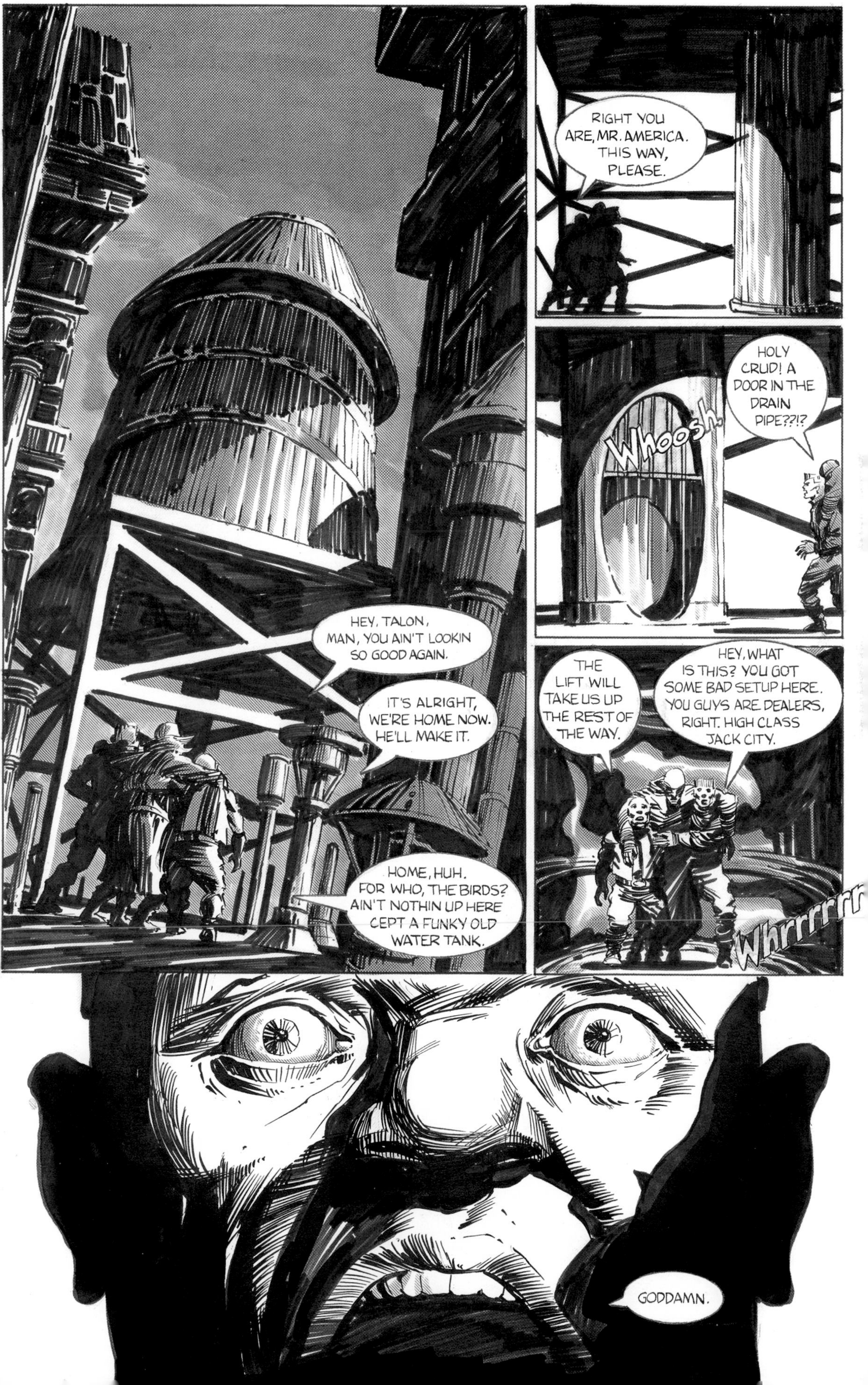
HEY, TALON, MAN, YOU AIN'T LOOKIN SO GOOD AGAIN.
IT'S ALRIGHT, WE'RE HOME NOW. HE'LL MAKE IT.
HOME, HUH. FOR WHO, THE BIRDS? AIN'T NOTHIN UP HERE CEPT A FUNKY OLD WATER TANK.
RIGHT YOU ARE, MR. AMERICA. THIS WAY, PLEASE.
WHOOSH
HOLY CRUD! A DOOR IN THE DRAIN PIPE??!?
THE LIFT WILL TAKE US UP THE REST OF THE WAY.
HEY, WHAT IS THIS? YOU GOT SOME BAD SETUP HERE. YOU GUYS ARE DEALERS, RIGHT. HIGH CLASS JACK CITY.
Whrrrrrr
GODDAMN.

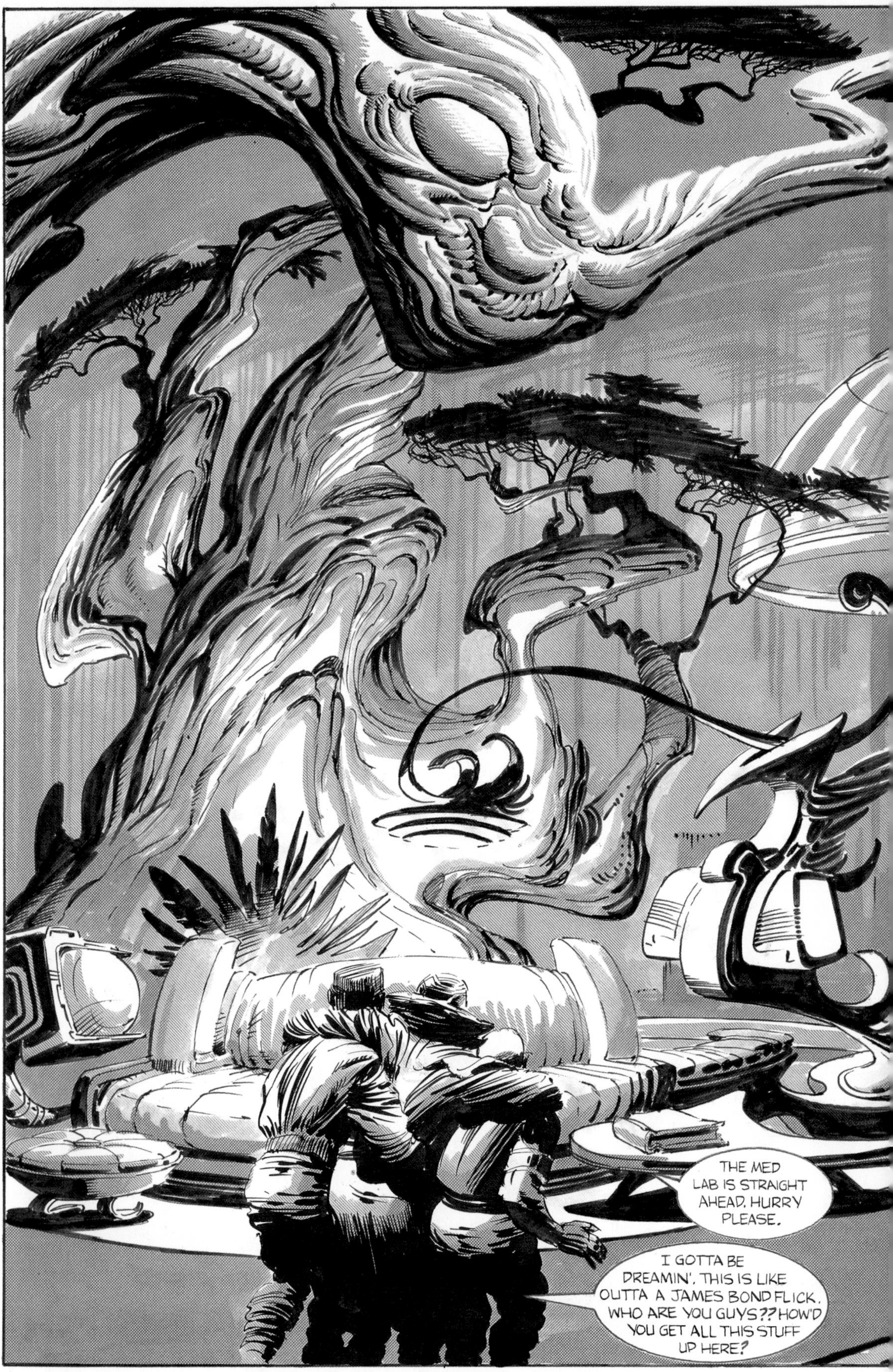
THE MED LAB IS STRAIGHT AHEAD. HURRY PLEASE.
I GOTTA BE DREAMIN'. THIS IS LIKE OUTTA A JAMES BOND FLICK. WHO ARE YOU GUYS?? HOW'D YOU GET ALL THIS STUFF UP HERE?

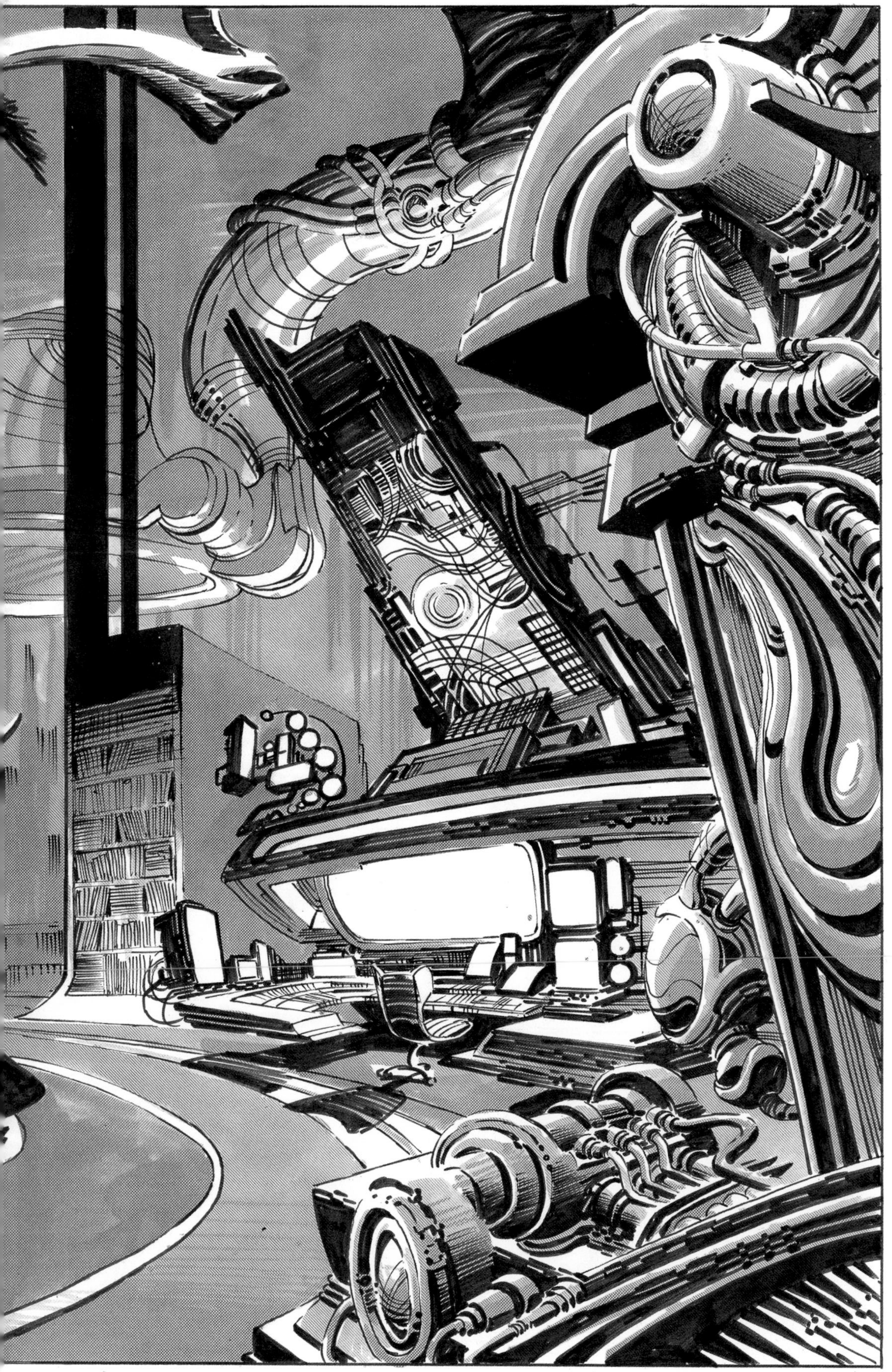

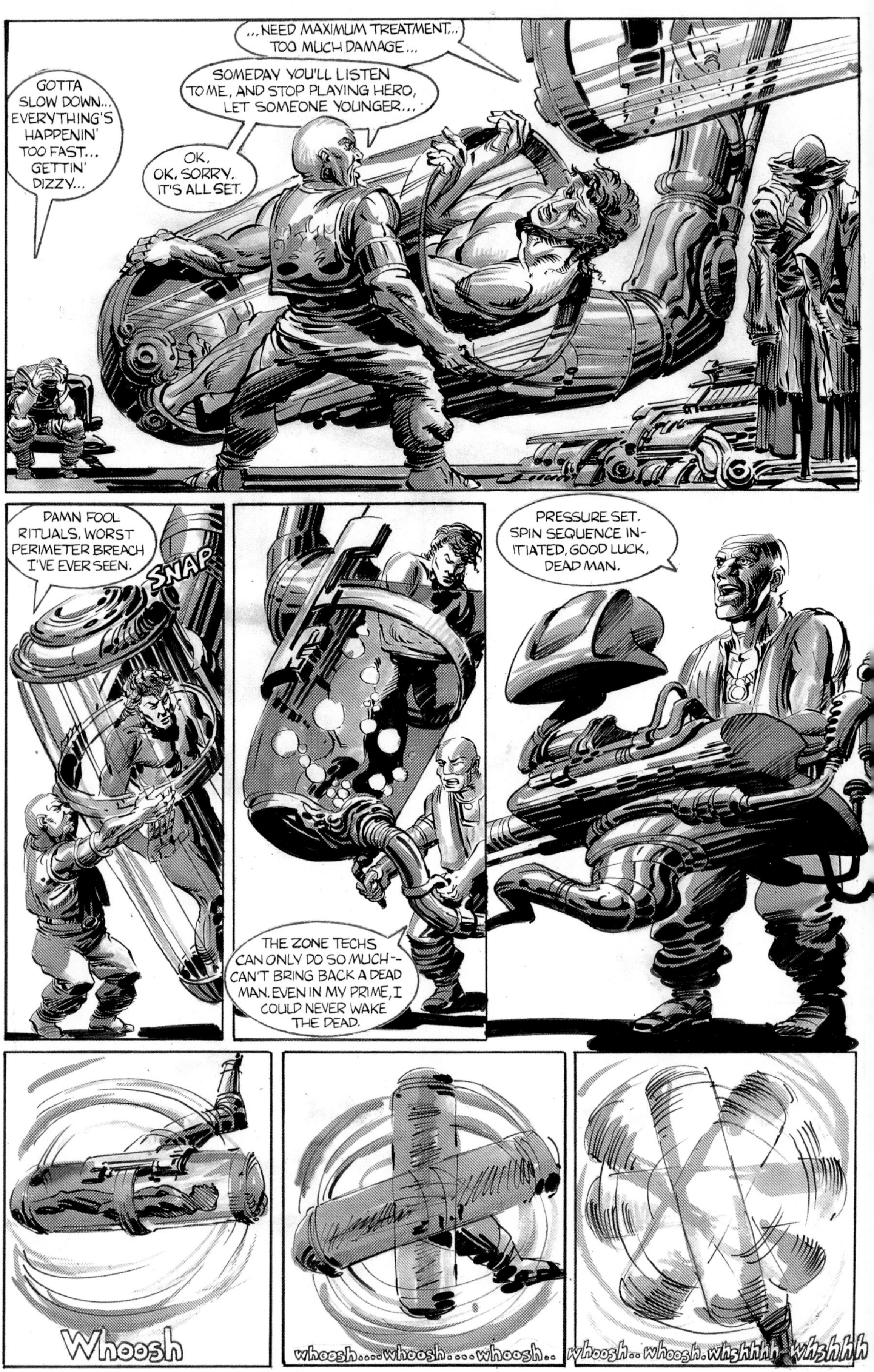
GOTTA SLOW DOWN... EVERYTHING'S HAPPENIN' TOO FAST... GETTIN' DIZZY...
...NEED MAXIMUM TREATMENT... TOO MUCH DAMAGE...
SOMEDAY YOU'LL LISTEN TO ME, AND STOP PLAYING HERO, LET SOMEONE YOUNGER...
OK, OK, SORRY. IT'S ALL SET.
DAMN FOOL RITUALS, WORST PERIMETER BREACH I'VE EVER SEEN.
SNAP
THE ZONE TECHS CAN ONLY DO SO MUCH-- CAN'T BRING BACK A DEAD MAN. EVEN IN MY PRIME, I COULD NEVER WAKE THE DEAD.
PRESSURE SET. SPIN SEQUENCE INITIATED, GOOD LUCK, DEAD MAN.
Whoosh
whoosh....whoosh....whoosh..
whoosh..whoosh.whshhhh whshhh

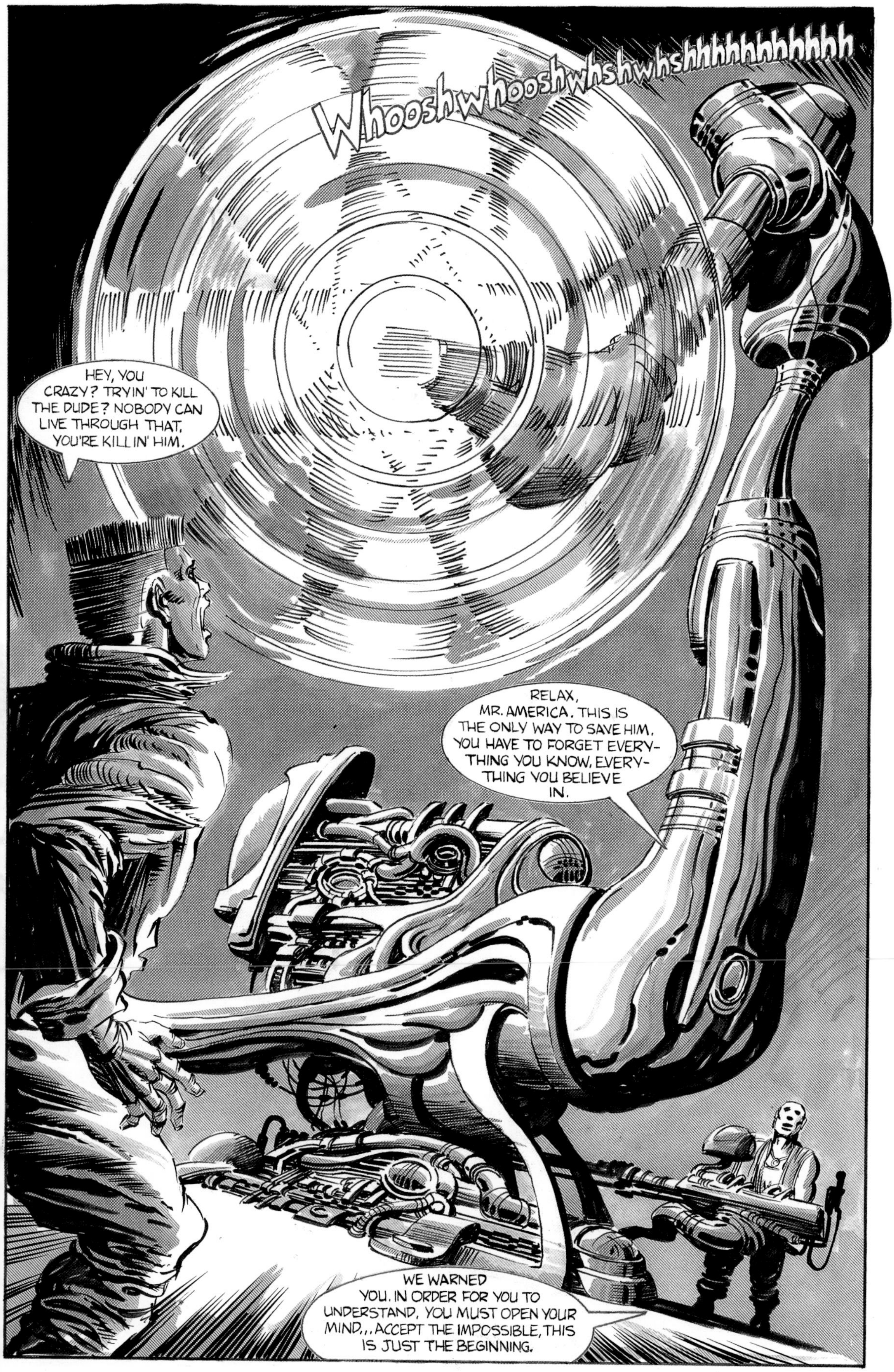
Whooshwhooshwhshwhshhhhhhhhhh
HEY, YOU CRAZY? TRYIN' TO KILL THE DUDE? NOBODY CAN LIVE THROUGH THAT. YOU'RE KILLIN' HIM.
RELAX, MR. AMERICA. THIS IS THE ONLY WAY TO SAVE HIM. YOU HAVE TO FORGET EVERYTHING YOU KNOW, EVERYTHING YOU BELIEVE IN.
WE WARNED YOU. IN ORDER FOR YOU TO UNDERSTAND, YOU MUST OPEN YOUR MIND,,, ACCEPT THE IMPOSSIBLE, THIS IS JUST THE BEGINNING.

YEAH, AND I'M BEGINNING TO GET SICK, NEVER FELT SO TIRED BEFORE. OK, MYSTERY MAN, YA GOT SOMETHIN' TO FIX ME UP WITH.

I COULD USE A LITTLE HELP TOO, YA KNOW?

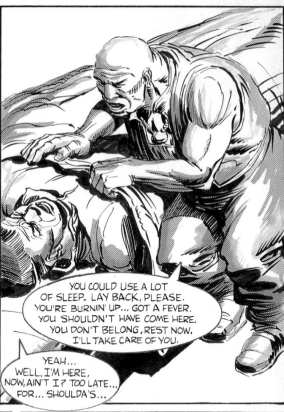

YOU COULD USE A LOT OF SLEEP. LAY BACK, PLEASE. YOU'RE BURNIN' UP... GOT A FEVER. YOU SHOULDN'T HAVE COME HERE, YOU DON'T BELONG, REST NOW. I'LL TAKE CARE OF YOU.

YEAH... WELL, I'M HERE, NOW, AIN'T I? TOO LATE... FOR... SHOULDA'S...

SLEEP, SLEEP, MR. AMERICA, YOU'LL FEEL FINE WHEN YOU WAKE UP.

...YER A REAL PAL... BETTER START GETTIN'... USED... TO... MEEEEE......

THE QUESTION IS, MY FRIEND, CAN YOU GET USED TO US?

I HOPE WE KNOW WHAT WE'RE DOING, TALON. THIS BOY COULD DESTROY US. THERE'S TOO MUCH AT STAKE TO RIDE IT ALL ON A GAMBLE.

YOU NEVER WOULD LISTEN TO ME. I'VE TRIED TO PROTECT YOU ALL THESE CENTURIES,,, BUT IT'S ALL SPINNING OUT OF CONTROL NOW. WHAT MUST I DO? IS IT ALREADY TOO LATE?

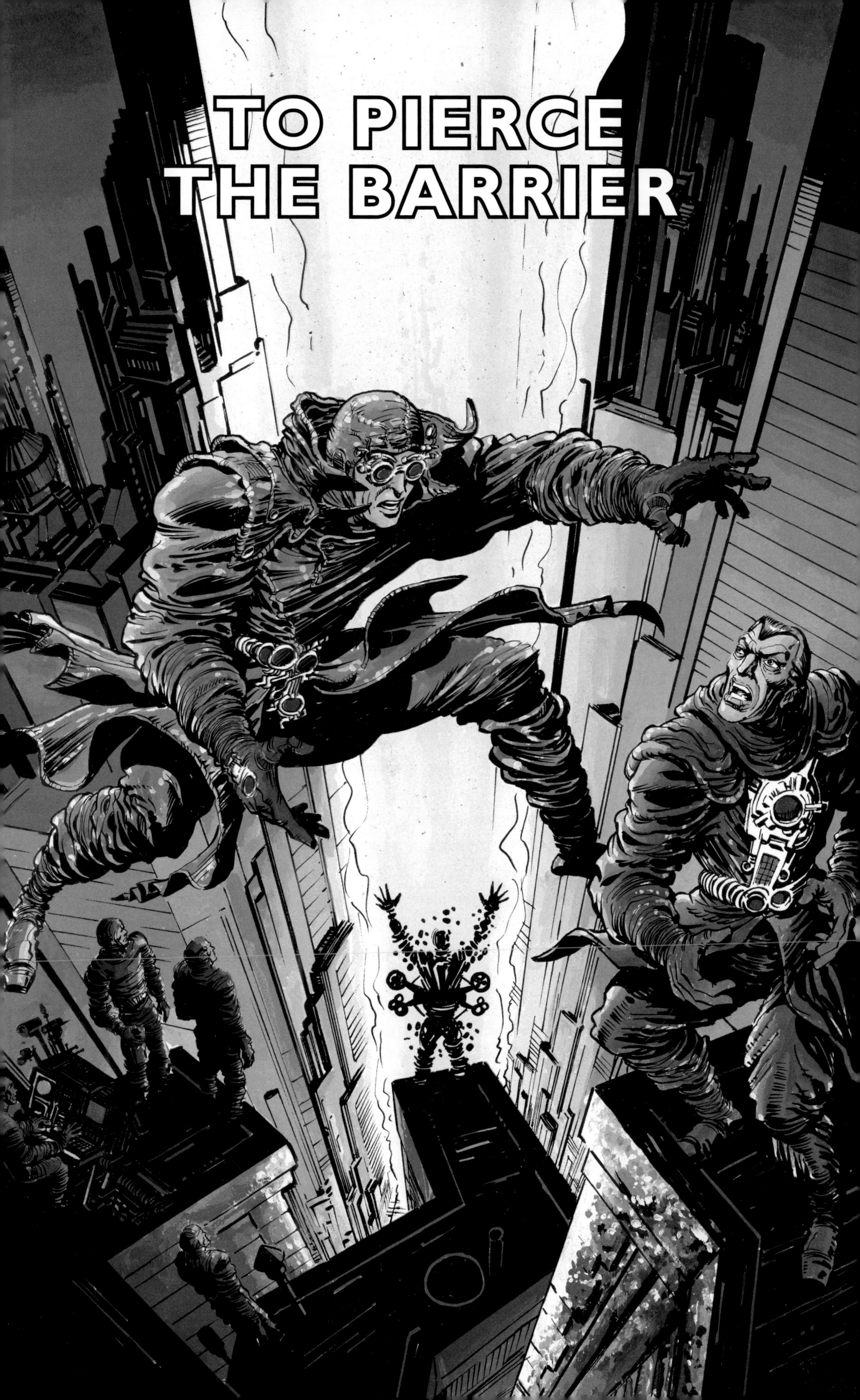
TO PIERCE THE BARRIER

ZONE GOGGLES represent a technology vastly superior to anything we have today. Our testing indicates that they detect magnetic field line disturbances similar to the way infrared lenses detect heat. According to Mr. Bronnis, the transistor-like parts around the frames are bitalic amplifiers, the goggles' power source.

Working on the principle of static field hyperization, electrical charges generated by the bitalic amplifiers sensitize the lenses to either a specific selected wavelength in Command Mode or optimum local wavelengths in Auto-Select.

The protruding device on the wearer's right side is the Auto-Select Sensor Array, which permits the passage of ambient light or any of the standard wavelengths, including infrared, ultraviolet, radio, and X-ray.

The extended device on the left side is the environmental sensor array (ESA), which detects and measures small changes in magnetic field conditions. The protrusion on the upper left is the distance-sensing OZMOS device, or Over-the-horizon Zone Magnetic Oscillation Sensor. Similar to backscatter radar, it allows the wearer to observe conditions in any Zone on Earth.

The device on the upper right is a Dimension Distortion Sensor (DDS). It is used to anticipate impending changes in perimeter field strength. All functions and data measurements can be viewed in the goggles' heads-up Peripheral Input Display (PID).

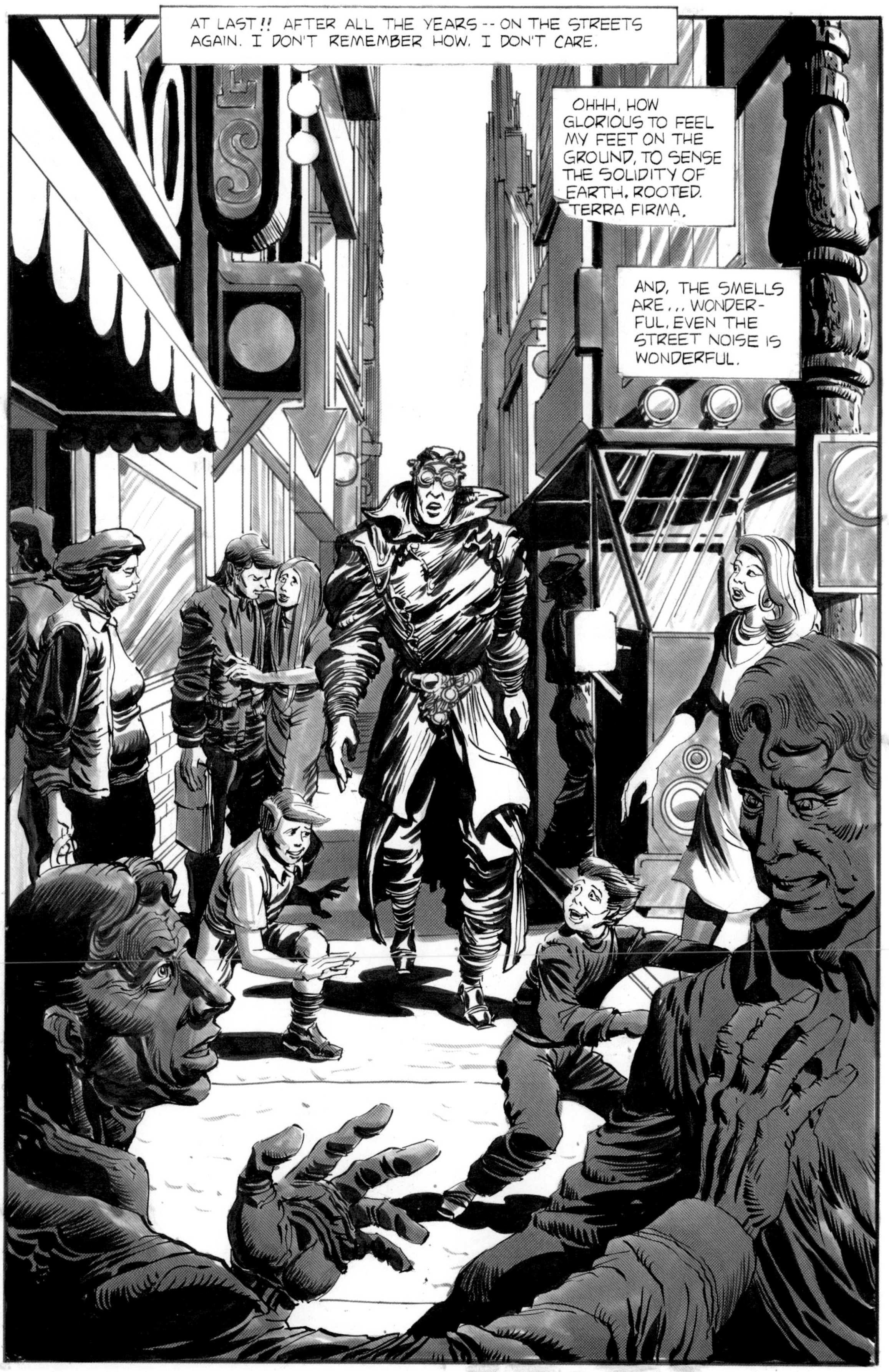
AT LAST!! AFTER ALL THE YEARS -- ON THE STREETS AGAIN. I DON'T REMEMBER HOW. I DON'T CARE.
OHHH, HOW GLORIOUS TO FEEL MY FEET ON THE GROUND, TO SENSE THE SOLIDITY OF EARTH. ROOTED. TERRA FIRMA.
AND, THE SMELLS ARE... WONDERFUL. EVEN THE STREET NOISE IS WONDERFUL.

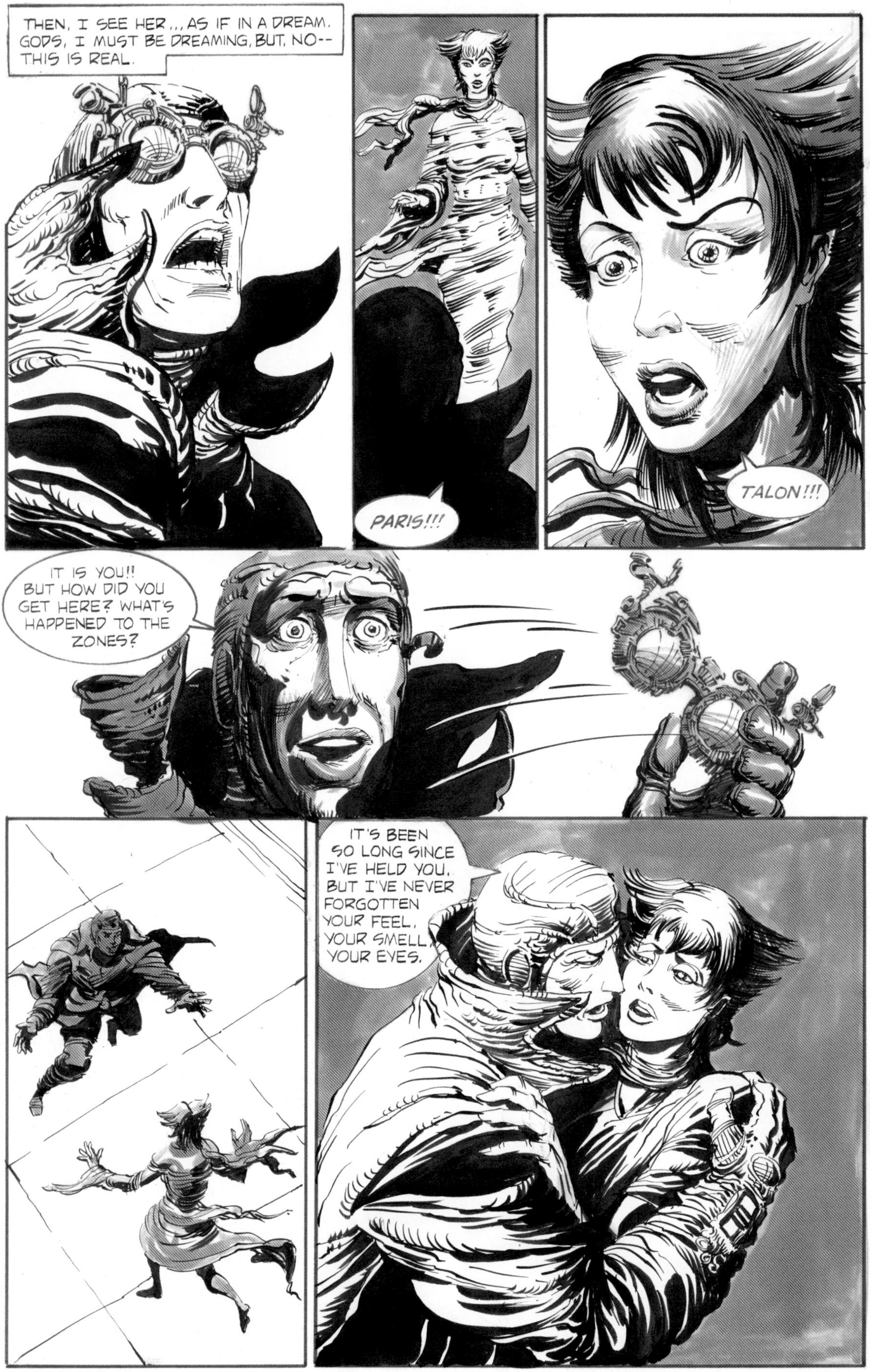
THEN, I SEE HER..., AS IF IN A DREAM. GODS, I MUST BE DREAMING, BUT, NO-- THIS IS REAL.
PARIS!!!
TALON!!!
IT IS YOU!! BUT HOW DID YOU GET HERE? WHAT'S HAPPENED TO THE ZONES?
IT'S BEEN SO LONG SINCE I'VE HELD YOU, BUT I'VE NEVER FORGOTTEN YOUR FEEL, YOUR SMELL, YOUR EYES.

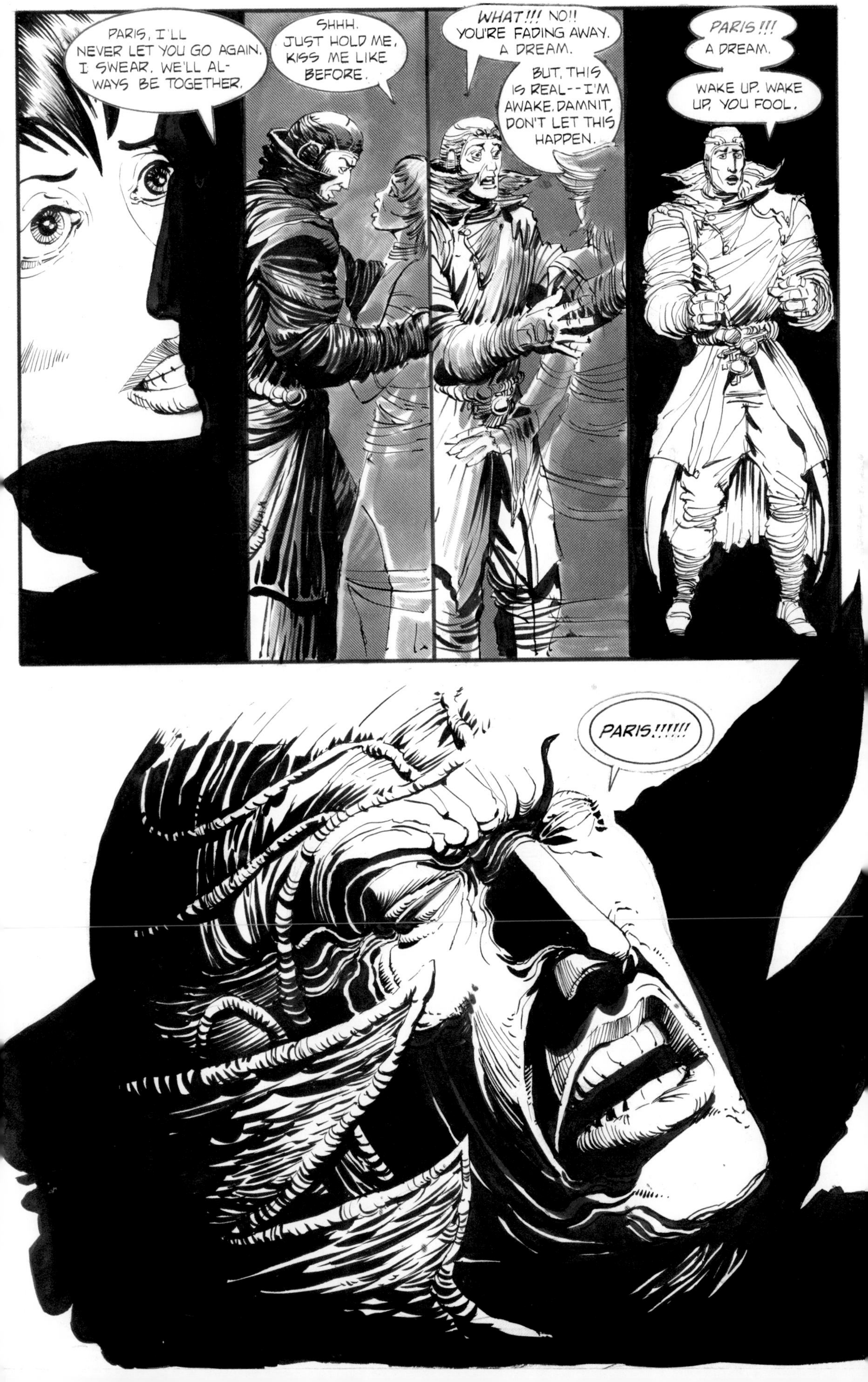
PARIS, I'LL NEVER LET YOU GO AGAIN. I SWEAR. WE'LL AL-WAYS BE TOGETHER.
SHHH. JUST HOLD ME, KISS ME LIKE BEFORE.
WHAT!!! NO!! YOU'RE FADING AWAY. A DREAM.
BUT, THIS IS REAL--I'M AWAKE. DAMNIT, DON'T LET THIS HAPPEN.
PARIS!!! A DREAM.
WAKE UP. WAKE UP, YOU FOOL.
PARIS!!!!!!

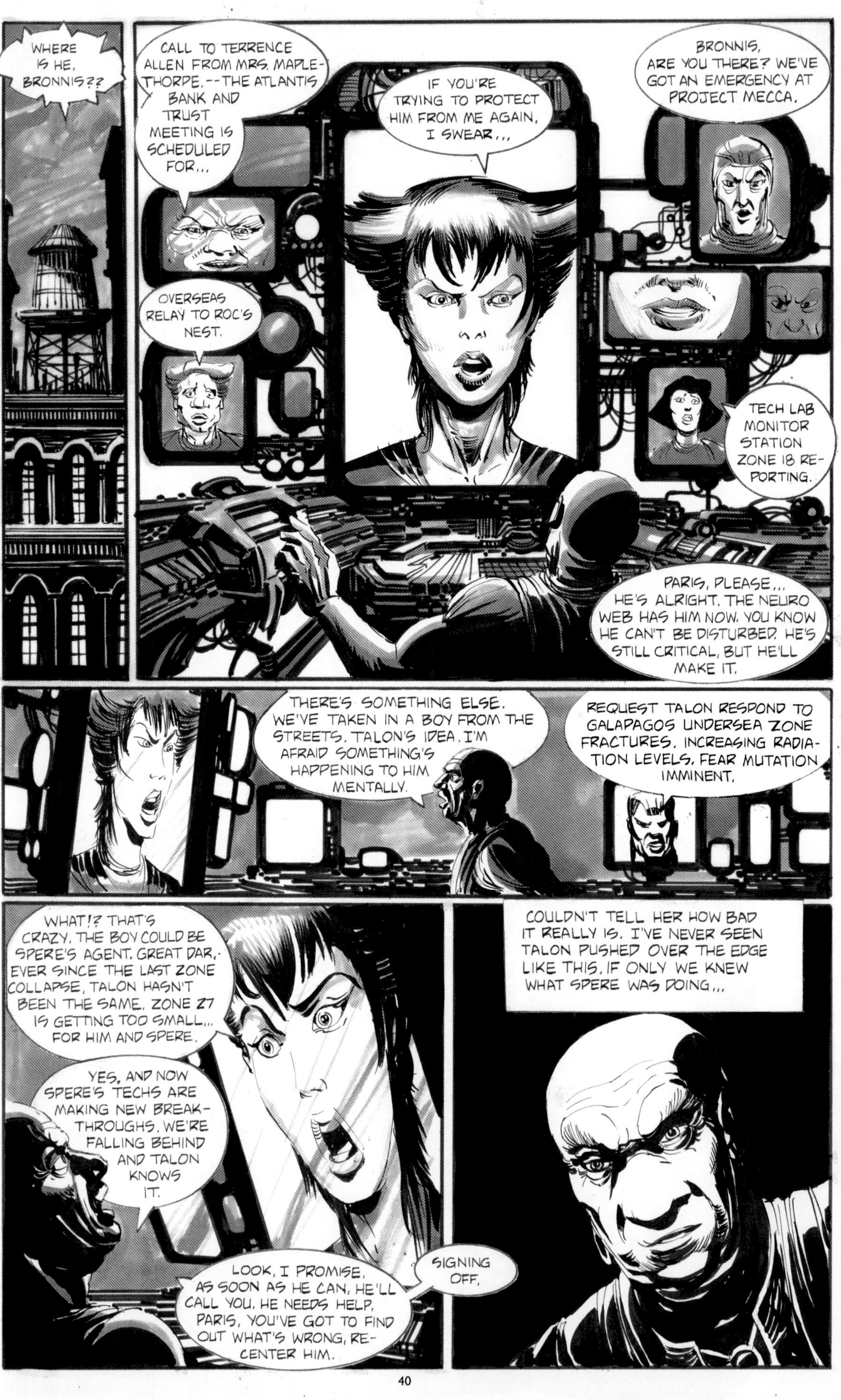
WHERE IS HE, BRONNIS??
CALL TO TERRENCE ALLEN FROM MRS. MAPLE-THORPE.--THE ATLANTIS BANK AND TRUST MEETING IS SCHEDULED FOR...
IF YOU'RE TRYING TO PROTECT HIM FROM ME AGAIN, I SWEAR...
BRONNIS, ARE YOU THERE? WE'VE GOT AN EMERGENCY AT PROJECT MECCA.
OVERSEAS RELAY TO ROC'S NEST.
TECH LAB MONITOR STATION ZONE 18 RE-PORTING.
PARIS, PLEASE... HE'S ALRIGHT. THE NEURO WEB HAS HIM NOW. YOU KNOW HE CAN'T BE DISTURBED. HE'S STILL CRITICAL, BUT HE'LL MAKE IT.
THERE'S SOMETHING ELSE. WE'VE TAKEN IN A BOY FROM THE STREETS. TALON'S IDEA. I'M AFRAID SOMETHING'S HAPPENING TO HIM MENTALLY.
REQUEST TALON RESPOND TO GALAPAGOS UNDERSEA ZONE FRACTURES. INCREASING RADIA-TION LEVELS. FEAR MUTATION IMMINENT.
WHAT!? THAT'S CRAZY. THE BOY COULD BE SPERE'S AGENT. GREAT DAR. EVER SINCE THE LAST ZONE COLLAPSE, TALON HASN'T BEEN THE SAME. ZONE 27 IS GETTING TOO SMALL... FOR HIM AND SPERE.
YES. AND NOW SPERE'S TECHS ARE MAKING NEW BREAK-THROUGHS. WE'RE FALLING BEHIND AND TALON KNOWS IT.
LOOK, I PROMISE. AS SOON AS HE CAN, HE'LL CALL YOU. HE NEEDS HELP. PARIS, YOU'VE GOT TO FIND OUT WHAT'S WRONG. RE-CENTER HIM.
SIGNING OFF.
COULDN'T TELL HER HOW BAD IT REALLY IS. I'VE NEVER SEEN TALON PUSHED OVER THE EDGE LIKE THIS. IF ONLY WE KNEW WHAT SPERE WAS DOING...

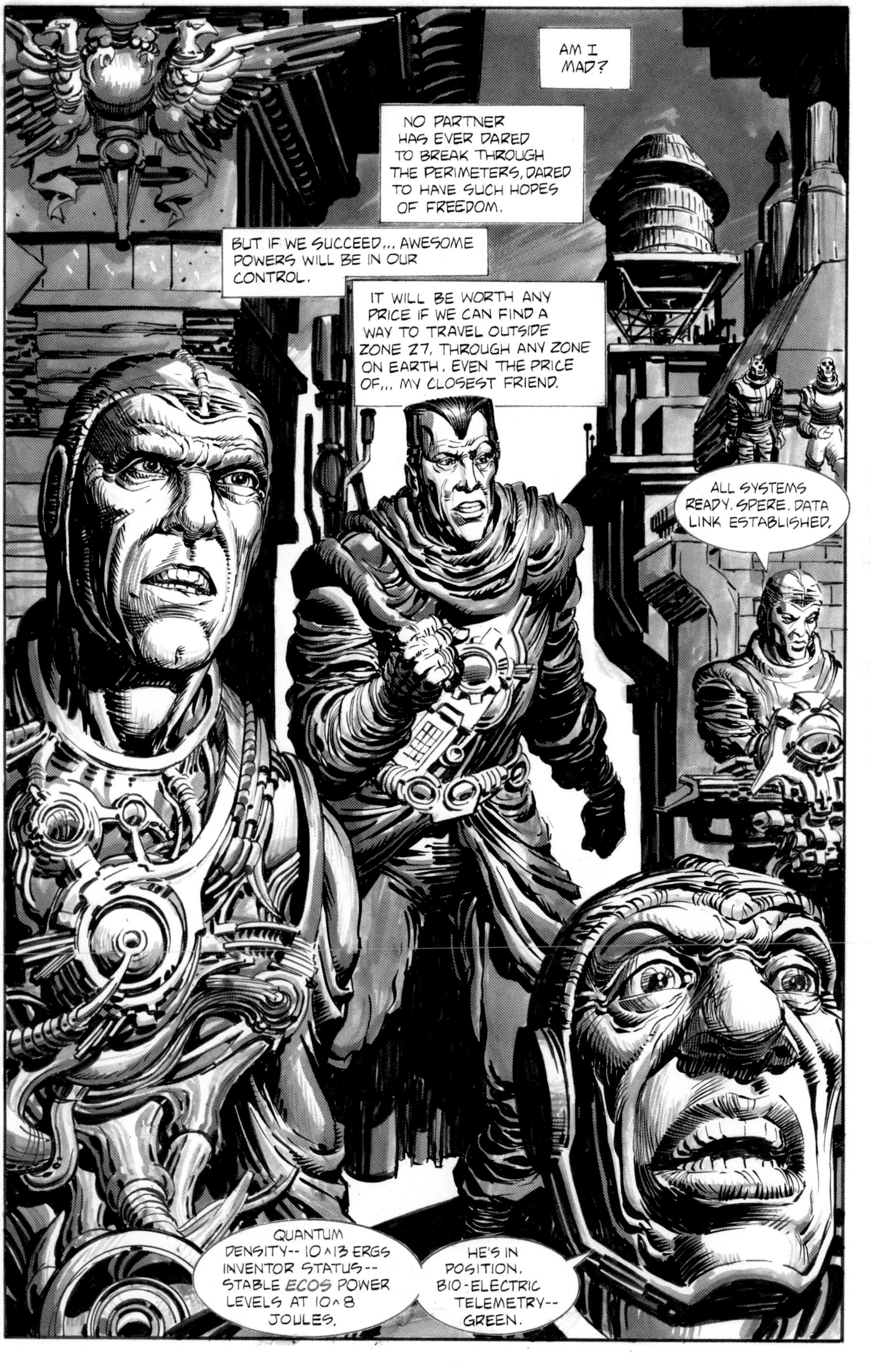
AM I MAD?
NO PARTNER HAS EVER DARED TO BREAK THROUGH THE PERIMETERS, DARED TO HAVE SUCH HOPES OF FREEDOM.
BUT IF WE SUCCEED... AWESOME POWERS WILL BE IN OUR CONTROL.
IT WILL BE WORTH ANY PRICE IF WE CAN FIND A WAY TO TRAVEL OUTSIDE ZONE 27, THROUGH ANY ZONE ON EARTH. EVEN THE PRICE OF... MY CLOSEST FRIEND.
ALL SYSTEMS READY, SPERE. DATA LINK ESTABLISHED.
QUANTUM DENSITY-- 10^13 ERGS INVENTOR STATUS-- STABLE ECOS POWER LEVELS AT 10^8 JOULES.
HE'S IN POSITION. BIO-ELECTRIC TELEMETRY-- GREEN.

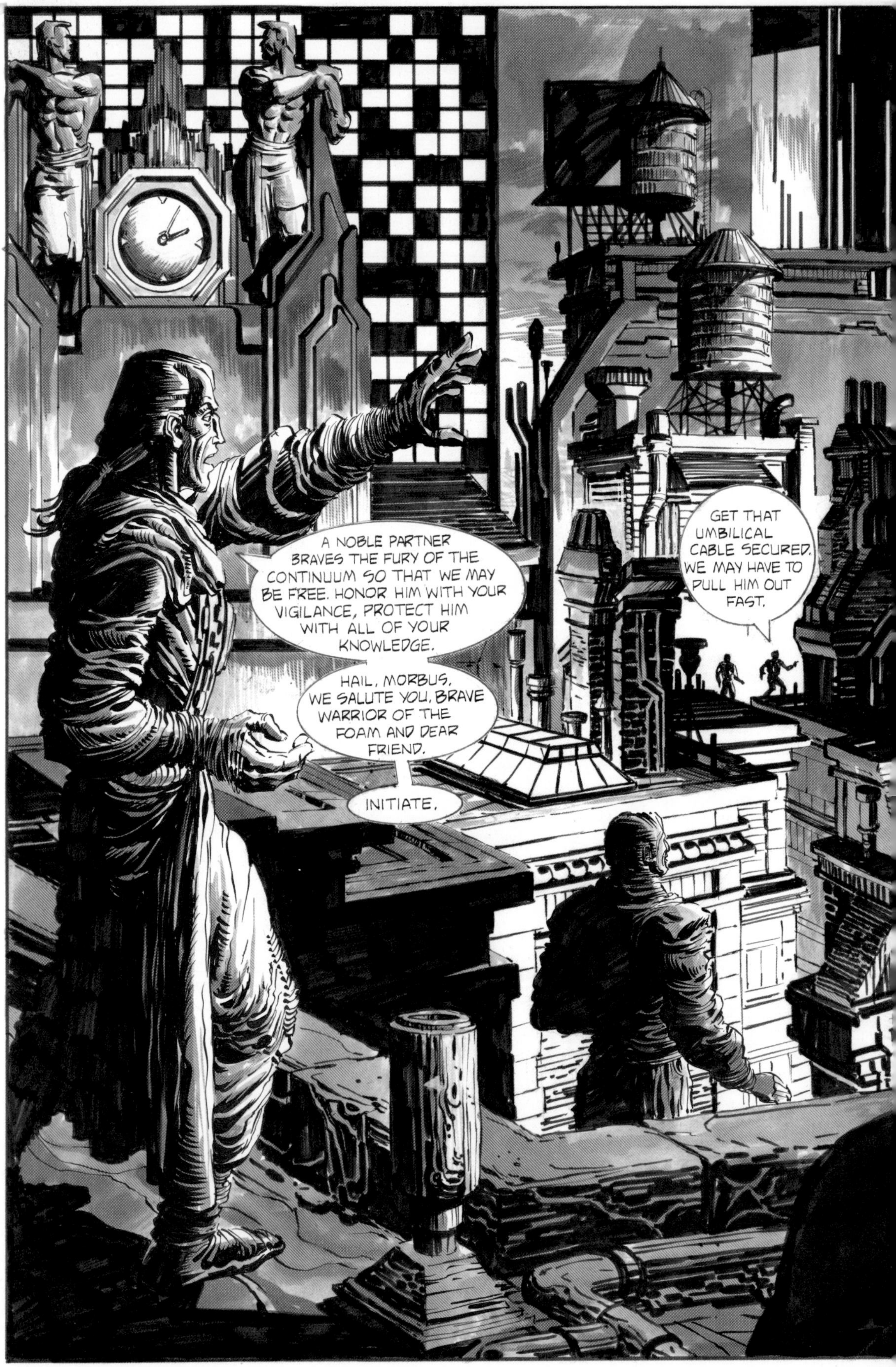
A NOBLE PARTNER BRAVES THE FURY OF THE CONTINUUM SO THAT WE MAY BE FREE. HONOR HIM WITH YOUR VIGILANCE, PROTECT HIM WITH ALL OF YOUR KNOWLEDGE.
HAIL, MORBUS, WE SALUTE YOU, BRAVE WARRIOR OF THE FOAM AND DEAR FRIEND.
INITIATE.
GET THAT UMBILICAL CABLE SECURED. WE MAY HAVE TO PULL HIM OUT FAST.

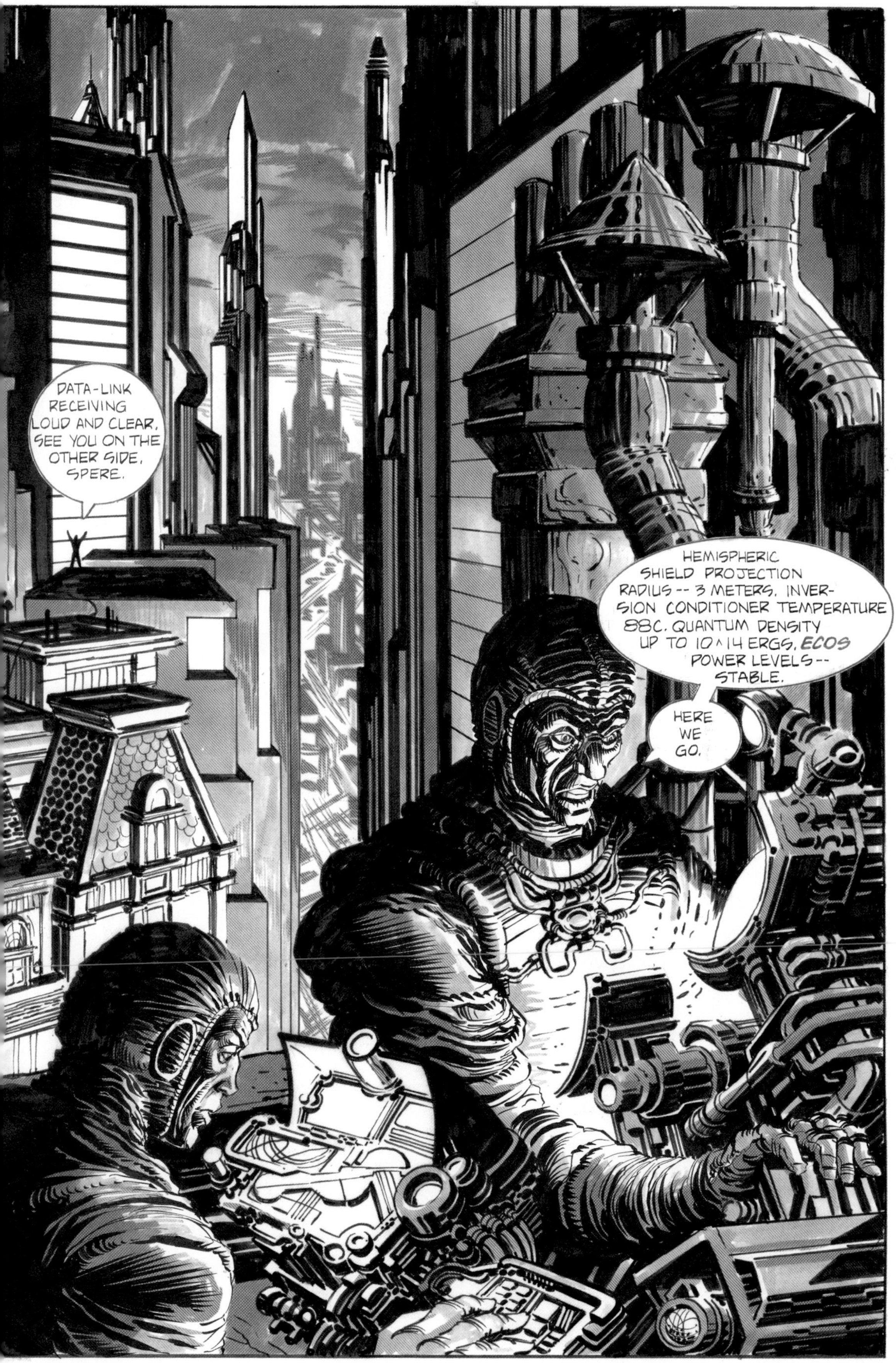
DATA-LINK RECEIVING LOUD AND CLEAR. SEE YOU ON THE OTHER SIDE, SPERE.
HEMISPHERIC SHIELD PROJECTION RADIUS -- 3 METERS. INVERSION CONDITIONER TEMPERATURE 88C. QUANTUM DENSITY UP TO 10^14 ERGS. ECOS POWER LEVELS -- STABLE.
HERE WE GO.

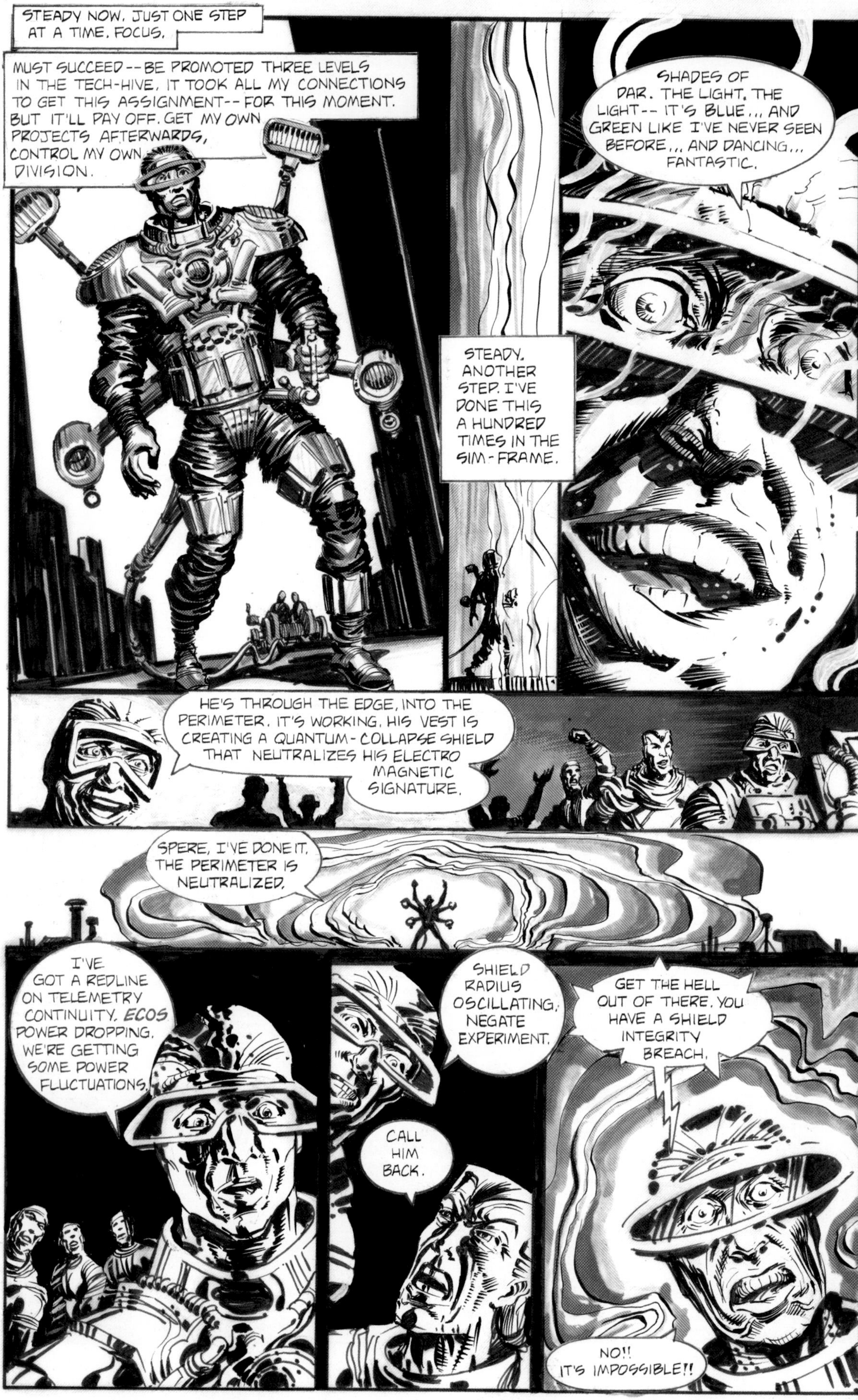
STEADY NOW. JUST ONE STEP AT A TIME. FOCUS.
MUST SUCCEED-- BE PROMOTED THREE LEVELS IN THE TECH-HIVE. IT TOOK ALL MY CONNECTIONS TO GET THIS ASSIGNMENT-- FOR THIS MOMENT. BUT IT'LL PAY OFF. GET MY OWN PROJECTS AFTERWARDS, CONTROL MY OWN DIVISION.
STEADY. ANOTHER STEP. I'VE DONE THIS A HUNDRED TIMES IN THE SIM-FRAME.
SHADES OF DAR. THE LIGHT. THE LIGHT-- IT'S BLUE... AND GREEN LIKE I'VE NEVER SEEN BEFORE... AND DANCING... FANTASTIC.
HE'S THROUGH THE EDGE, INTO THE PERIMETER. IT'S WORKING. HIS VEST IS CREATING A QUANTUM-COLLAPSE SHIELD THAT NEUTRALIZES HIS ELECTRO MAGNETIC SIGNATURE.
SPERE, I'VE DONE IT. THE PERIMETER IS NEUTRALIZED.
I'VE GOT A REDLINE ON TELEMETRY CONTINUITY. ECOS POWER DROPPING. WE'RE GETTING SOME POWER FLUCTUATIONS.
SHIELD RADIUS OSCILLATING. NEGATE EXPERIMENT.
CALL HIM BACK.
GET THE HELL OUT OF THERE. YOU HAVE A SHIELD INTEGRITY BREACH.
NO!! IT'S IMPOSSIBLE!!

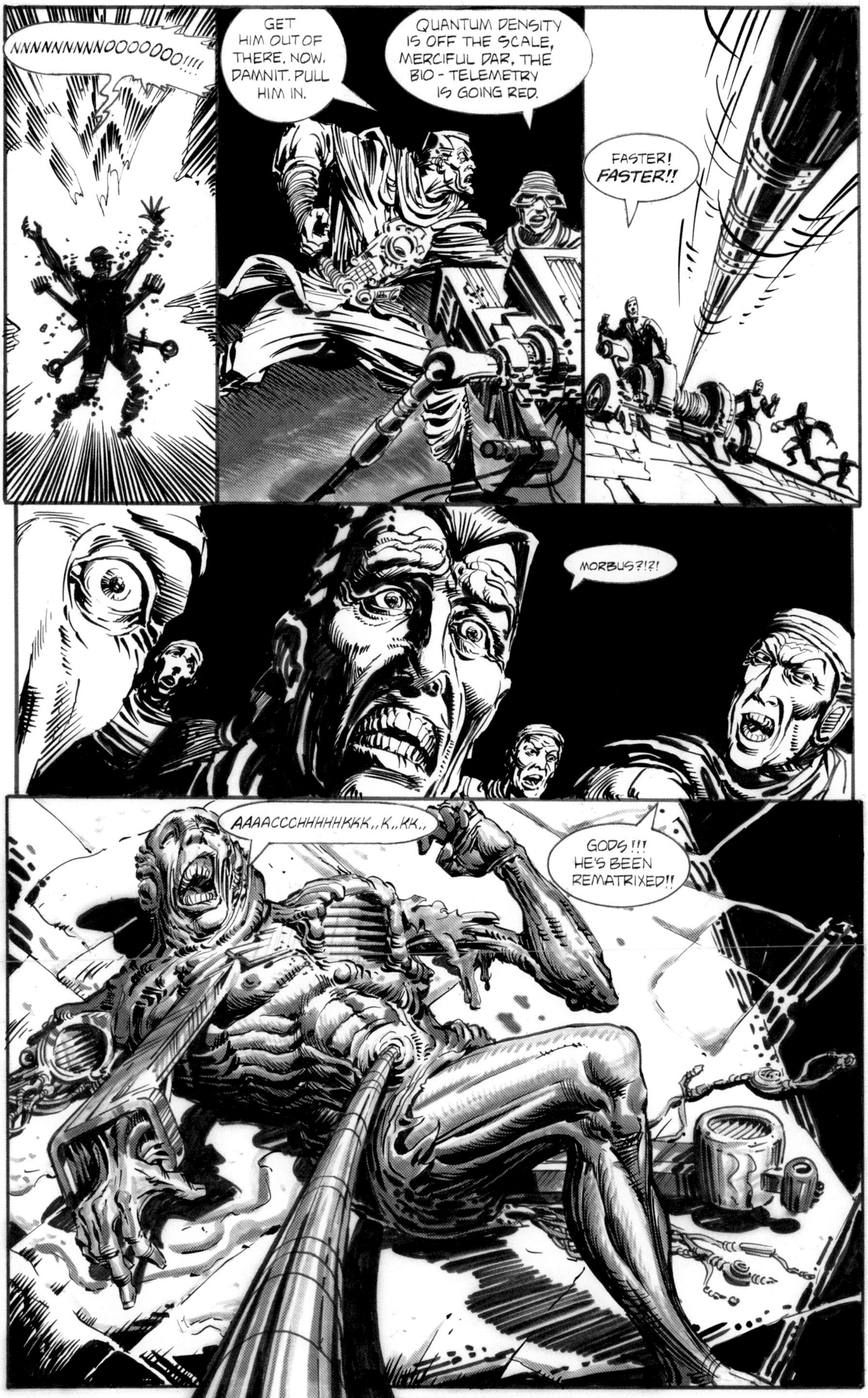
NNNNNNNNNOOOOOOO!!!!
GET HIM OUT OF THERE. NOW. DAMNIT. PULL HIM IN.
QUANTUM DENSITY IS OFF THE SCALE, MERCIFUL DAR. THE BIO - TELEMETRY IS GOING RED.
FASTER! FASTER!!
MORBUS?!?!
AAAACCCHHHHHHKKK,,K,,KK,,
GODS!!! HE'S BEEN REMATRIXED!!

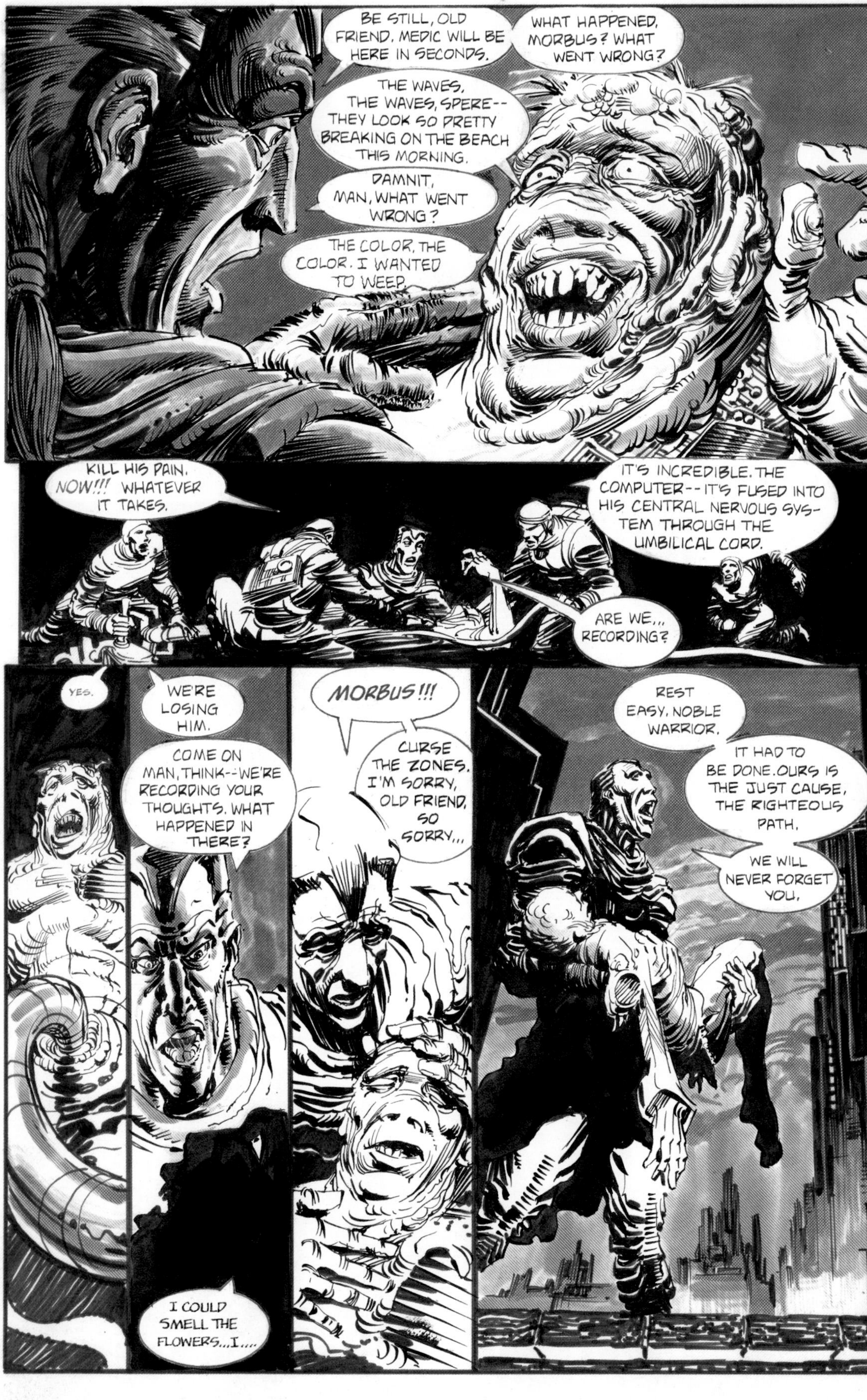
BE STILL, OLD FRIEND. MEDIC WILL BE HERE IN SECONDS.
WHAT HAPPENED, MORBUS? WHAT WENT WRONG?
THE WAVES, THE WAVES, SPERE-- THEY LOOK SO PRETTY BREAKING ON THE BEACH THIS MORNING.
DAMNIT, MAN, WHAT WENT WRONG?
THE COLOR, THE COLOR. I WANTED TO WEEP.
KILL HIS PAIN. NOW!!! WHATEVER IT TAKES.
IT'S INCREDIBLE. THE COMPUTER-- IT'S FUSED INTO HIS CENTRAL NERVOUS SYS-TEM THROUGH THE UMBILICAL CORD.
ARE WE... RECORDING?
YES.
WE'RE LOSING HIM.
COME ON MAN, THINK--WE'RE RECORDING YOUR THOUGHTS. WHAT HAPPENED IN THERE?
I COULD SMELL THE FLOWERS...I....
MORBUS!!!
CURSE THE ZONES. I'M SORRY, OLD FRIEND, SO SORRY...
REST EASY, NOBLE WARRIOR.
IT HAD TO BE DONE. OURS IS THE JUST CAUSE, THE RIGHTEOUS PATH.
WE WILL NEVER FORGET YOU.

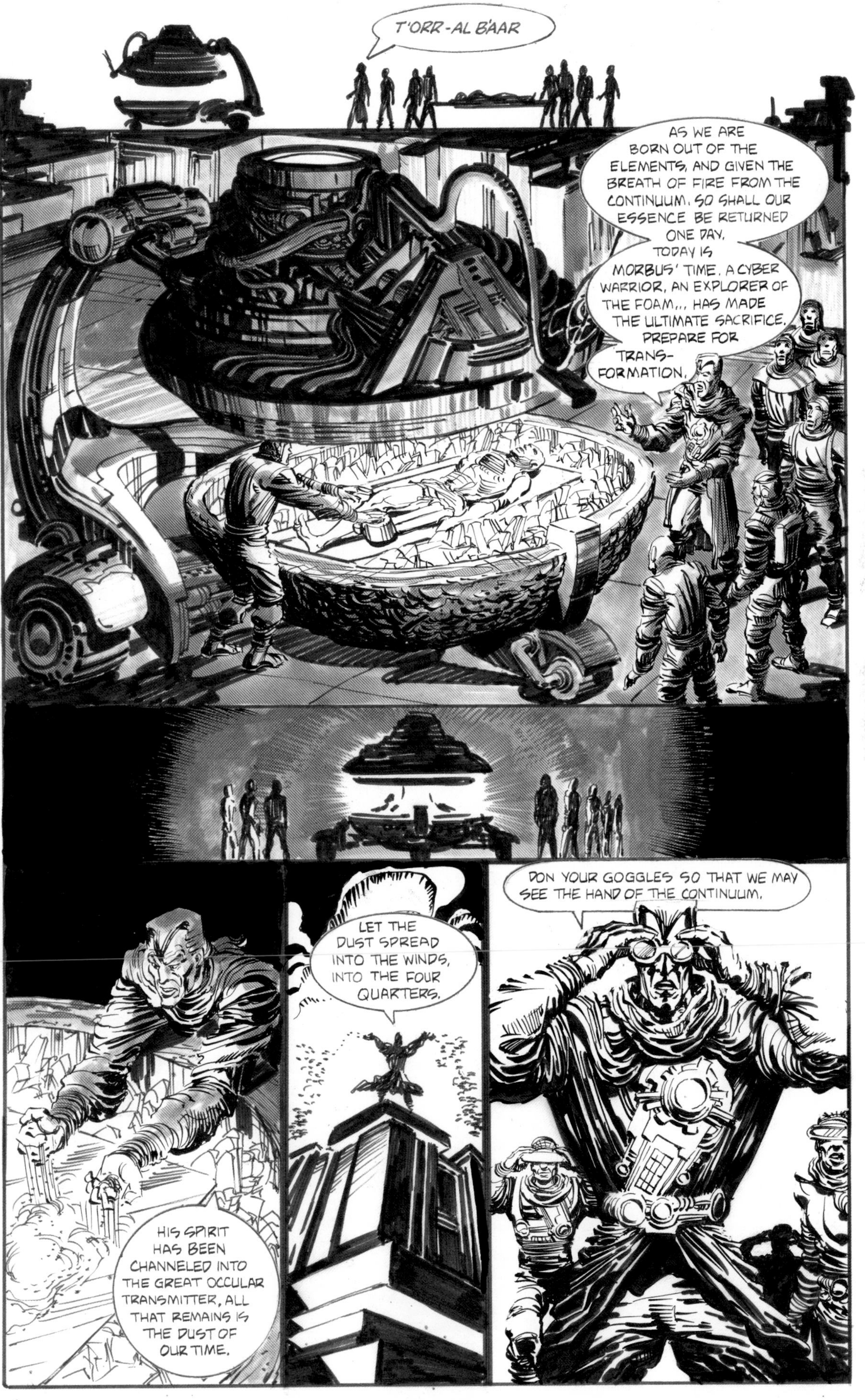
T'ORR-AL B'AAR
AS WE ARE BORN OUT OF THE ELEMENTS, AND GIVEN THE BREATH OF FIRE FROM THE CONTINUUM. SO SHALL OUR ESSENCE BE RETURNED ONE DAY.
TODAY IS MORBUS' TIME. A CYBER WARRIOR, AN EXPLORER OF THE FOAM... HAS MADE THE ULTIMATE SACRIFICE. PREPARE FOR TRANS-FORMATION.
HIS SPIRIT HAS BEEN CHANNELED INTO THE GREAT OCCULAR TRANSMITTER, ALL THAT REMAINS IS THE DUST OF OUR TIME.
LET THE DUST SPREAD INTO THE WINDS, INTO THE FOUR QUARTERS.
DON YOUR GOGGLES SO THAT WE MAY SEE THE HAND OF THE CONTINUUM.

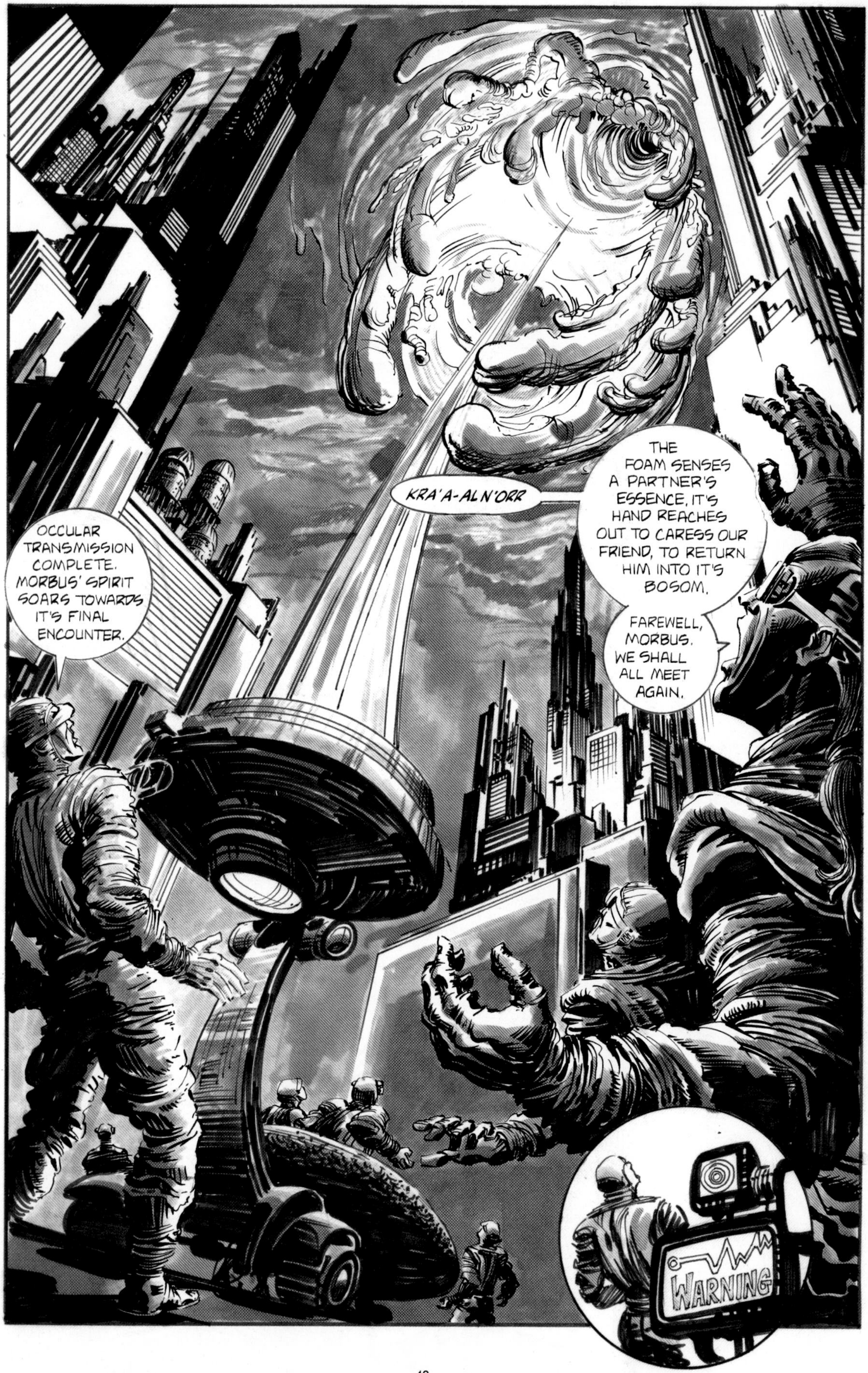
KRA'A-AL N'ORR
THE FOAM SENSES A PARTNER'S ESSENCE, IT'S HAND REACHES OUT TO CARESS OUR FRIEND, TO RETURN HIM INTO IT'S BOSOM.
OCCULAR TRANSMISSION COMPLETE. MORBUS' SPIRIT SOARS TOWARDS IT'S FINAL ENCOUNTER.
FAREWELL, MORBUS. WE SHALL ALL MEET AGAIN.
WARNING

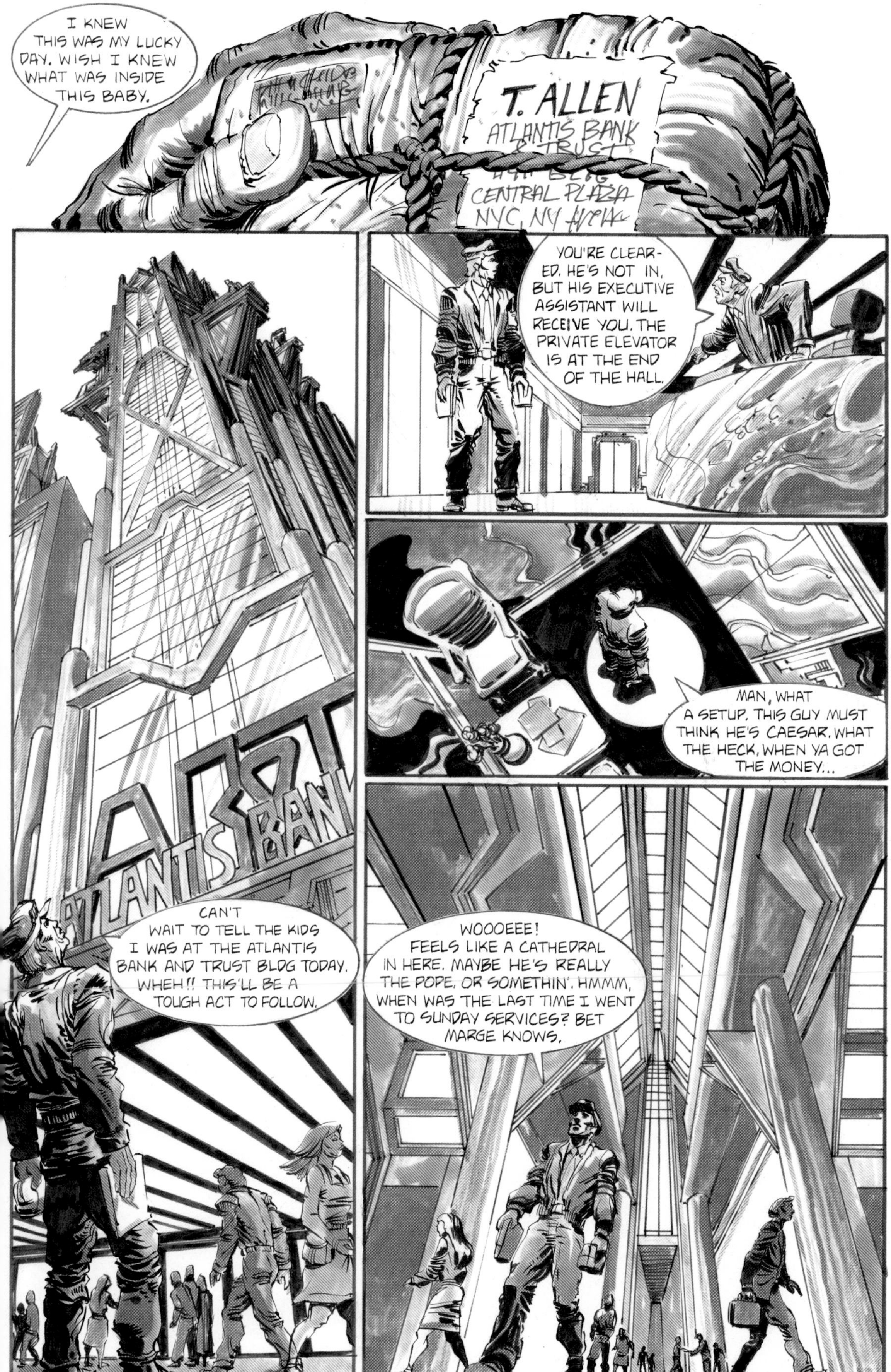
I KNEW THIS WAS MY LUCKY DAY. WISH I KNEW WHAT WAS INSIDE THIS BABY.
T. ALLEN
ATLANTIS BANK & TRUST
CENTRAL PLAZA
NYC, NY
YOU'RE CLEAR-ED. HE'S NOT IN, BUT HIS EXECUTIVE ASSISTANT WILL RECEIVE YOU. THE PRIVATE ELEVATOR IS AT THE END OF THE HALL.
MAN, WHAT A SETUP. THIS GUY MUST THINK HE'S CAESAR. WHAT THE HECK, WHEN YA GOT THE MONEY...
ATLANTIS BANK
CAN'T WAIT TO TELL THE KIDS I WAS AT THE ATLANTIS BANK AND TRUST BLDG TODAY. WHEH!! THIS'LL BE A TOUGH ACT TO FOLLOW.
WOOOEEE! FEELS LIKE A CATHEDRAL IN HERE. MAYBE HE'S REALLY THE POPE, OR SOMETHIN'. HMMM, WHEN WAS THE LAST TIME I WENT TO SUNDAY SERVICES? BET MARGE KNOWS.

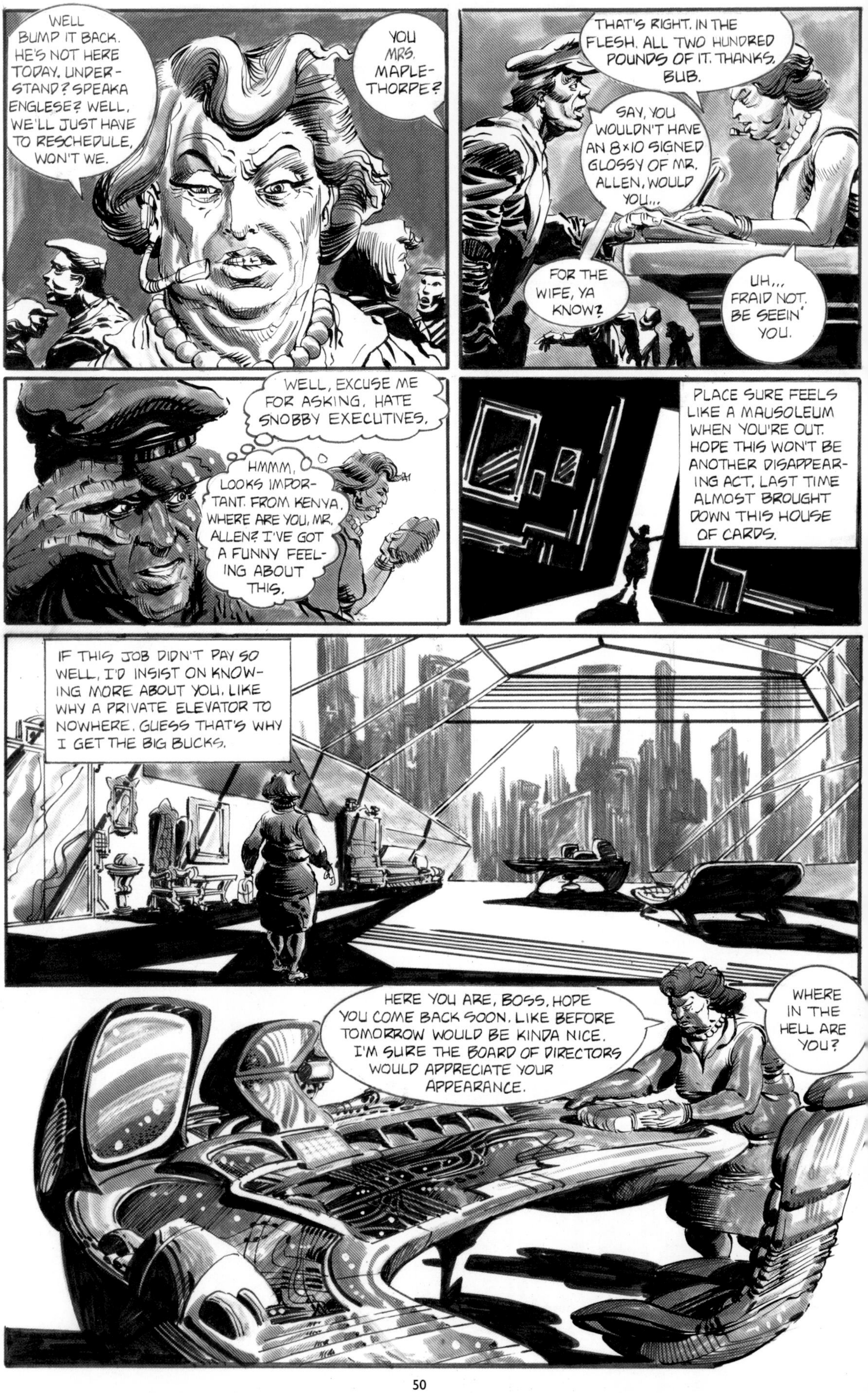
WELL BUMP IT BACK. HE'S NOT HERE TODAY. UNDERSTAND? SPEAKA ENGLESE? WELL, WE'LL JUST HAVE TO RESCHEDULE, WON'T WE.
YOU MRS. MAPLETHORPE?
THAT'S RIGHT. IN THE FLESH. ALL TWO HUNDRED POUNDS OF IT. THANKS, BUB.
SAY, YOU WOULDN'T HAVE AN 8×10 SIGNED GLOSSY OF MR. ALLEN, WOULD YOU...
FOR THE WIFE, YA KNOW?
UH... FRAID NOT. BE SEEIN' YOU.
WELL, EXCUSE ME FOR ASKING. HATE SNOBBY EXECUTIVES.
HMMM, LOOKS IMPORTANT. FROM KENYA. WHERE ARE YOU, MR. ALLEN? I'VE GOT A FUNNY FEELING ABOUT THIS.
PLACE SURE FEELS LIKE A MAUSOLEUM WHEN YOU'RE OUT. HOPE THIS WON'T BE ANOTHER DISAPPEARING ACT. LAST TIME ALMOST BROUGHT DOWN THIS HOUSE OF CARDS.
IF THIS JOB DIDN'T PAY SO WELL, I'D INSIST ON KNOWING MORE ABOUT YOU. LIKE WHY A PRIVATE ELEVATOR TO NOWHERE. GUESS THAT'S WHY I GET THE BIG BUCKS.
HERE YOU ARE, BOSS. HOPE YOU COME BACK SOON. LIKE BEFORE TOMORROW WOULD BE KINDA NICE. I'M SURE THE BOARD OF DIRECTORS WOULD APPRECIATE YOUR APPEARANCE.
WHERE IN THE HELL ARE YOU?

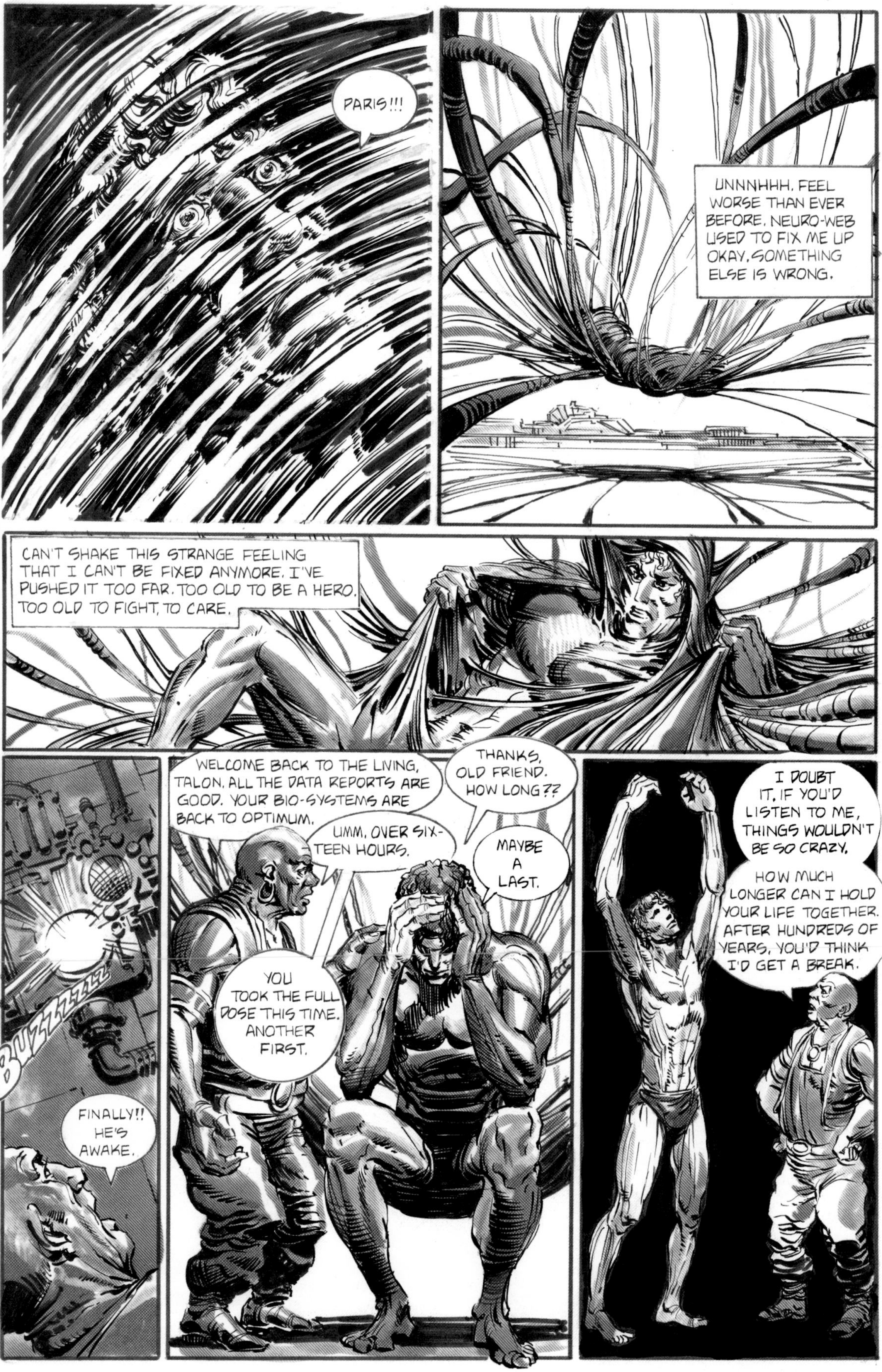
PARIS!!!
UNNNHHH. FEEL WORSE THAN EVER BEFORE. NEURO-WEB USED TO FIX ME UP OKAY. SOMETHING ELSE IS WRONG.
CAN'T SHAKE THIS STRANGE FEELING THAT I CAN'T BE FIXED ANYMORE. I'VE PUSHED IT TOO FAR. TOO OLD TO BE A HERO. TOO OLD TO FIGHT, TO CARE.
BUZZZZZZ
FINALLY!! HE'S AWAKE.
WELCOME BACK TO THE LIVING, TALON. ALL THE DATA REPORTS ARE GOOD. YOUR BIO-SYSTEMS ARE BACK TO OPTIMUM.
THANKS, OLD FRIEND. HOW LONG??
UMM, OVER SIX-TEEN HOURS.
MAYBE A LAST.
YOU TOOK THE FULL DOSE THIS TIME. ANOTHER FIRST.
I DOUBT IT. IF YOU'D LISTEN TO ME, THINGS WOULDN'T BE SO CRAZY.
HOW MUCH LONGER CAN I HOLD YOUR LIFE TOGETHER. AFTER HUNDREDS OF YEARS, YOU'D THINK I'D GET A BREAK.

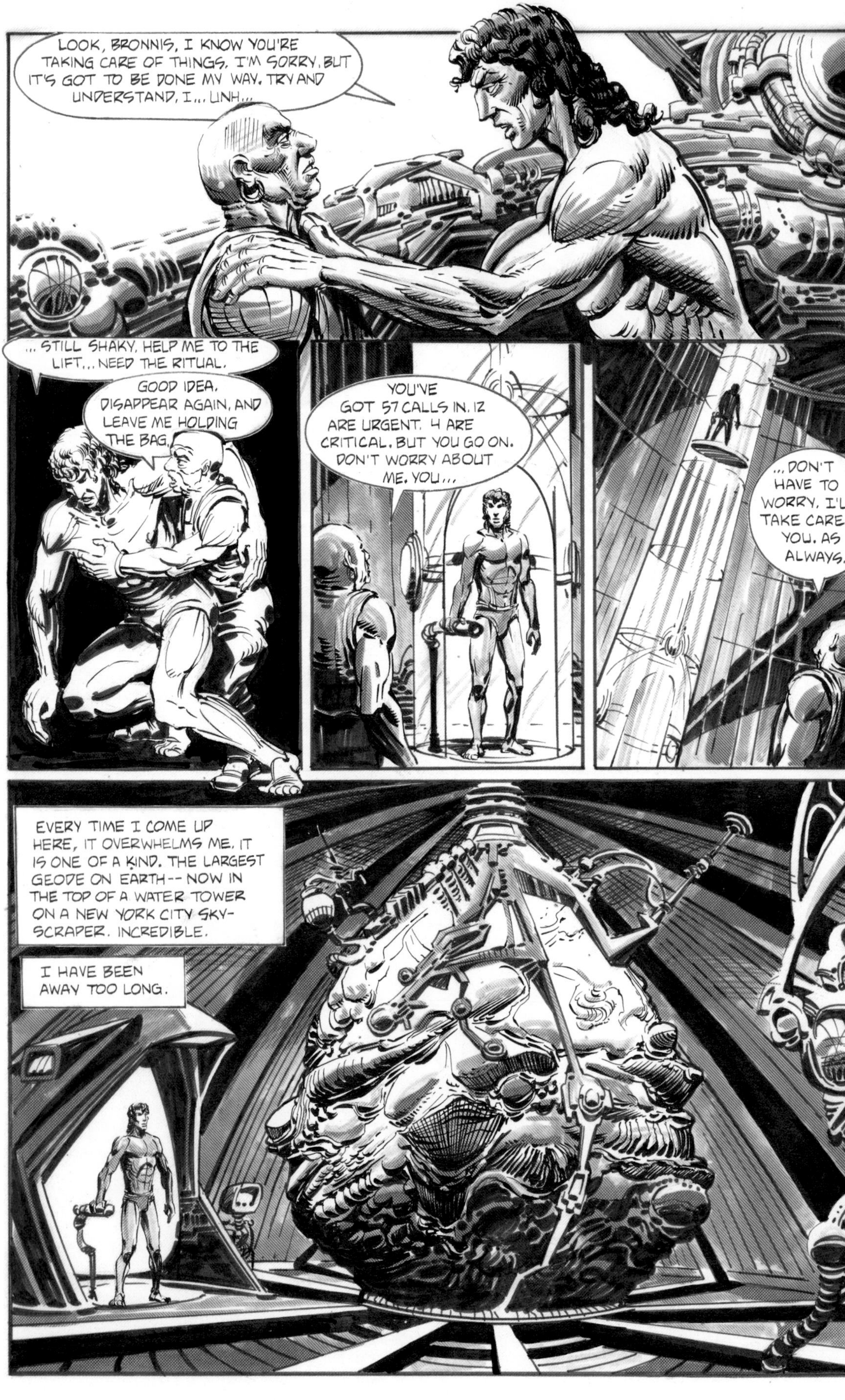
LOOK, BRONNIS, I KNOW YOU'RE TAKING CARE OF THINGS. I'M SORRY, BUT IT'S GOT TO BE DONE MY WAY. TRY AND UNDERSTAND. I... UNH...
... STILL SHAKY. HELP ME TO THE LIFT... NEED THE RITUAL.
GOOD IDEA. DISAPPEAR AGAIN, AND LEAVE ME HOLDING THE BAG.
YOU'VE GOT 57 CALLS IN. 12 ARE URGENT. 4 ARE CRITICAL. BUT YOU GO ON. DON'T WORRY ABOUT ME. YOU...
... DON'T HAVE TO WORRY. I'LL TAKE CARE OF YOU. AS ALWAYS.
EVERY TIME I COME UP HERE, IT OVERWHELMS ME. IT IS ONE OF A KIND. THE LARGEST GEODE ON EARTH -- NOW IN THE TOP OF A WATER TOWER ON A NEW YORK CITY SKY-SCRAPER. INCREDIBLE.
I HAVE BEEN AWAY TOO LONG.

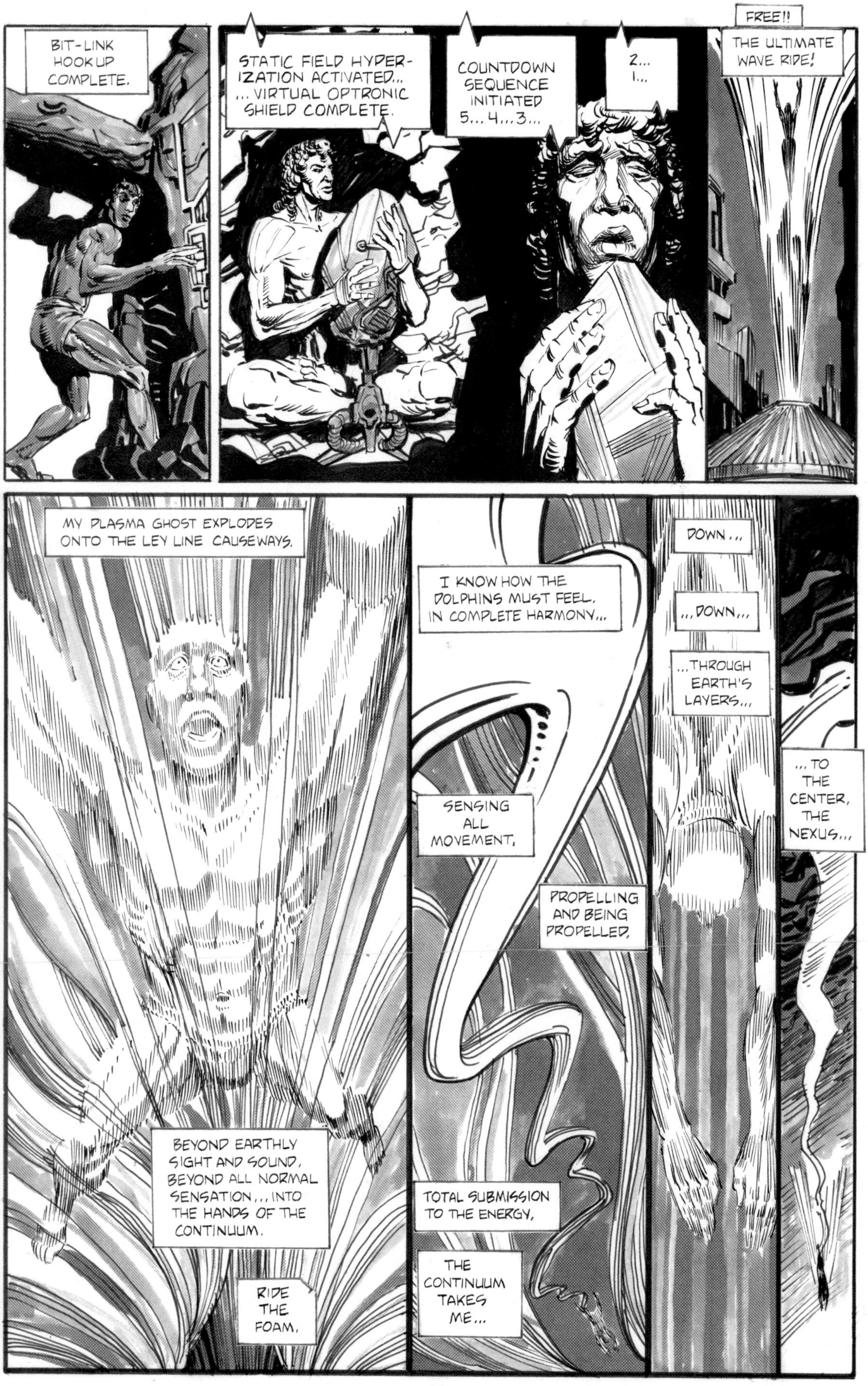
BIT-LINK HOOKUP COMPLETE.
STATIC FIELD HYPER-IZATION ACTIVATED... ...VIRTUAL OPTRONIC SHIELD COMPLETE.
COUNTDOWN SEQUENCE INITIATED 5...4...3...
2... 1...
FREE!!
THE ULTIMATE WAVE RIDE!
MY PLASMA GHOST EXPLODES ONTO THE LEY LINE CAUSEWAYS.
BEYOND EARTHLY SIGHT AND SOUND, BEYOND ALL NORMAL SENSATION... INTO THE HANDS OF THE CONTINUUM.
RIDE THE FOAM.
I KNOW HOW THE DOLPHINS MUST FEEL, IN COMPLETE HARMONY...
SENSING ALL MOVEMENT,
PROPELLING AND BEING PROPELLED,
TOTAL SUBMISSION TO THE ENERGY,
THE CONTINUUM TAKES ME...
DOWN...
...DOWN...
...THROUGH EARTH'S LAYERS...
...TO THE CENTER, THE NEXUS...

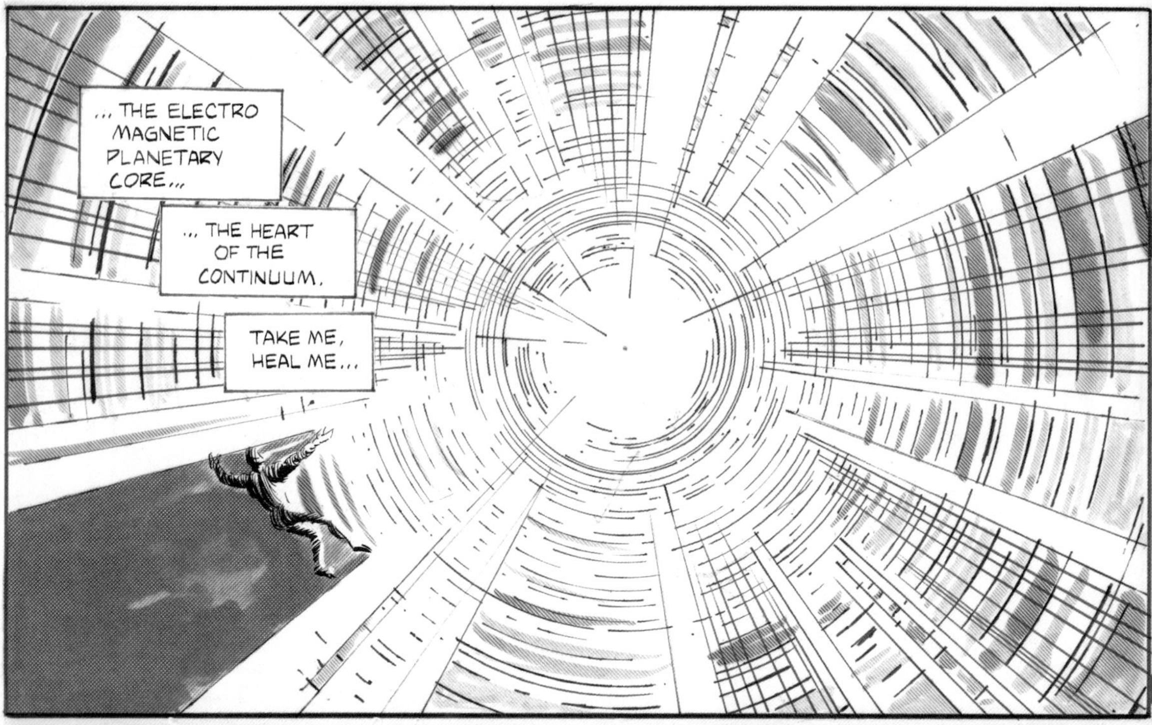

...THE ELECTRO MAGNETIC PLANETARY CORE...
...THE HEART OF THE CONTINUUM.
TAKE ME, HEAL ME...

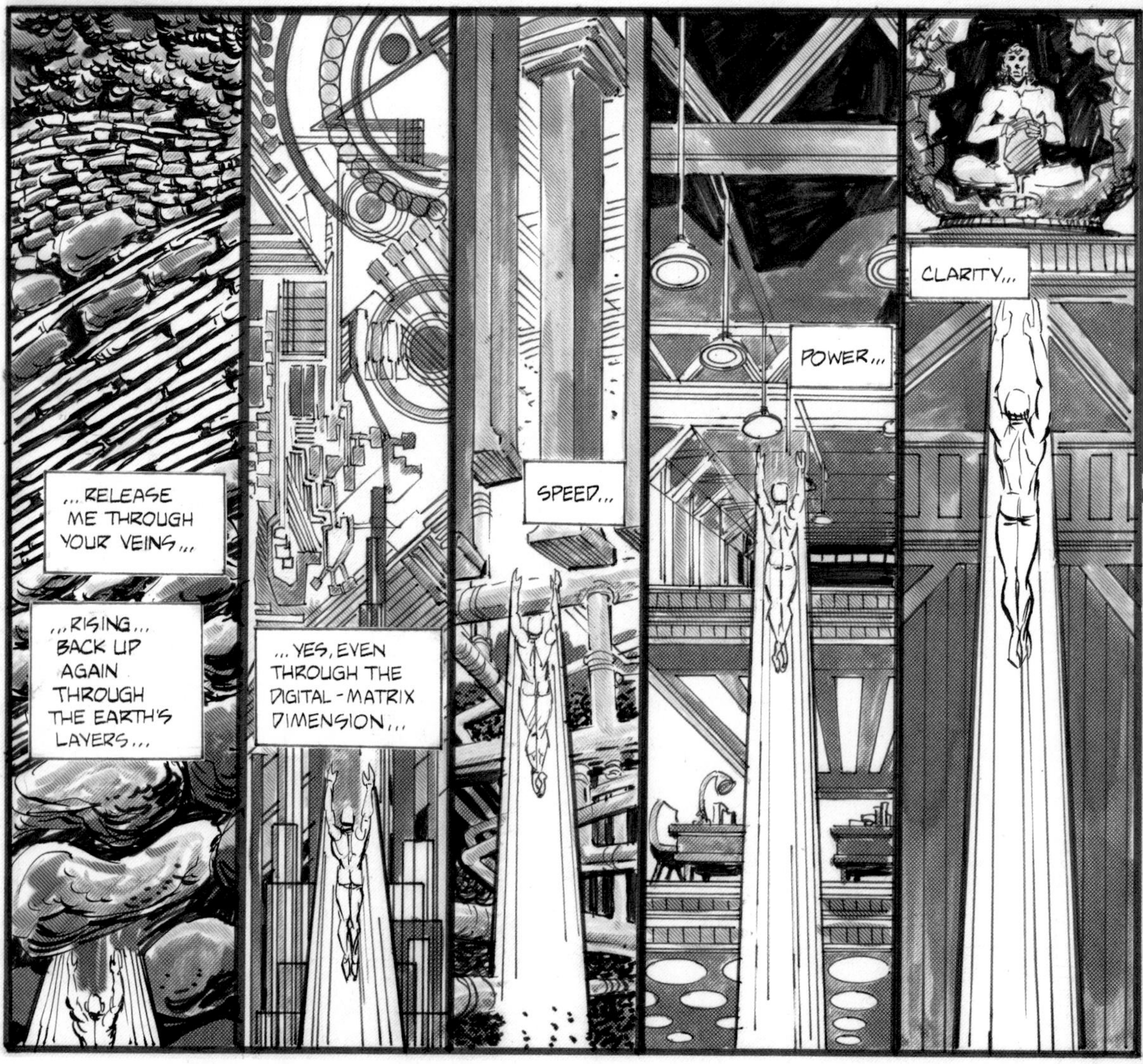

...RELEASE ME THROUGH YOUR VEINS...
...RISING... BACK UP AGAIN THROUGH THE EARTH'S LAYERS...
...YES, EVEN THROUGH THE DIGITAL-MATRIX DIMENSION...
SPEED...
POWER...
CLARITY...

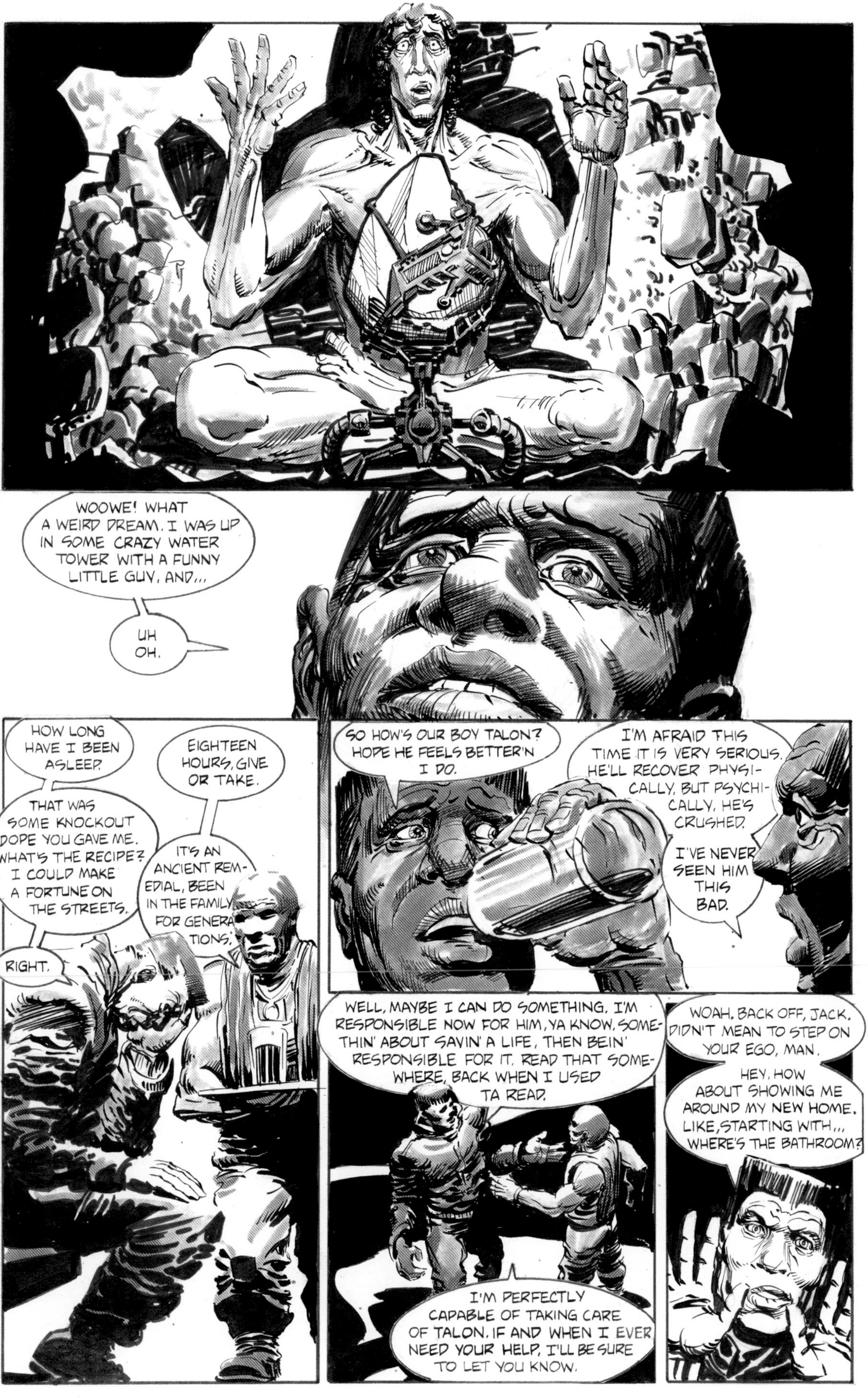
WOOWE! WHAT A WEIRD DREAM. I WAS UP IN SOME CRAZY WATER TOWER WITH A FUNNY LITTLE GUY, AND...
UH OH.
HOW LONG HAVE I BEEN ASLEEP?
EIGHTEEN HOURS, GIVE OR TAKE.
THAT WAS SOME KNOCKOUT DOPE YOU GAVE ME. WHAT'S THE RECIPE? I COULD MAKE A FORTUNE ON THE STREETS.
IT'S AN ANCIENT REM-EDIAL, BEEN IN THE FAMILY FOR GENERA-TIONS.
RIGHT.
SO HOW'S OUR BOY TALON? HOPE HE FEELS BETTER'N I DO.
I'M AFRAID THIS TIME IT IS VERY SERIOUS. HE'LL RECOVER PHYSI-CALLY, BUT PSYCHI-CALLY, HE'S CRUSHED.
I'VE NEVER SEEN HIM THIS BAD.
WELL, MAYBE I CAN DO SOMETHING. I'M RESPONSIBLE NOW FOR HIM, YA KNOW. SOME-THIN' ABOUT SAVIN' A LIFE, THEN BEIN' RESPONSIBLE FOR IT. READ THAT SOME-WHERE, BACK WHEN I USED TA READ.
I'M PERFECTLY CAPABLE OF TAKING CARE OF TALON. IF AND WHEN I EVER NEED YOUR HELP, I'LL BE SURE TO LET YOU KNOW.
WOAH. BACK OFF, JACK. DIDN'T MEAN TO STEP ON YOUR EGO, MAN.
HEY, HOW ABOUT SHOWING ME AROUND MY NEW HOME. LIKE, STARTING WITH... WHERE'S THE BATHROOM?

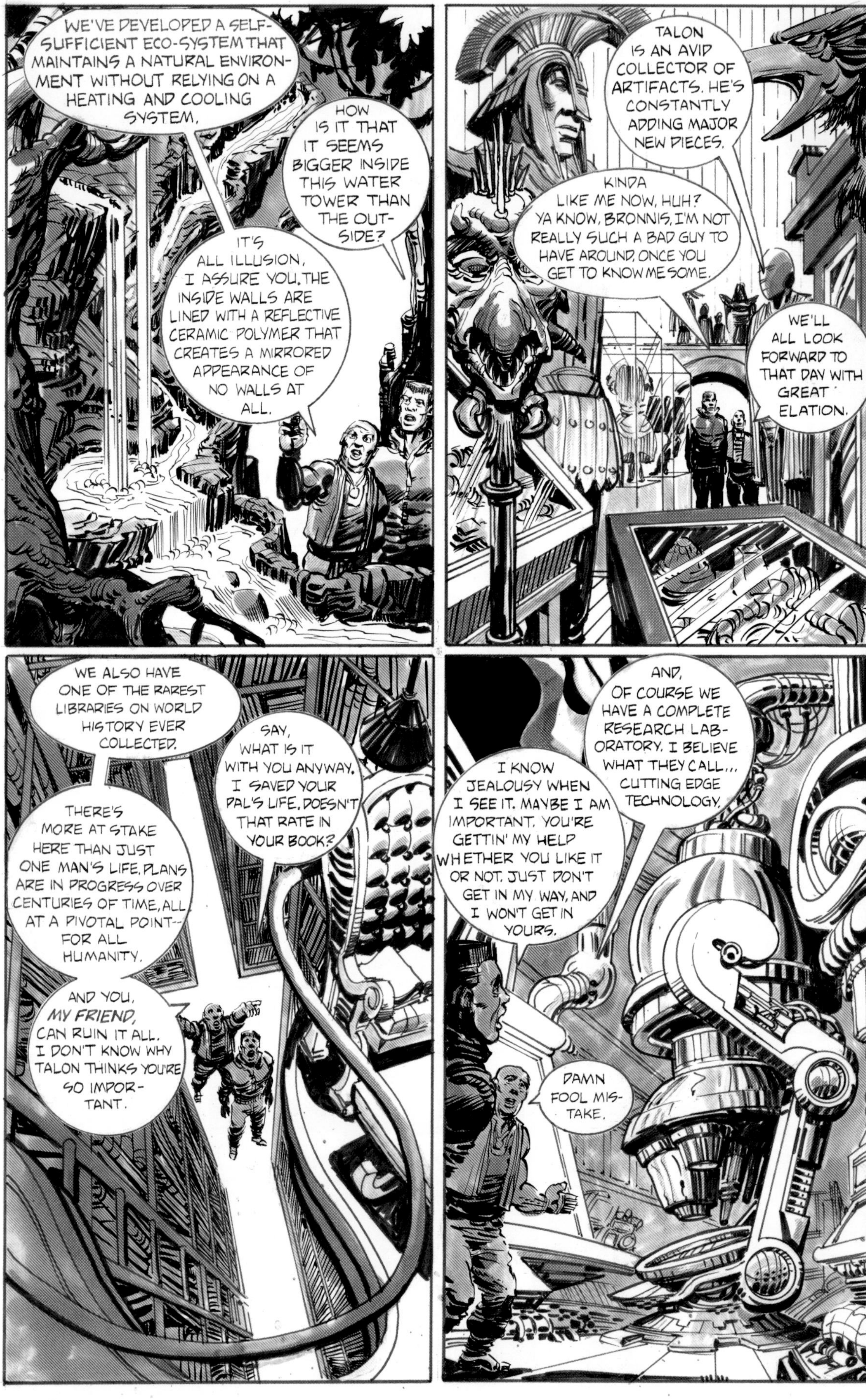
WE'VE DEVELOPED A SELF-SUFFICIENT ECO-SYSTEM THAT MAINTAINS A NATURAL ENVIRONMENT WITHOUT RELYING ON A HEATING AND COOLING SYSTEM.
HOW IS IT THAT IT SEEMS BIGGER INSIDE THIS WATER TOWER THAN THE OUTSIDE?
IT'S ALL ILLUSION, I ASSURE YOU. THE INSIDE WALLS ARE LINED WITH A REFLECTIVE CERAMIC POLYMER THAT CREATES A MIRRORED APPEARANCE OF NO WALLS AT ALL.
TALON IS AN AVID COLLECTOR OF ARTIFACTS. HE'S CONSTANTLY ADDING MAJOR NEW PIECES.
KINDA LIKE ME NOW, HUH? YA KNOW, BRONNIS, I'M NOT REALLY SUCH A BAD GUY TO HAVE AROUND, ONCE YOU GET TO KNOW ME SOME.
WE'LL ALL LOOK FORWARD TO THAT DAY WITH GREAT ELATION.
WE ALSO HAVE ONE OF THE RAREST LIBRARIES ON WORLD HISTORY EVER COLLECTED.
SAY, WHAT IS IT WITH YOU ANYWAY. I SAVED YOUR PAL'S LIFE, DOESN'T THAT RATE IN YOUR BOOK?
THERE'S MORE AT STAKE HERE THAN JUST ONE MAN'S LIFE. PLANS ARE IN PROGRESS OVER CENTURIES OF TIME, ALL AT A PIVOTAL POINT--FOR ALL HUMANITY.
AND YOU, MY FRIEND, CAN RUIN IT ALL. I DON'T KNOW WHY TALON THINKS YOU'RE SO IMPORTANT.
AND, OF COURSE WE HAVE A COMPLETE RESEARCH LABORATORY. I BELIEVE WHAT THEY CALL... CUTTING EDGE TECHNOLOGY.
I KNOW JEALOUSY WHEN I SEE IT. MAYBE I AM IMPORTANT. YOU'RE GETTIN' MY HELP WHETHER YOU LIKE IT OR NOT. JUST DON'T GET IN MY WAY, AND I WON'T GET IN YOURS.
DAMN FOOL MISTAKE.

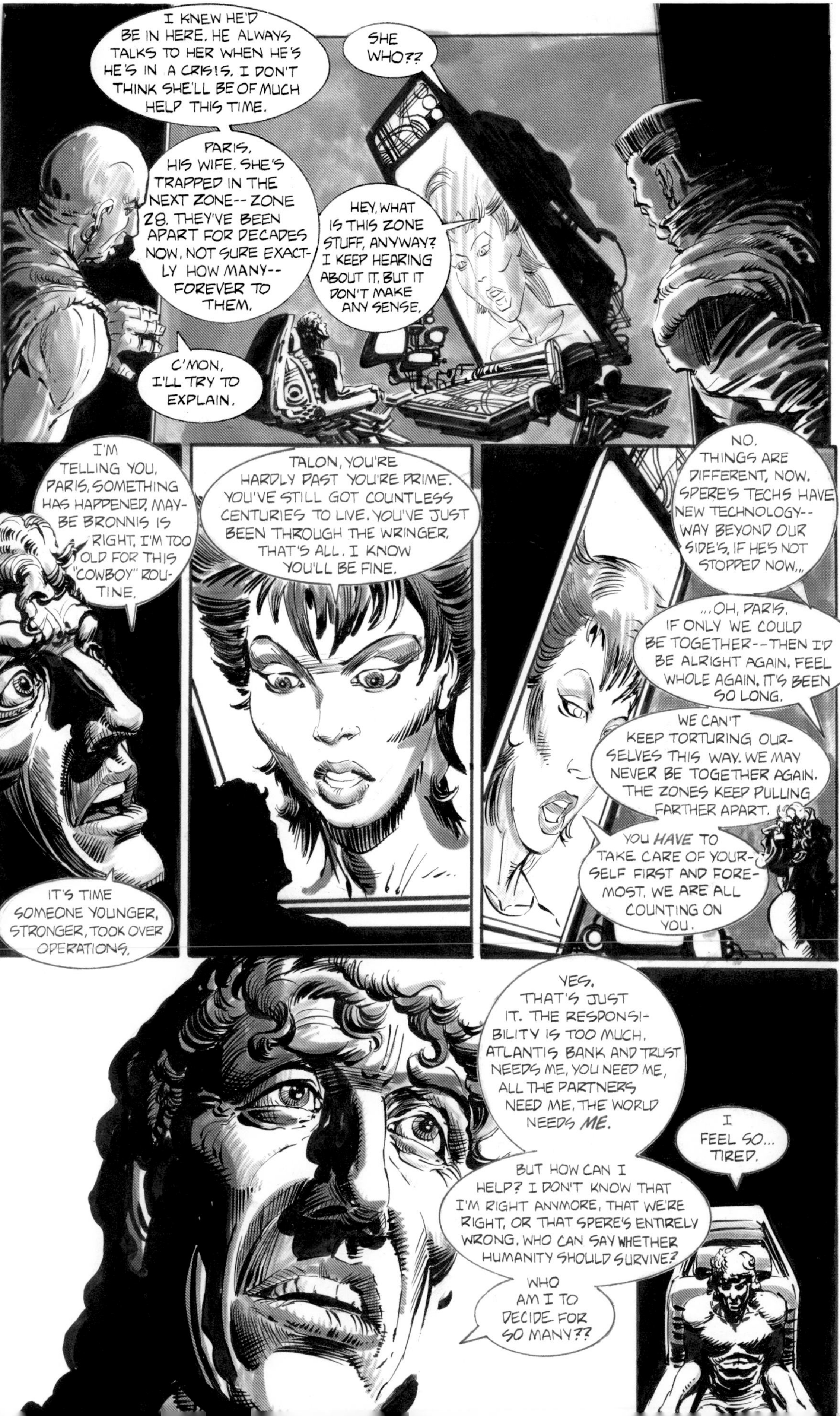
I KNEW HE'D BE IN HERE. HE ALWAYS TALKS TO HER WHEN HE'S HE'S IN A CRISIS. I DON'T THINK SHE'LL BE OF MUCH HELP THIS TIME.
SHE WHO??
PARIS. HIS WIFE. SHE'S TRAPPED IN THE NEXT ZONE-- ZONE 28. THEY'VE BEEN APART FOR DECADES NOW. NOT SURE EXACTLY HOW MANY-- FOREVER TO THEM.
HEY, WHAT IS THIS ZONE STUFF, ANYWAY? I KEEP HEARING ABOUT IT, BUT IT DON'T MAKE ANY SENSE.
C'MON, I'LL TRY TO EXPLAIN.
I'M TELLING YOU, PARIS, SOMETHING HAS HAPPENED. MAYBE BRONNIS IS RIGHT. I'M TOO OLD FOR THIS "COWBOY" ROUTINE.
IT'S TIME SOMEONE YOUNGER, STRONGER, TOOK OVER OPERATIONS.
TALON, YOU'RE HARDLY PAST YOU'RE PRIME. YOU'VE STILL GOT COUNTLESS CENTURIES TO LIVE. YOU'VE JUST BEEN THROUGH THE WRINGER, THAT'S ALL. I KNOW YOU'LL BE FINE.
NO. THINGS ARE DIFFERENT, NOW. SPERE'S TECHS HAVE NEW TECHNOLOGY-- WAY BEYOND OUR SIDE'S. IF HE'S NOT STOPPED NOW...
...OH, PARIS, IF ONLY WE COULD BE TOGETHER--THEN I'D BE ALRIGHT AGAIN. FEEL WHOLE AGAIN. IT'S BEEN SO LONG.
WE CAN'T KEEP TORTURING OURSELVES THIS WAY. WE MAY NEVER BE TOGETHER AGAIN. THE ZONES KEEP PULLING FARTHER APART.
YOU HAVE TO TAKE CARE OF YOURSELF FIRST AND FOREMOST. WE ARE ALL COUNTING ON YOU.
YES. THAT'S JUST IT. THE RESPONSIBILITY IS TOO MUCH. ATLANTIS BANK AND TRUST NEEDS ME, YOU NEED ME, ALL THE PARTNERS NEED ME, THE WORLD NEEDS ME.
BUT HOW CAN I HELP? I DON'T KNOW THAT I'M RIGHT ANYMORE, THAT WE'RE RIGHT, OR THAT SPERE'S ENTIRELY WRONG. WHO CAN SAY WHETHER HUMANITY SHOULD SURVIVE?
WHO AM I TO DECIDE FOR SO MANY??
I FEEL SO... TIRED.

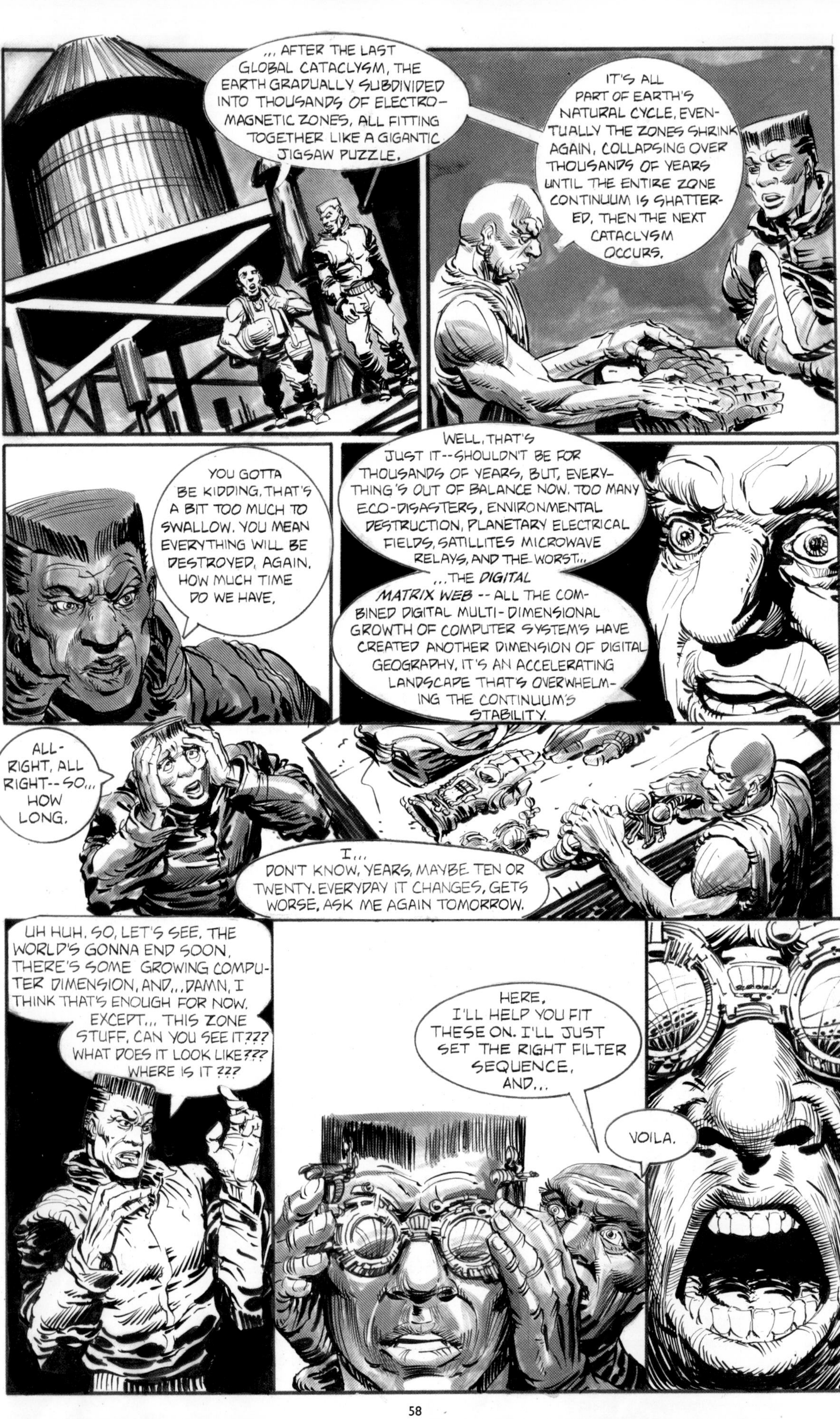
... AFTER THE LAST GLOBAL CATACLYSM, THE EARTH GRADUALLY SUBDIVIDED INTO THOUSANDS OF ELECTRO-MAGNETIC ZONES, ALL FITTING TOGETHER LIKE A GIGANTIC JIGSAW PUZZLE.
IT'S ALL PART OF EARTH'S NATURAL CYCLE. EVENTUALLY THE ZONES SHRINK AGAIN, COLLAPSING OVER THOUSANDS OF YEARS UNTIL THE ENTIRE ZONE CONTINUUM IS SHATTERED, THEN THE NEXT CATACLYSM OCCURS.
YOU GOTTA BE KIDDING. THAT'S A BIT TOO MUCH TO SWALLOW. YOU MEAN EVERYTHING WILL BE DESTROYED, AGAIN. HOW MUCH TIME DO WE HAVE.
WELL, THAT'S JUST IT--SHOULDN'T BE FOR THOUSANDS OF YEARS, BUT, EVERYTHING'S OUT OF BALANCE NOW. TOO MANY ECO-DISASTERS, ENVIRONMENTAL DESTRUCTION, PLANETARY ELECTRICAL FIELDS, SATILLITES MICROWAVE RELAYS, AND THE WORST...
...THE *DIGITAL MATRIX WEB* -- ALL THE COMBINED DIGITAL MULTI-DIMENSIONAL GROWTH OF COMPUTER SYSTEM'S HAVE CREATED ANOTHER DIMENSION OF DIGITAL GEOGRAPHY. IT'S AN ACCELERATING LANDSCAPE THAT'S OVERWHELMING THE CONTINUUM'S STABILITY.
ALL-RIGHT, ALL RIGHT--SO... HOW LONG.
I... DON'T KNOW. YEARS. MAYBE TEN OR TWENTY. EVERYDAY IT CHANGES, GETS WORSE. ASK ME AGAIN TOMORROW.
UH HUH. SO, LET'S SEE. THE WORLD'S GONNA END SOON, THERE'S SOME GROWING COMPUTER DIMENSION, AND,..DAMN, I THINK THAT'S ENOUGH FOR NOW. EXCEPT... THIS ZONE STUFF. CAN YOU SEE IT??? WHAT DOES IT LOOK LIKE??? WHERE IS IT ???
HERE, I'LL HELP YOU FIT THESE ON. I'LL JUST SET THE RIGHT FILTER SEQUENCE, AND...
VOILA.

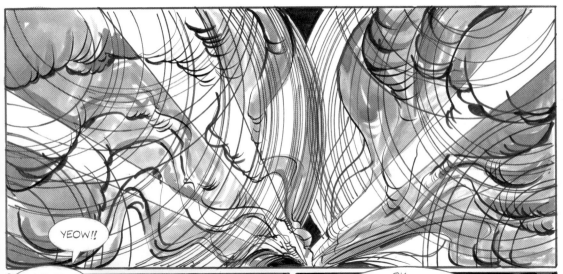

YEOW!!

CAN'T... TAKE IT... TOO INTENSE!!

OK, REALITY CHECK. I'M MANX AMERICA, FROM THE PLANET EARTH. BORN ON THE EAST SIDE. UHHH... AND, I DON'T THINK I'M IN KANSAS ANYMORE.

DAMN, WHAT A MESS. I THOUGHT I HAD SOME PROBLEMS BEFORE, BUT NOW...

SOMEHOW MY WORLD SEEMS SO FAR AWAY, SO SMALL AND UNIMPORTANT. ALMOST UNREAL. IT'S LIKE AS LONG AS I'M UP HERE, NOTHING IS GOING ON DOWN IN THE REAL WORLD ANYMORE.

BUT, HOW LONG CAN I HIDE FROM THINGS. SOONER OR LATER IT'LL CATCH UP TO ME... THEY'LL CATCH UP TO ME. BUT FOR NOW, IT DOESN'T SEEM TO MATTER.

I FINALLY CAN MAKE A DIFFERENCE UP HERE. DON'T EXACTLY KNOW WHAT'S GOING ON, BUT FOR THE FIRST TIME I FEEL LIKE I'VE GOT SOMETHING IMPORTANT TO DO, THAT I'M IMPORTANT.

NOBODY'S EVER TAKEN CARE OF ME... BEEN THERE WHEN I NEEDED THEM. I COULD NEVER COUNT ON PEOPLE, OR BELIEVE SOMETHING GOOD COULD EVER HAPPEN.

BUT NOW SOMEONE BELIEVES IN ME, AND NEEDS ME. I CAN'T LET HIM DOWN. IF HE FAILS, I FAIL.

YOU KNOW ME TOO WELL, BRONNIS, BUT I KNOW YOU TOO. YOU'RE AFRAID I'M GOING OUT AGAIN TO CLEAR MY HEAD. CLEAN MY SOUL IN THE FIRES OF COMBAT, RIGHT? TO THROW MYSELF INTO BATTLE...

I THOUGHT YOU MIGHT WANT TO GO OUT AGAIN, SO I SET UP YOUR EQUIPMENT.

CAN YOU DENY IT?

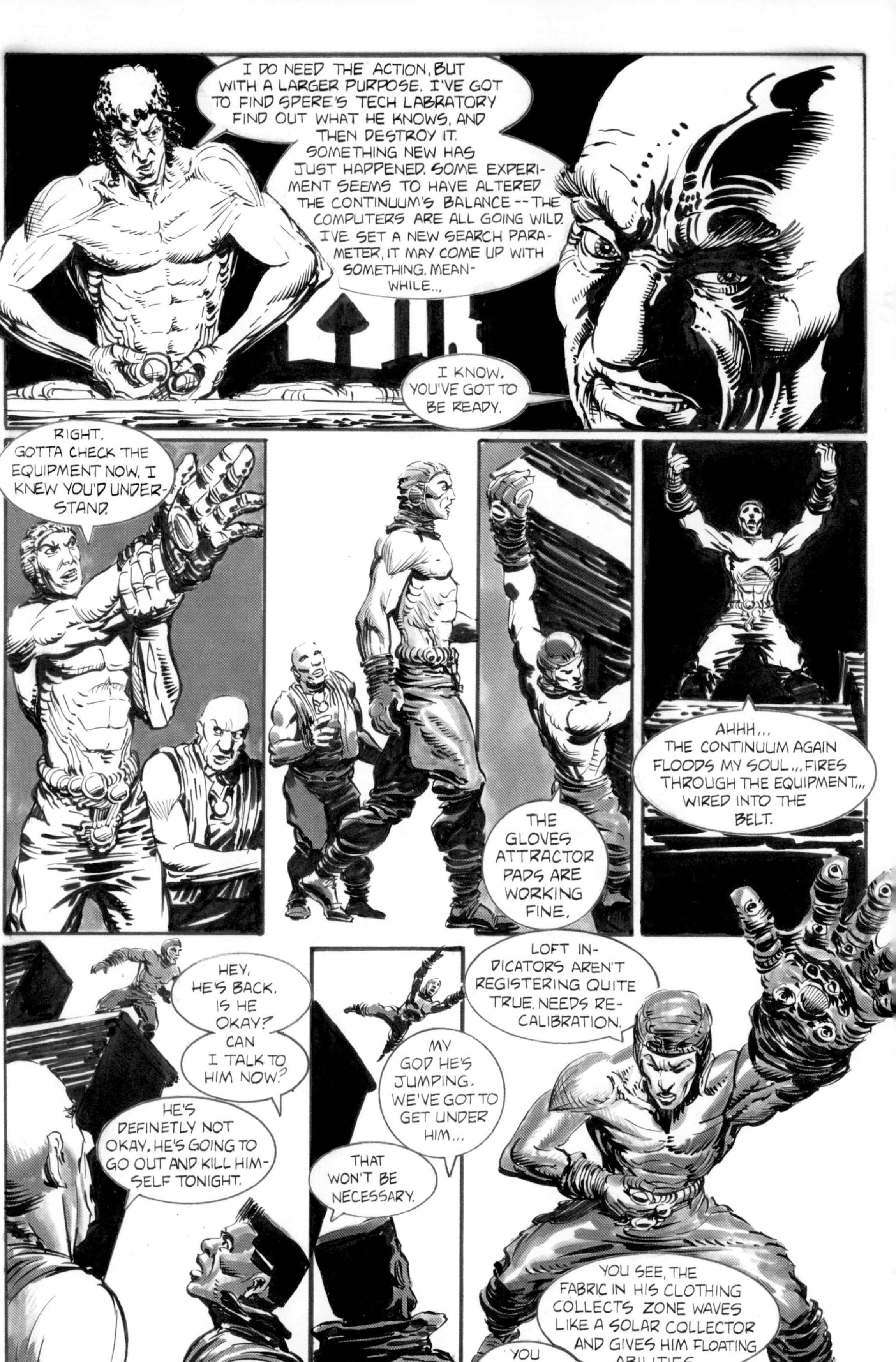
I DO NEED THE ACTION, BUT WITH A LARGER PURPOSE. I'VE GOT TO FIND SPERE'S TECH LABRATORY FIND OUT WHAT HE KNOWS, AND THEN DESTROY IT.
SOMETHING NEW HAS JUST HAPPENED. SOME EXPERIMENT SEEMS TO HAVE ALTERED THE CONTINUUM'S BALANCE -- THE COMPUTERS ARE ALL GOING WILD. IVE SET A NEW SEARCH PARAMETER, IT MAY COME UP WITH SOMETHING. MEANWHILE...
I KNOW, YOU'VE GOT TO BE READY.
RIGHT. GOTTA CHECK THE EQUIPMENT NOW. I KNEW YOU'D UNDERSTAND.
THE GLOVES ATTRACTOR PADS ARE WORKING FINE.
AHHH... THE CONTINUUM AGAIN FLOODS MY SOUL... FIRES THROUGH THE EQUIPMENT... WIRED INTO THE BELT.
HEY, HE'S BACK. IS HE OKAY?
CAN I TALK TO HIM NOW?
HE'S DEFINETLY NOT OKAY. HE'S GOING TO GO OUT AND KILL HIMSELF TONIGHT.
MY GOD HE'S JUMPING. WE'VE GOT TO GET UNDER HIM...
THAT WON'T BE NECESSARY.
LOFT INDICATORS AREN'T REGISTERING QUITE TRUE. NEEDS RECALIBRATION.
YOU SEE, THE FABRIC IN HIS CLOTHING COLLECTS ZONE WAVES LIKE A SOLAR COLLECTOR AND GIVES HIM FLOATING ABILITIES.
YOU MEAN... HE CAN FLY?
NOT QUITE. JUST FLOAT A BIT. DEPENDS ON THE WAVES... THE CURRENTS ARE CONSTANTLY IN FLUX.

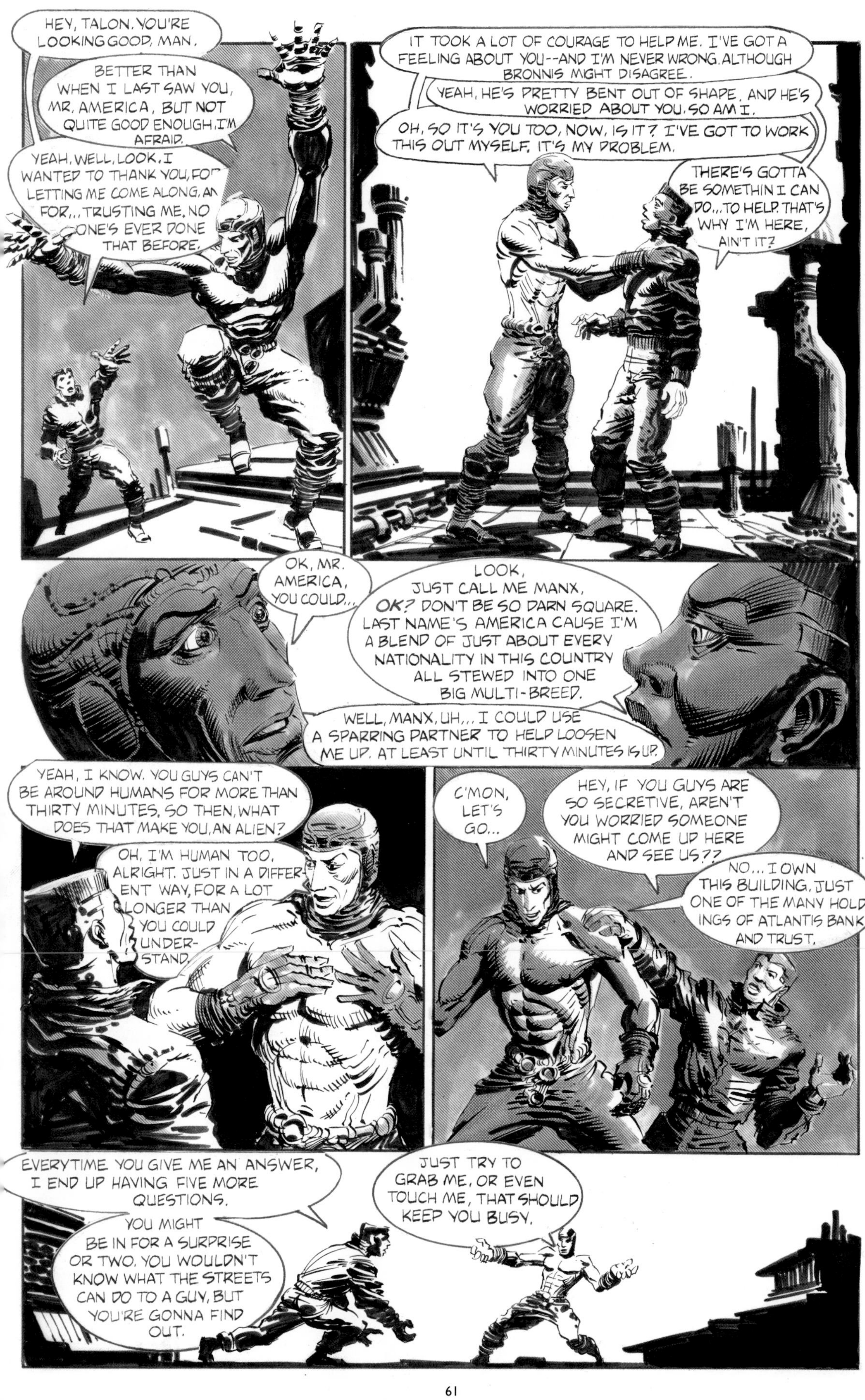
HEY, TALON. YOU'RE LOOKING GOOD, MAN.
BETTER THAN WHEN I LAST SAW YOU, MR. AMERICA, BUT NOT QUITE GOOD ENOUGH, I'M AFRAID.
YEAH, WELL, LOOK, I WANTED TO THANK YOU, FOR LETTING ME COME ALONG, AN FOR... TRUSTING ME. NO ONE'S EVER DONE THAT BEFORE.
IT TOOK A LOT OF COURAGE TO HELP ME. I'VE GOT A FEELING ABOUT YOU--AND I'M NEVER WRONG. ALTHOUGH BRONNIS MIGHT DISAGREE.
YEAH, HE'S PRETTY BENT OUT OF SHAPE, AND HE'S WORRIED ABOUT YOU. SO AM I.
OH, SO IT'S YOU TOO, NOW, IS IT? I'VE GOT TO WORK THIS OUT MYSELF. IT'S MY PROBLEM.
THERE'S GOTTA BE SOMETHIN I CAN DO... TO HELP. THAT'S WHY I'M HERE, AIN'T IT?
OK, MR. AMERICA, YOU COULD...
LOOK, JUST CALL ME MANX, OK? DON'T BE SO DARN SQUARE. LAST NAME'S AMERICA CAUSE I'M A BLEND OF JUST ABOUT EVERY NATIONALITY IN THIS COUNTRY ALL STEWED INTO ONE BIG MULTI-BREED.
WELL, MANX, UH... I COULD USE A SPARRING PARTNER TO HELP LOOSEN ME UP. AT LEAST UNTIL THIRTY MINUTES IS UP.
YEAH, I KNOW. YOU GUYS CAN'T BE AROUND HUMANS FOR MORE THAN THIRTY MINUTES. SO THEN, WHAT DOES THAT MAKE YOU, AN ALIEN?
OH, I'M HUMAN TOO, ALRIGHT. JUST IN A DIFFERENT WAY, FOR A LOT LONGER THAN YOU COULD UNDERSTAND.
C'MON, LET'S GO...
HEY, IF YOU GUYS ARE SO SECRETIVE, AREN'T YOU WORRIED SOMEONE MIGHT COME UP HERE AND SEE US??
NO... I OWN THIS BUILDING. JUST ONE OF THE MANY HOLDINGS OF ATLANTIS BANK AND TRUST.
EVERYTIME YOU GIVE ME AN ANSWER, I END UP HAVING FIVE MORE QUESTIONS.
YOU MIGHT BE IN FOR A SURPRISE OR TWO. YOU WOULDN'T KNOW WHAT THE STREETS CAN DO TO A GUY, BUT YOU'RE GONNA FIND OUT.
JUST TRY TO GRAB ME, OR EVEN TOUCH ME, THAT SHOULD KEEP YOU BUSY.

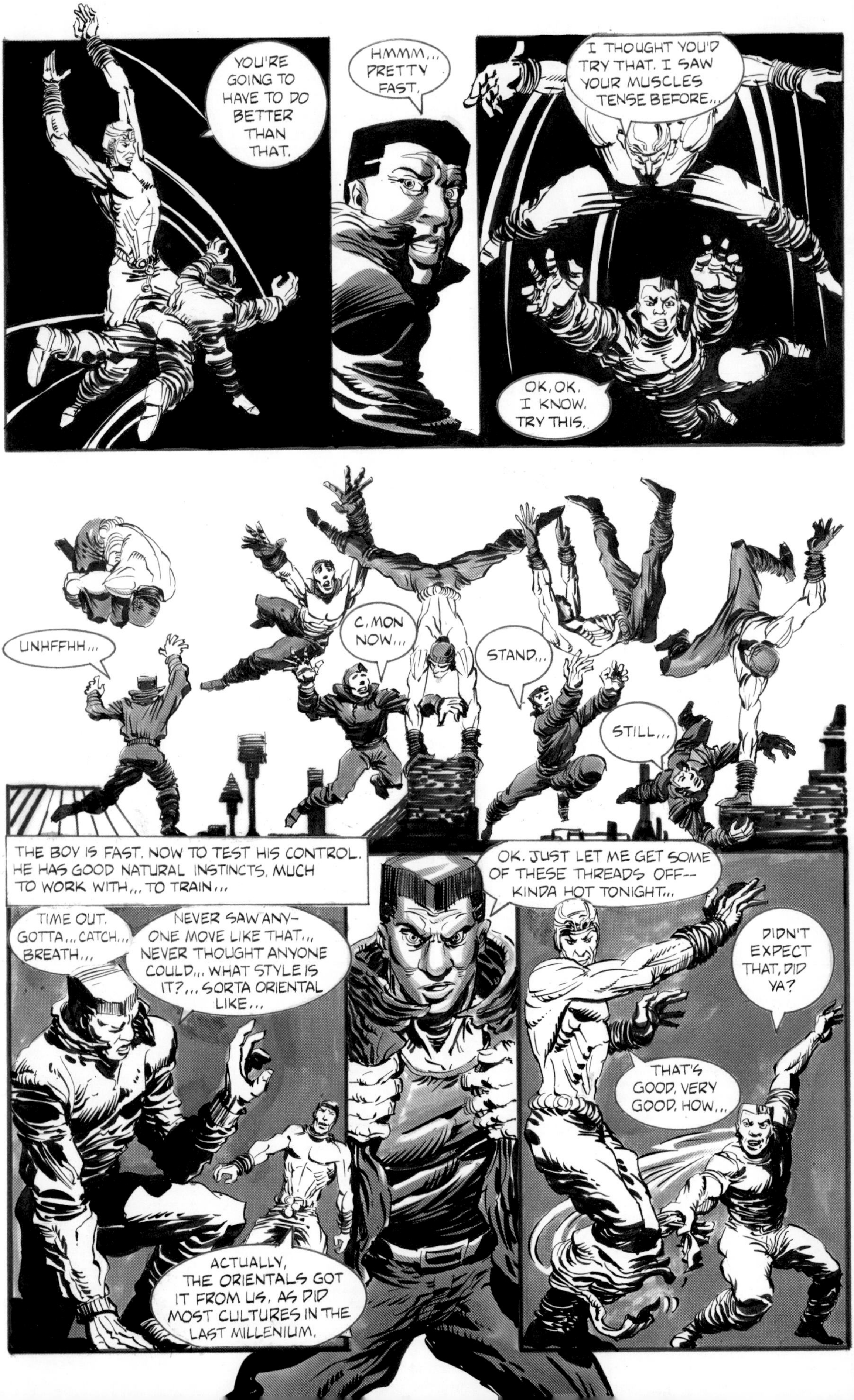
YOU'RE GOING TO HAVE TO DO BETTER THAN THAT.
HMMM... PRETTY FAST.
I THOUGHT YOU'D TRY THAT. I SAW YOUR MUSCLES TENSE BEFORE...
OK, OK. I KNOW. TRY THIS.
UNHFFHH...
C,MON NOW...
STAND...
STILL...
THE BOY IS FAST. NOW TO TEST HIS CONTROL. HE HAS GOOD NATURAL INSTINCTS, MUCH TO WORK WITH... TO TRAIN...
TIME OUT. GOTTA... CATCH... BREATH...
NEVER SAW ANY-ONE MOVE LIKE THAT... NEVER THOUGHT ANYONE COULD... WHAT STYLE IS IT?... SORTA ORIENTAL LIKE...
ACTUALLY, THE ORIENTALS GOT IT FROM US, AS DID MOST CULTURES IN THE LAST MILLENIUM.
OK. JUST LET ME GET SOME OF THESE THREADS OFF-- KINDA HOT TONIGHT...
DIDN'T EXPECT THAT, DID YA?
THAT'S GOOD, VERY GOOD. HOW...

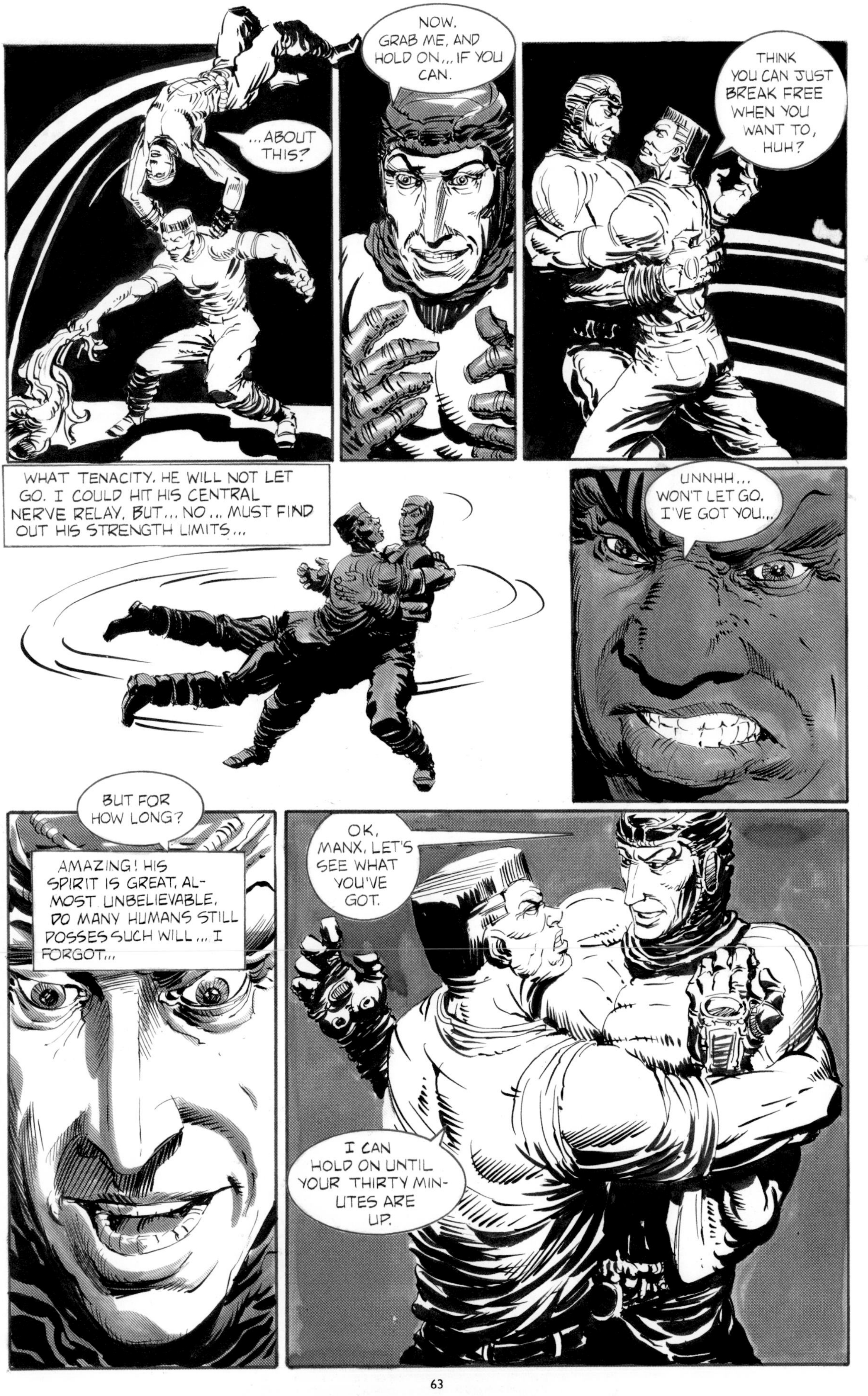

...ABOUT THIS?
NOW. GRAB ME, AND HOLD ON... IF YOU CAN.
THINK YOU CAN JUST BREAK FREE WHEN YOU WANT TO, HUH?
WHAT TENACITY. HE WILL NOT LET GO. I COULD HIT HIS CENTRAL NERVE RELAY, BUT... NO... MUST FIND OUT HIS STRENGTH LIMITS...
UNNHH... WON'T LET GO. I'VE GOT YOU...
BUT FOR HOW LONG?
AMAZING! HIS SPIRIT IS GREAT, AL-MOST UNBELIEVABLE. DO MANY HUMANS STILL POSSES SUCH WILL... I FORGOT...
OK, MANX, LET'S SEE WHAT YOU'VE GOT.
I CAN HOLD ON UNTIL YOUR THIRTY MIN-UTES ARE UP.

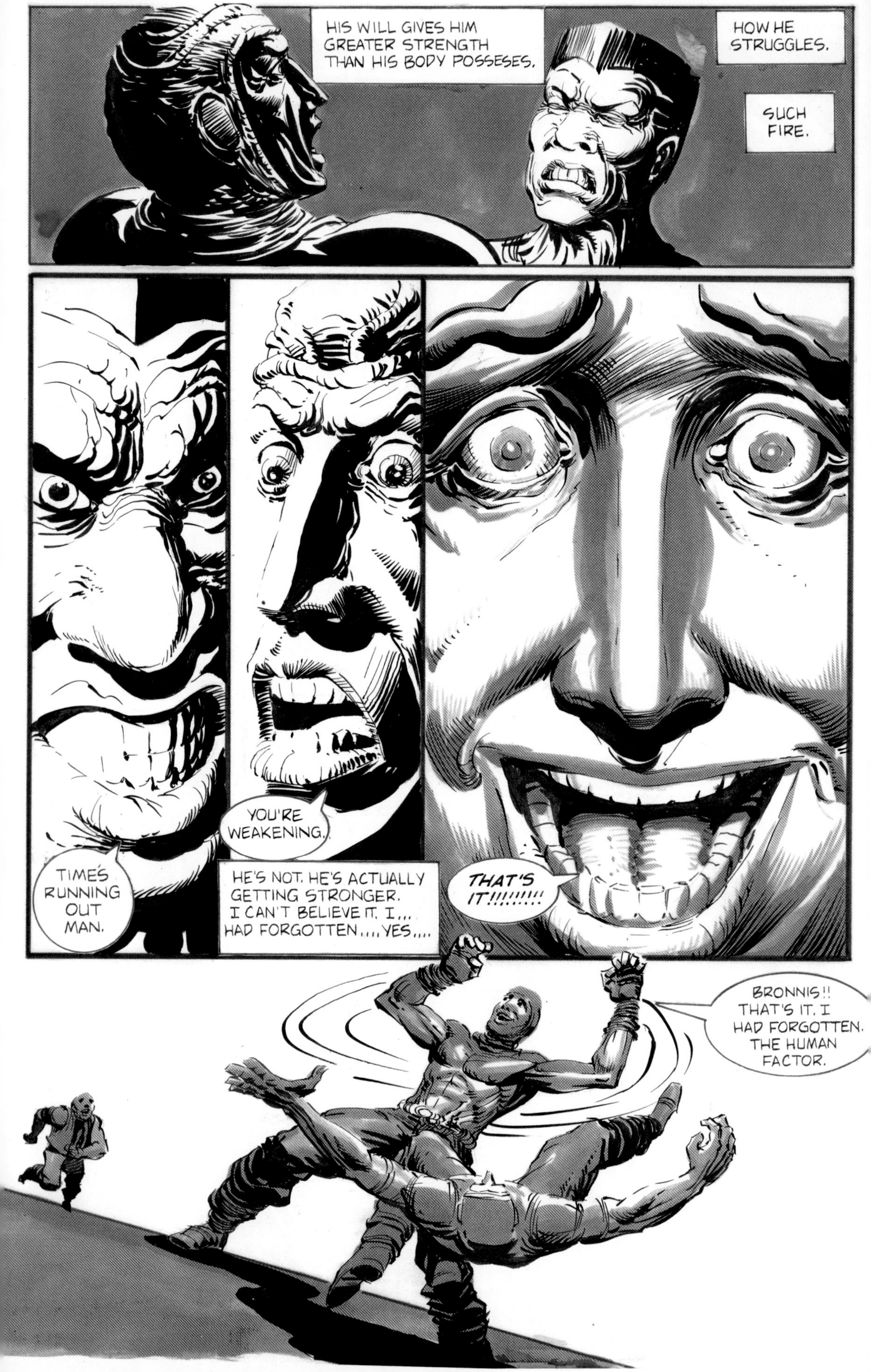
HIS WILL GIVES HIM GREATER STRENGTH THAN HIS BODY POSSESES.
HOW HE STRUGGLES.
SUCH FIRE.
TIME'S RUNNING OUT MAN.
YOU'RE WEAKENING.
HE'S NOT. HE'S ACTUALLY GETTING STRONGER. I CAN'T BELIEVE IT. I... HAD FORGOTTEN.... YES....
THAT'S IT!!!!!!!!!
BRONNIS!! THAT'S IT. I HAD FORGOTTEN. THE HUMAN FACTOR.

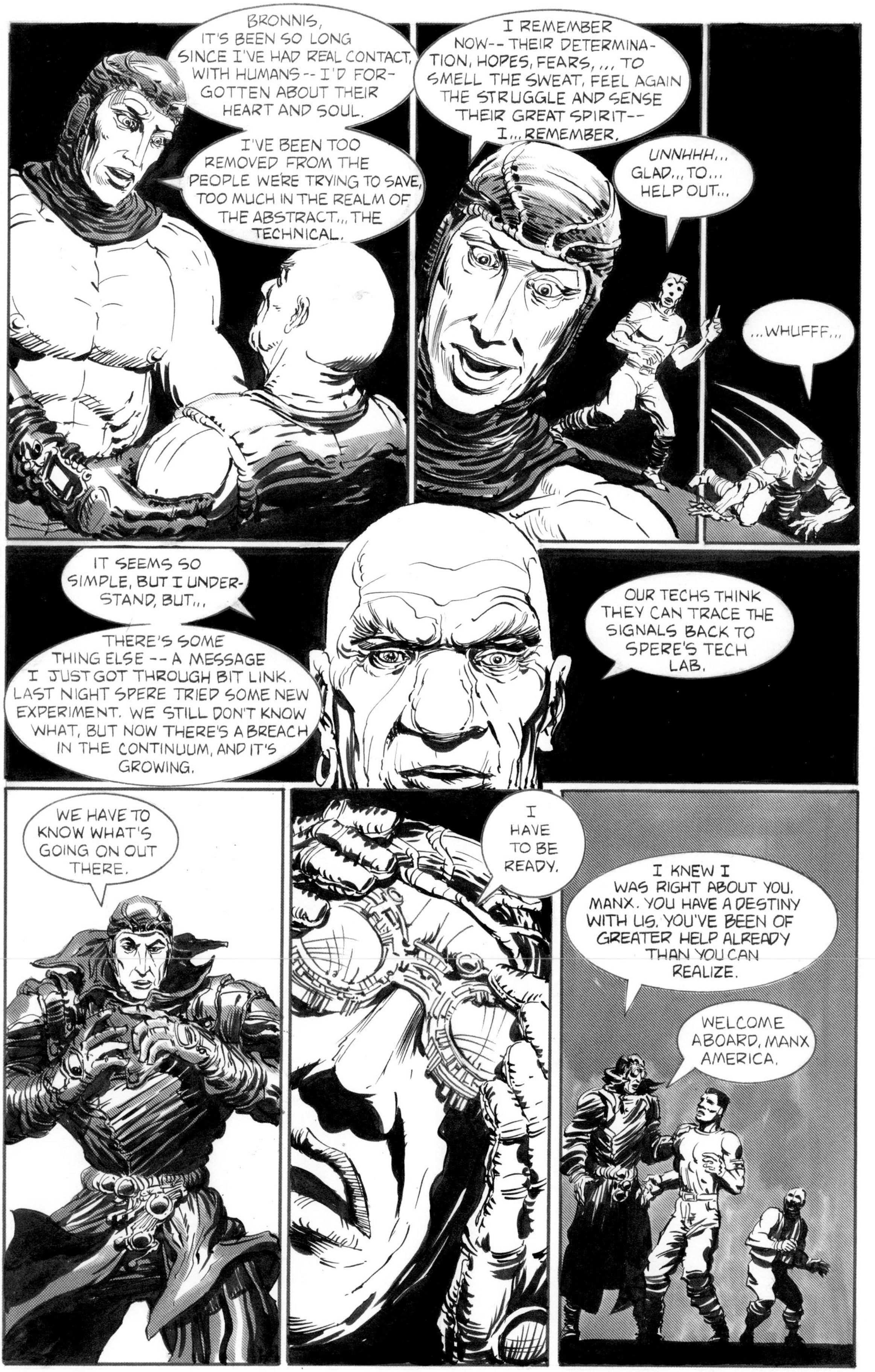
BRONNIS, IT'S BEEN SO LONG SINCE I'VE HAD REAL CONTACT WITH HUMANS -- I'D FORGOTTEN ABOUT THEIR HEART AND SOUL.
I'VE BEEN TOO REMOVED FROM THE PEOPLE WE'RE TRYING TO SAVE, TOO MUCH IN THE REALM OF THE ABSTRACT... THE TECHNICAL.
I REMEMBER NOW-- THEIR DETERMINATION, HOPES, FEARS,... TO SMELL THE SWEAT, FEEL AGAIN THE STRUGGLE AND SENSE THEIR GREAT SPIRIT-- I... REMEMBER.
UNNHHH... GLAD... TO... HELP OUT...
...WHUFFF...
IT SEEMS SO SIMPLE, BUT I UNDERSTAND, BUT...
THERE'S SOME THING ELSE -- A MESSAGE I JUST GOT THROUGH BIT LINK. LAST NIGHT SPERE TRIED SOME NEW EXPERIMENT. WE STILL DON'T KNOW WHAT, BUT NOW THERE'S A BREACH IN THE CONTINUUM, AND IT'S GROWING.
OUR TECHS THINK THEY CAN TRACE THE SIGNALS BACK TO SPERE'S TECH LAB.
WE HAVE TO KNOW WHAT'S GOING ON OUT THERE.
I HAVE TO BE READY.
I KNEW I WAS RIGHT ABOUT YOU, MANX. YOU HAVE A DESTINY WITH US. YOU'VE BEEN OF GREATER HELP ALREADY THAN YOU CAN REALIZE.
WELCOME ABOARD, MANX AMERICA.

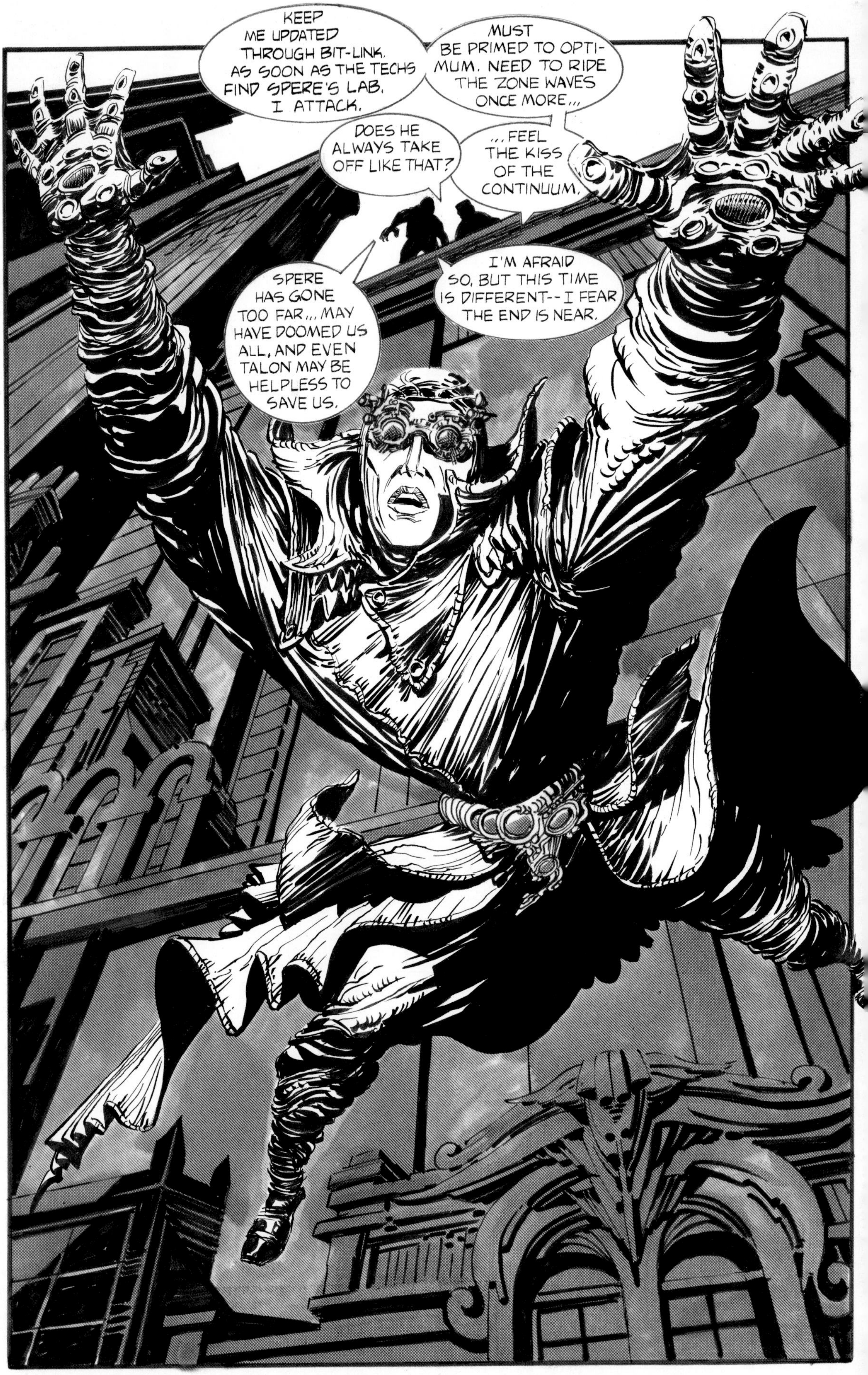
KEEP ME UPDATED THROUGH BIT-LINK. AS SOON AS THE TECHS FIND SPERE'S LAB, I ATTACK.
MUST BE PRIMED TO OPTI-MUM. NEED TO RIDE THE ZONE WAVES ONCE MORE...
DOES HE ALWAYS TAKE OFF LIKE THAT?
...FEEL THE KISS OF THE CONTINUUM.
SPERE HAS GONE TOO FAR... MAY HAVE DOOMED US ALL, AND EVEN TALON MAY BE HELPLESS TO SAVE US.
I'M AFRAID SO, BUT THIS TIME IS DIFFERENT--I FEAR THE END IS NEAR.

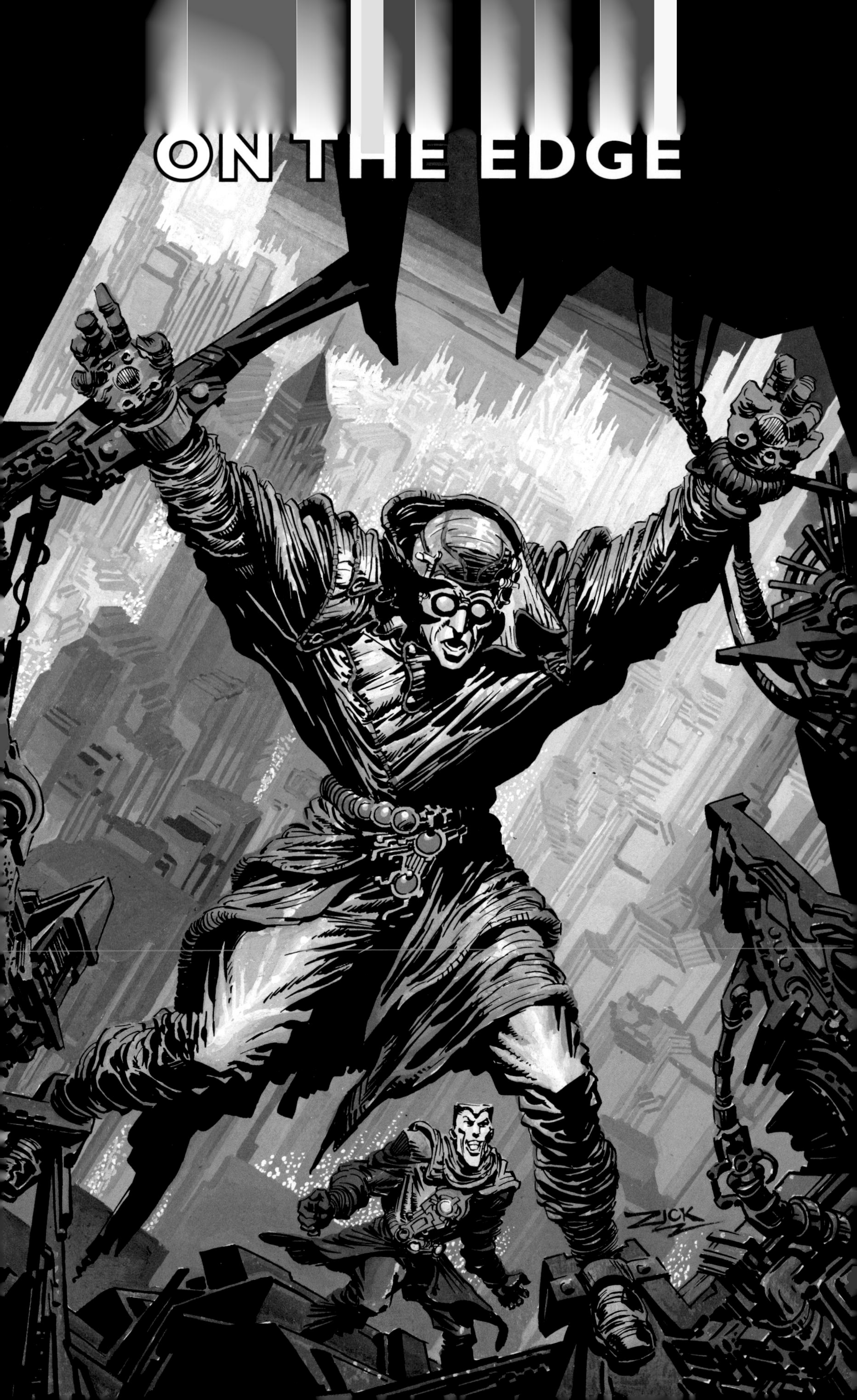
ON THE EDGE
ZICK

HOT GLOVES are the primary control devices which directly interact with the Zone Goggles and all other components of Talon's Zone Suit. They are constructed of Wavelite and Carbon 60 ("bucky ball" composite material) precipitated into an acrylic polymer.

Both gloves feature microdisplay liquid crystal screens which reveal any condition, function, or power consumption of Talon's Zone Suit—including variances in the local magnetic levitation field strength, which enables Talon's ability to glide. They can also display video images of incredible resolution.

The large pads on the back of the gloves are MCMs, or Magnetic Counter-Measure devices. With these, Talon can create a degree of magnetic invisibility or hide any field signature his opponents are capable of detecting.

The small pads on the palm side are contact sensors of various types. The large palm pads are powerful Micro ElectroMagnets (MEMs), which, when activated, produce a slight repulsive force that can brake a fall or cushion a landing. Conversely, the magnetic polarity can be reversed to help "grip" any object.

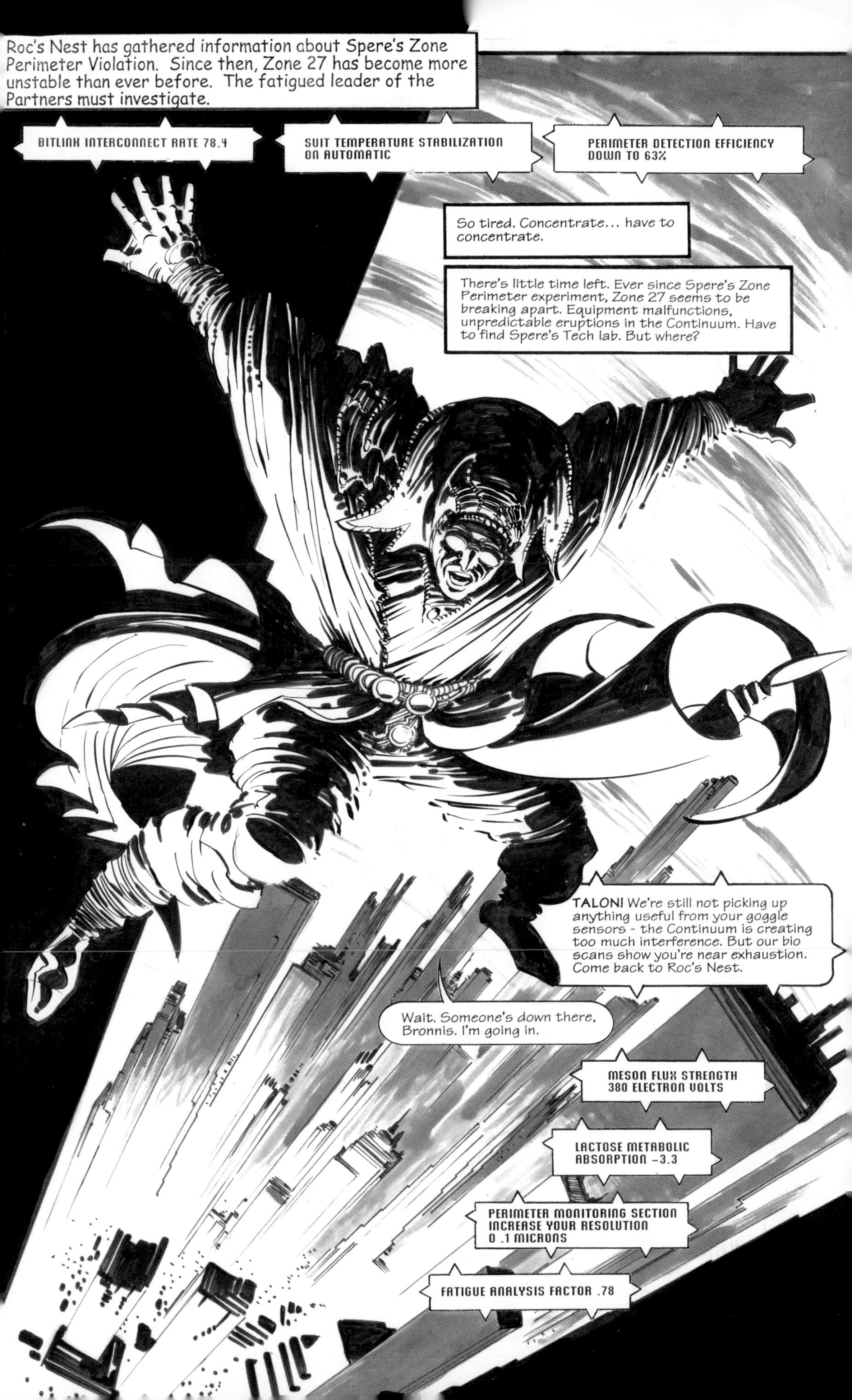
Roc's Nest has gathered information about Spere's Zone Perimeter Violation. Since then, Zone 27 has become more unstable than ever before. The fatigued leader of the Partners must investigate.
BITLINK INTERCONNECT RATE 78.4
SUIT TEMPERATURE STABILIZATION ON AUTOMATIC
PERIMETER DETECTION EFFICIENCY DOWN TO 63%
So tired. Concentrate... have to concentrate.
There's little time left. Ever since Spere's Zone Perimeter experiment, Zone 27 seems to be breaking apart. Equipment malfunctions, unpredictable eruptions in the Continuum. Have to find Spere's Tech lab. But where?
TALON! We're still not picking up anything useful from your goggle sensors - the Continuum is creating too much interference. But our bio scans show you're near exhaustion. Come back to Roc's Nest.
Wait. Someone's down there, Bronnis. I'm going in.
MESON FLUX STRENGTH 380 ELECTRON VOLTS
LACTOSE METABOLIC ABSORPTION -3.3
PERIMETER MONITORING SECTION INCREASE YOUR RESOLUTION 0 .1 MICRONS
FATIGUE ANALYSIS FACTOR .78

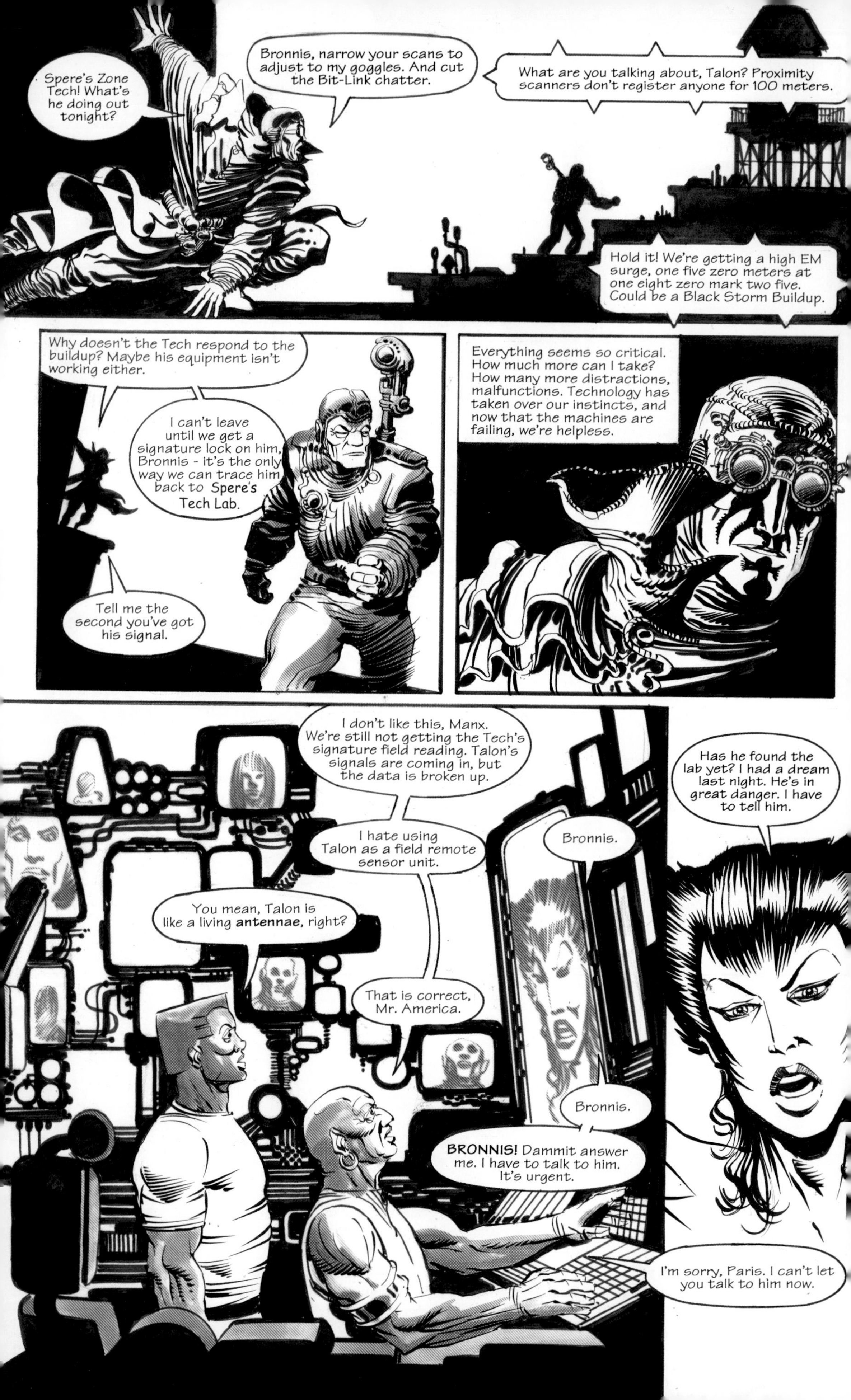
Spere's Zone Tech! What's he doing out tonight?
Bronnis, narrow your scans to adjust to my goggles. And cut the Bit-Link chatter.
What are you talking about, Talon? Proximity scanners don't register anyone for 100 meters.
Hold it! We're getting a high EM surge, one five zero meters at one eight zero mark two five. Could be a Black Storm Buildup.
Why doesn't the Tech respond to the buildup? Maybe his equipment isn't working either.
I can't leave until we get a signature lock on him, Bronnis - it's the only way we can trace him back to Spere's Tech Lab.
Tell me the second you've got his signal.
Everything seems so critical. How much more can I take? How many more distractions, malfunctions. Technology has taken over our instincts, and now that the machines are failing, we're helpless.
I don't like this, Manx. We're still not getting the Tech's signature field reading. Talon's signals are coming in, but the data is broken up.
I hate using Talon as a field remote sensor unit.
You mean, Talon is like a living **antennae**, right?
That is correct, Mr. America.
Has he found the lab yet? I had a dream last night. He's in great danger. I have to tell him.
Bronnis.
Bronnis.
BRONNIS! Dammit answer me. I have to talk to him. It's urgent.
I'm sorry, Paris. I can't let you talk to him now.

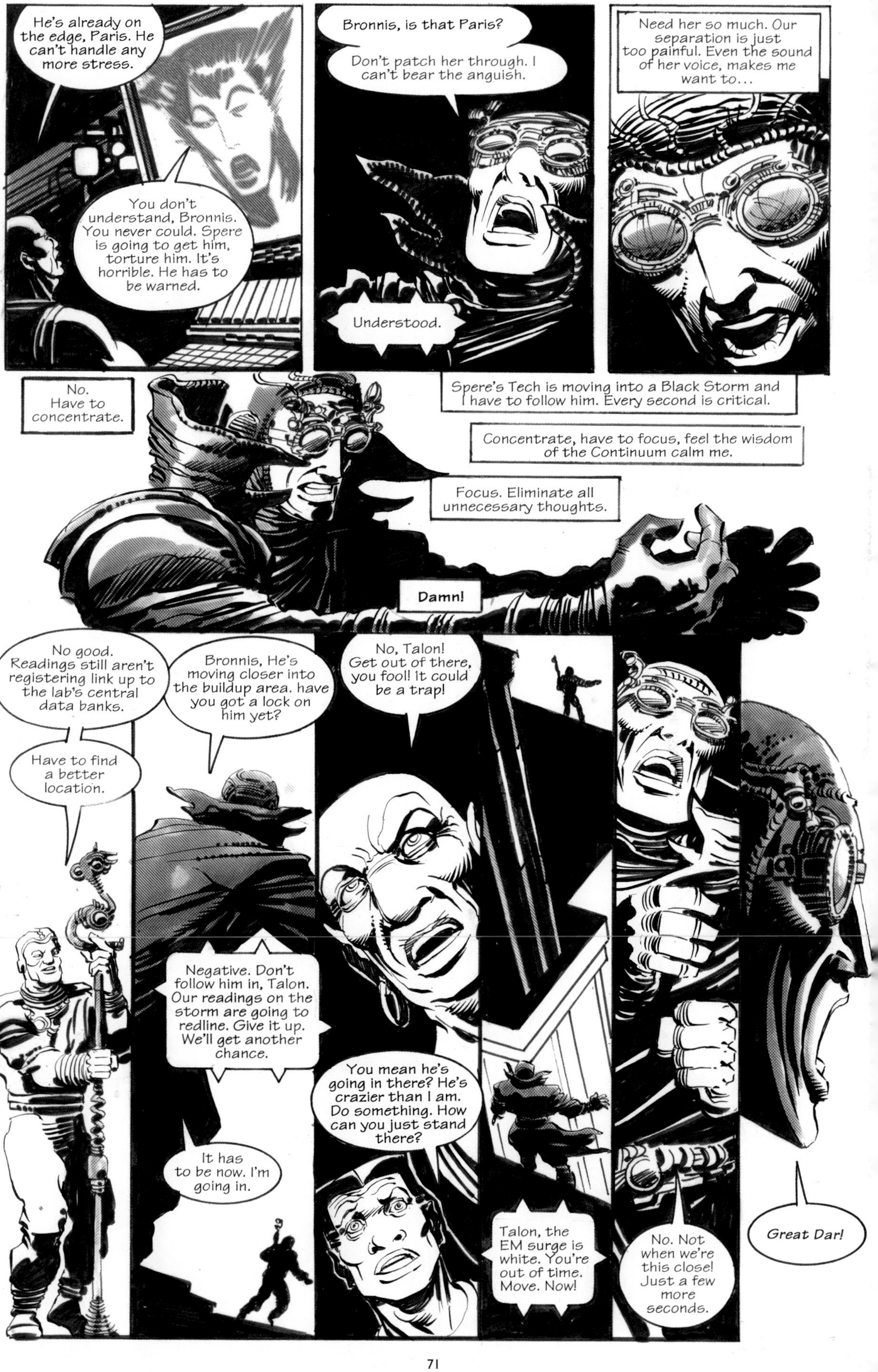
He's already on the edge, Paris. He can't handle any more stress.
You don't understand, Bronnis. You never could. Spere is going to get him, torture him. It's horrible. He has to be warned.
Bronnis, is that Paris?
Don't patch her through. I can't bear the anguish.
Understood.
Need her so much. Our separation is just too painful. Even the sound of her voice, makes me want to...
No. Have to concentrate.
Spere's Tech is moving into a Black Storm and I have to follow him. Every second is critical.
Concentrate, have to focus, feel the wisdom of the Continuum calm me.
Focus. Eliminate all unnecessary thoughts.
Damn!
No good. Readings still aren't registering link up to the lab's central data banks.
Have to find a better location.
Bronnis, He's moving closer into the buildup area. have you got a lock on him yet?
Negative. Don't follow him in, Talon. Our readings on the storm are going to redline. Give it up. We'll get another chance.
It has to be now. I'm going in.
No, Talon! Get out of there, you fool! It could be a trap!
You mean he's going in there? He's crazier than I am. Do something. How can you just stand there?
Talon, the EM surge is white. You're out of time. Move. Now!
No. Not when we're this close! Just a few more seconds.
Great Dar!

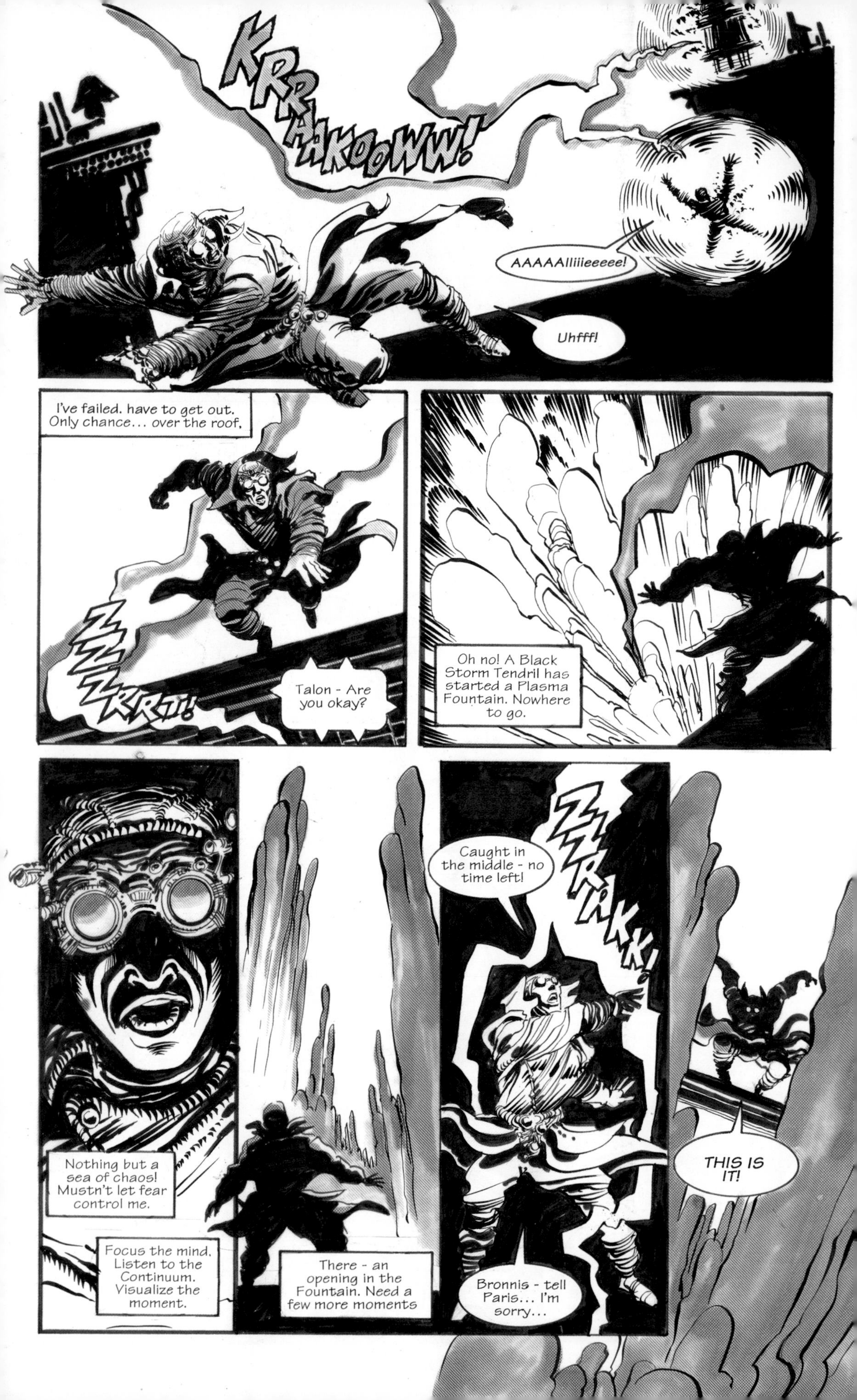
KRRAAKOOOWW!
AAAAAIIiiieeeee!
Uhfff!
I've failed. have to get out. Only chance... over the roof,
ZZZZRRT!
Talon - Are you okay?
Oh no! A Black Storm Tendril has started a Plasma Fountain. Nowhere to go.
Nothing but a sea of chaos! Mustn't let fear control me.
Focus the mind. Listen to the Continuum. Visualize the moment.
There - an opening in the Fountain. Need a few more moments
Caught in the middle - no time left!
ZZRAKK!
Bronnis - tell Paris... I'm sorry...
THIS IS IT!

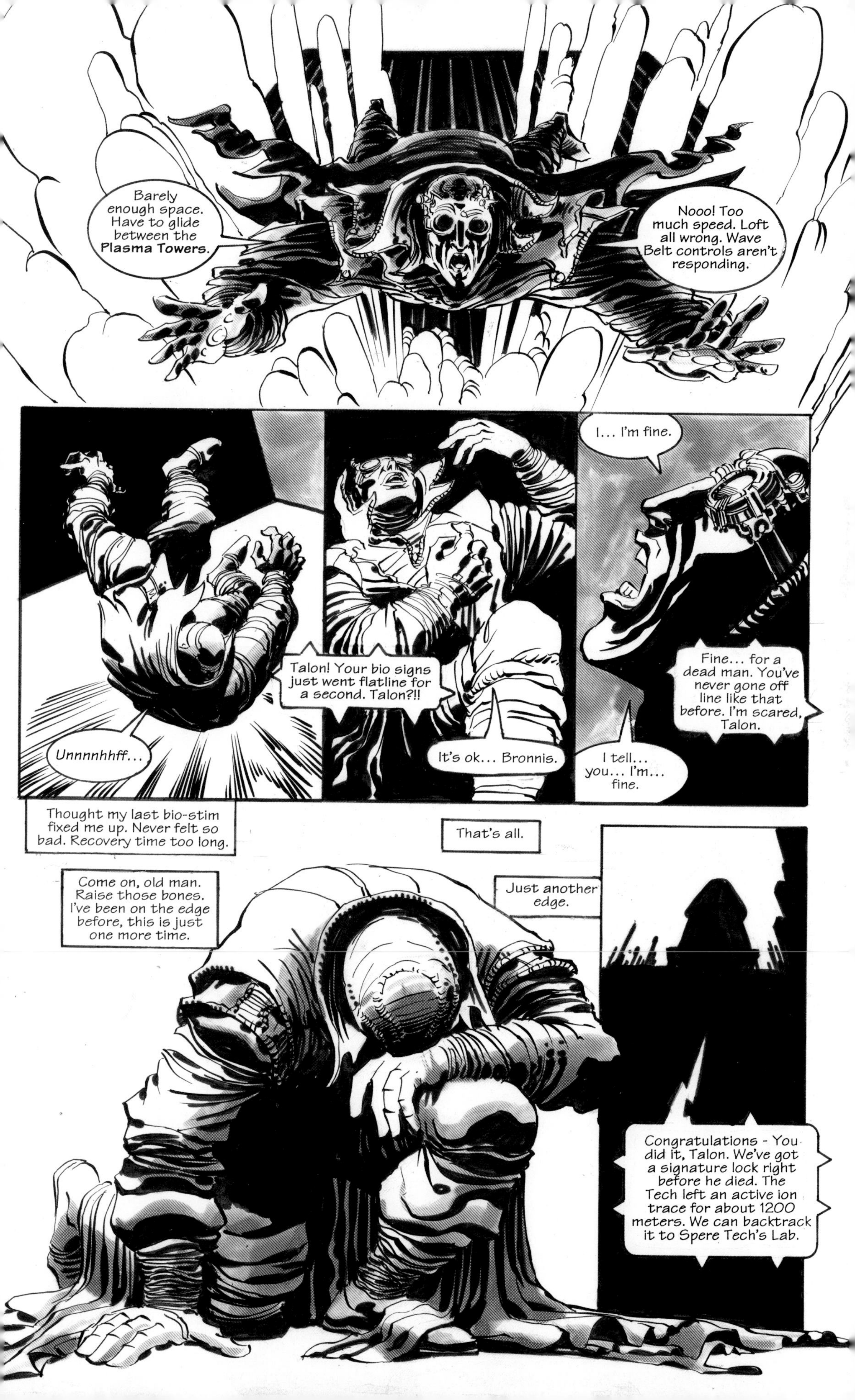
Barely enough space. Have to glide between the **Plasma Towers.**
Nooo! Too much speed. Loft all wrong. Wave Belt controls aren't responding.
Unnnnhhff...
Talon! Your bio signs just went flatline for a second. Talon?!!
It's ok... Bronnis.
I... I'm fine.
Fine... for a dead man. You've never gone off line like that before. I'm scared, Talon.
I tell... you... I'm... fine.
Thought my last bio-stim fixed me up. Never felt so bad. Recovery time too long.
That's all.
Come on, old man. Raise those bones. I've been on the edge before, this is just one more time.
Just another edge.
Congratulations - You did it, Talon. We've got a signature lock right before he died. The Tech left an active ion trace for about 1200 meters. We can backtrack it to Spere Tech's Lab.

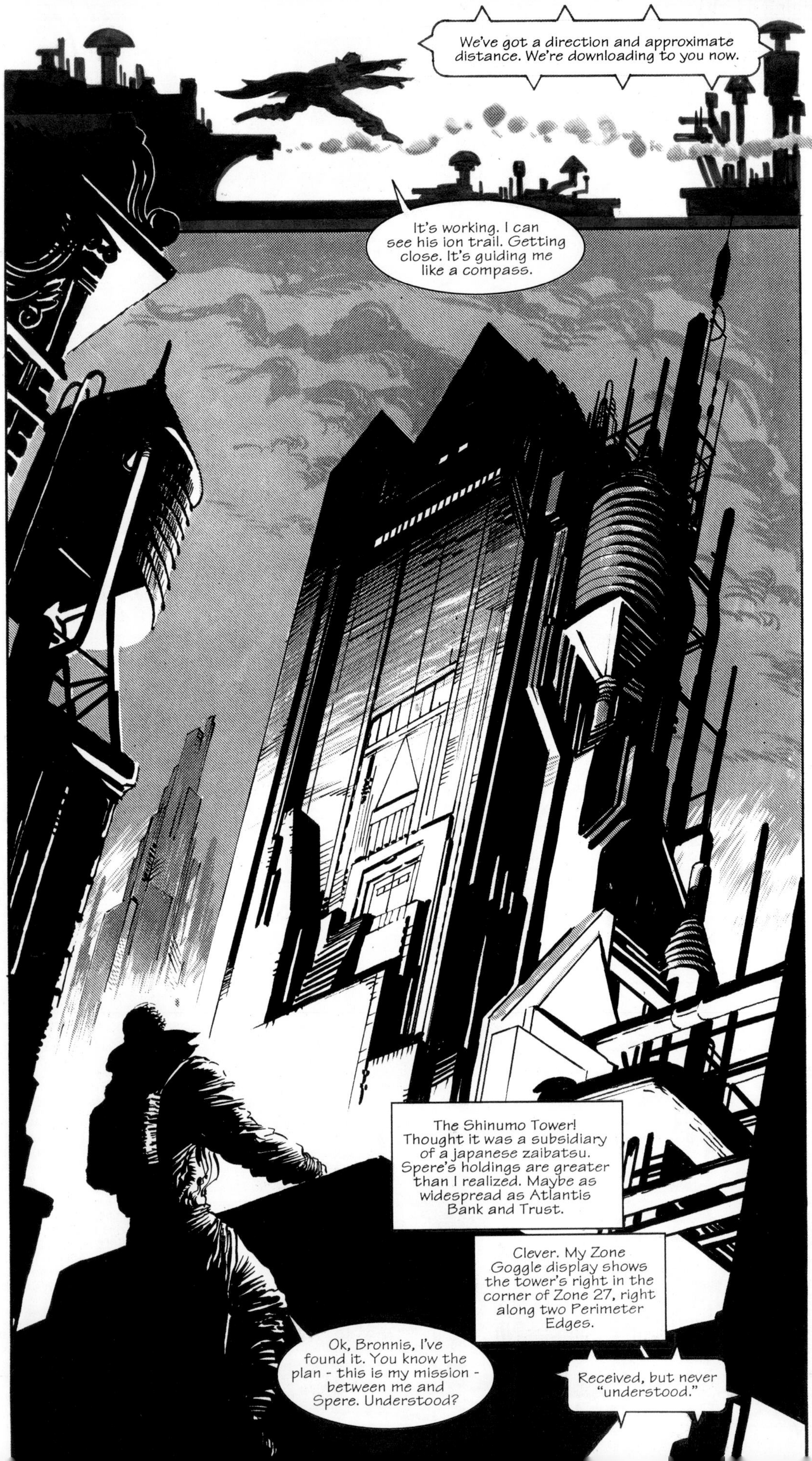
We've got a direction and approximate distance. We're downloading to you now.
It's working. I can see his ion trail. Getting close. It's guiding me like a compass.
The Shinumo Tower! Thought it was a subsidiary of a japanese zaibatsu. Spere's holdings are greater than I realized. Maybe as widespread as Atlantis Bank and Trust.
Clever. My Zone Goggle display shows the tower's right in the corner of Zone 27, right along two Perimeter Edges.
Ok, Bronnis, I've found it. You know the plan - this is my mission - between me and Spere. Understood?
Received, but never "understood."

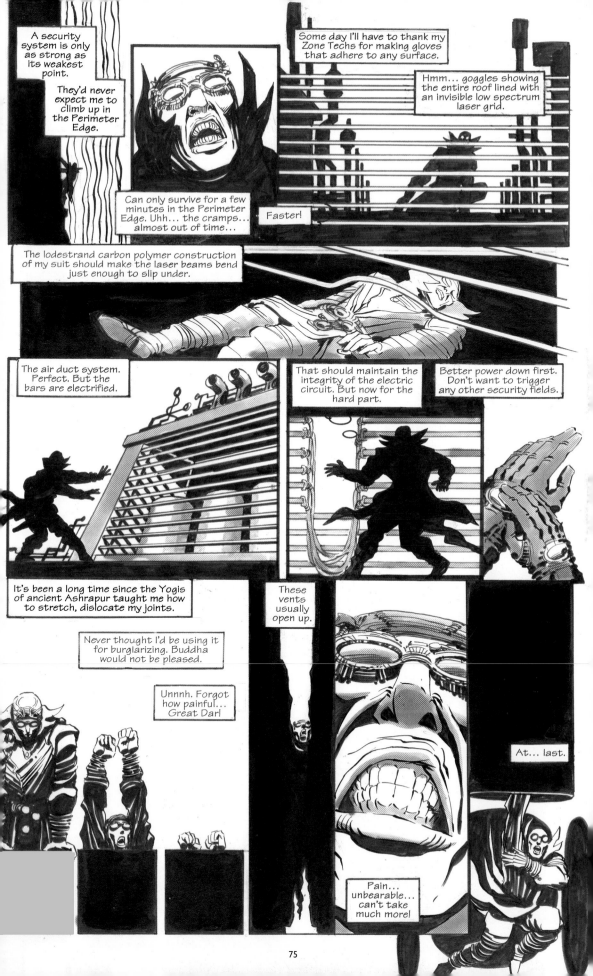

A security system is only as strong as its weakest point.

They'd never expect me to climb up in the Perimeter Edge.

Some day I'll have to thank my Zone Techs for making gloves that adhere to any surface.

Hmm... goggles showing the entire roof lined with an invisible low spectrum laser grid.

Can only survive for a few minutes in the Perimeter Edge. Uhh... the cramps... almost out of time...

Faster!

The lodestrand carbon polymer construction of my suit should make the laser beams bend just enough to slip under.

The air duct system. Perfect. But the bars are electrified.

That should maintain the integrity of the electric circuit. But now for the hard part.

Better power down first. Don't want to trigger any other security fields.

It's been a long time since the Yogis of ancient Ashrapur taught me how to stretch, dislocate my joints.

These vents usually open up.

Never thought I'd be using it for burglarizing. Buddha would not be pleased.

Unnnh. Forgot how painful... Great Dar!

At... last.

Pain... unbearable... can't take much more!

75

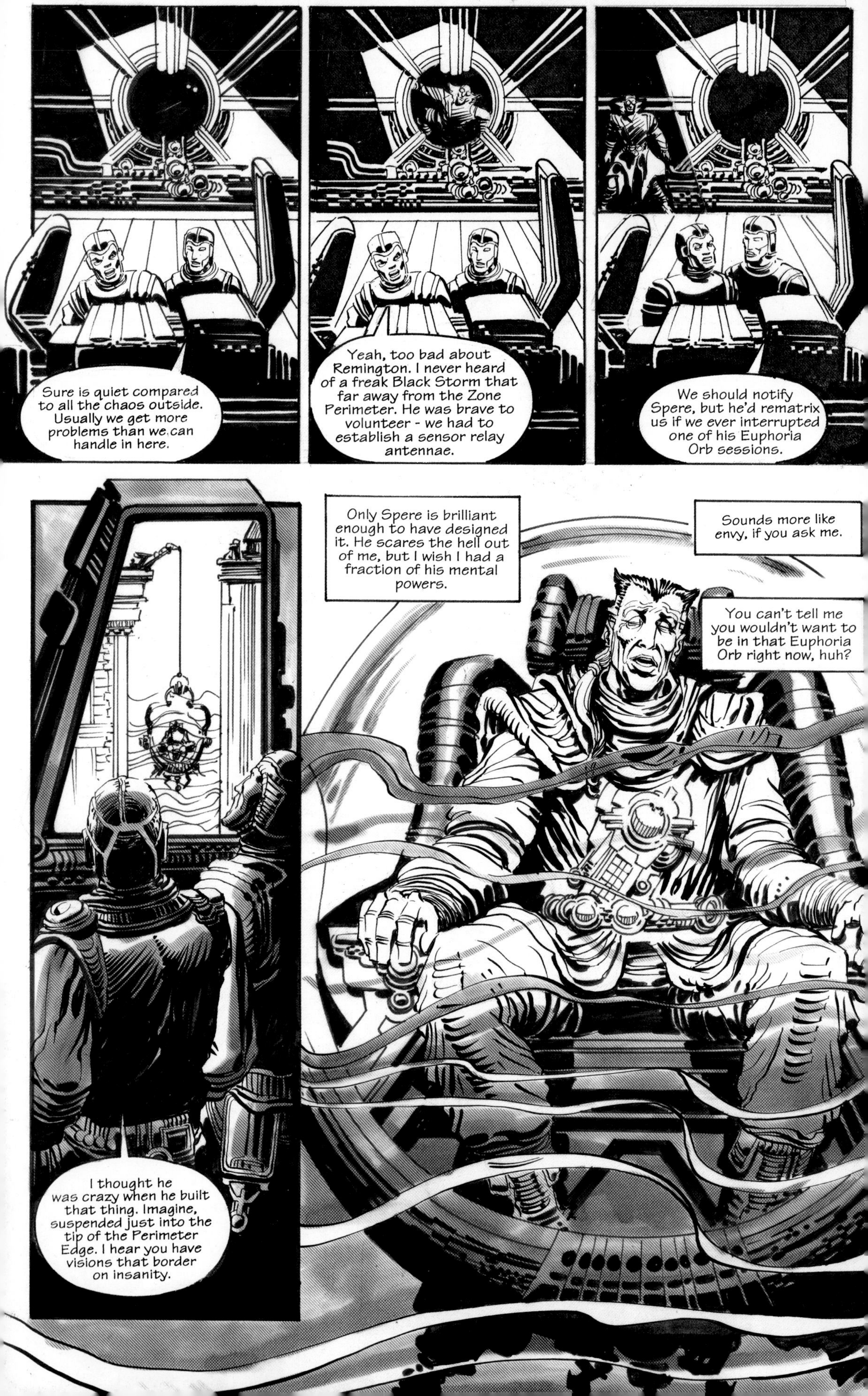

Sure is quiet compared to all the chaos outside. Usually we get more problems than we can handle in here.
Yeah, too bad about Remington. I never heard of a freak Black Storm that far away from the Zone Perimeter. He was brave to volunteer - we had to establish a sensor relay antennae.
We should notify Spere, but he'd rematrix us if we ever interrupted one of his Euphoria Orb sessions.
Only Spere is brilliant enough to have designed it. He scares the hell out of me, but I wish I had a fraction of his mental powers.
Sounds more like envy, if you ask me.
You can't tell me you wouldn't want to be in that Euphoria Orb right now, huh?
I thought he was crazy when he built that thing. Imagine, suspended just into the tip of the Perimeter Edge. I hear you have visions that border on insanity.

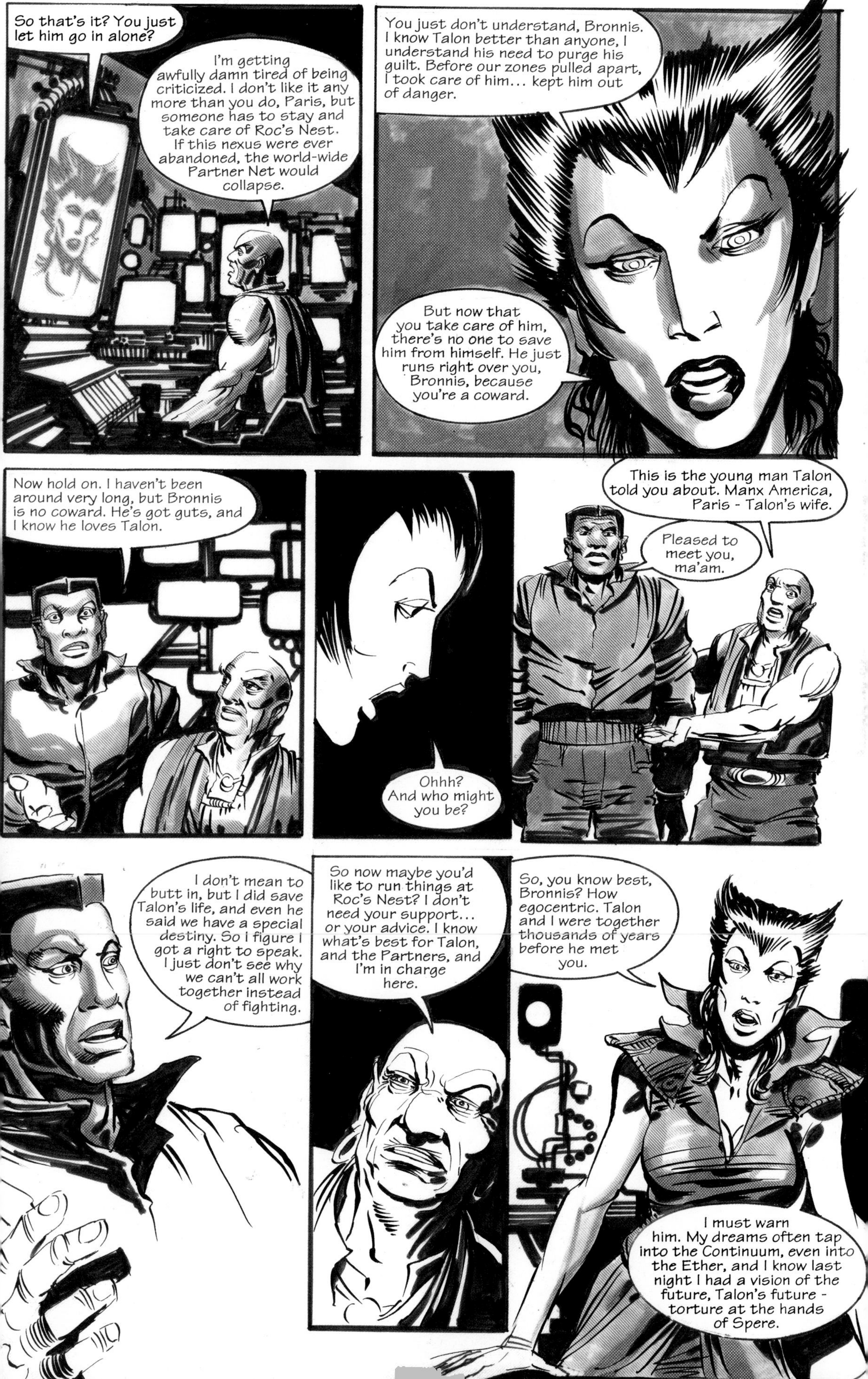

So that's it? You just let him go in alone?
I'm getting awfully damn tired of being criticized. I don't like it any more than you do, Paris, but someone has to stay and take care of Roc's Nest. If this nexus were ever abandoned, the world-wide Partner Net would collapse.
You just don't understand, Bronnis. I know Talon better than anyone, I understand his need to purge his guilt. Before our zones pulled apart, I took care of him... kept him out of danger.
But now that you take care of him, there's no one to save him from himself. He just runs right over you, Bronnis, because you're a coward.
Now hold on. I haven't been around very long, but Bronnis is no coward. He's got guts, and I know he loves Talon.
Ohhh? And who might you be?
This is the young man Talon told you about. Manx America, Paris - Talon's wife.
Pleased to meet you, ma'am.
I don't mean to butt in, but I did save Talon's life, and even he said we have a special destiny. So I figure I got a right to speak. I just don't see why we can't all work together instead of fighting.
So now maybe you'd like to run things at Roc's Nest? I don't need your support... or your advice. I know what's best for Talon, and the Partners, and I'm in charge here.
So, you know best, Bronnis? How egocentric. Talon and I were together thousands of years before he met you.
I must warn him. My dreams often tap into the Continuum, even into the Ether, and I know last night I had a vision of the future, Talon's future - torture at the hands of Spere.

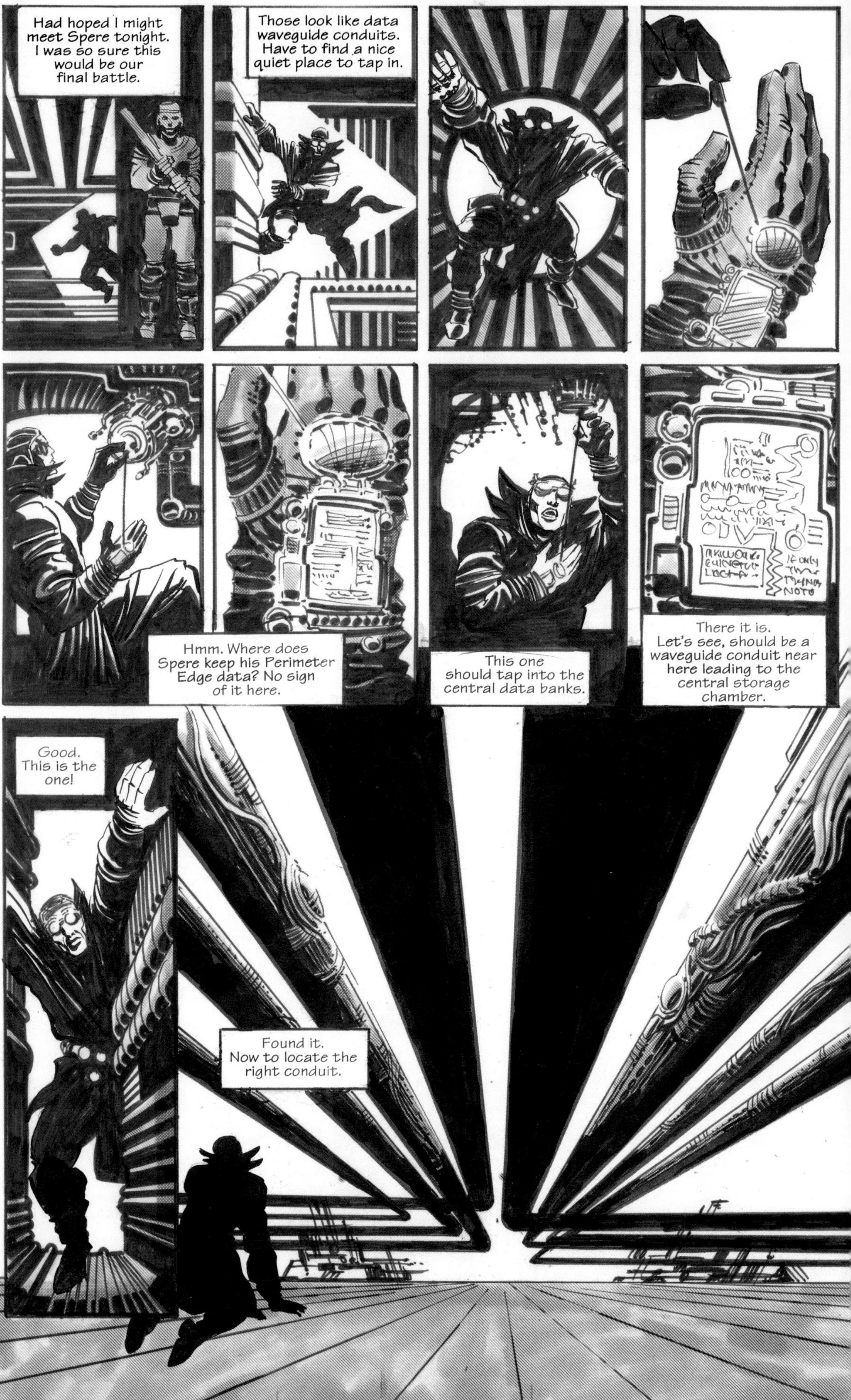
Had hoped I might meet Spere tonight. I was so sure this would be our final battle.
Those look like data waveguide conduits. Have to find a nice quiet place to tap in.
Hmm. Where does Spere keep his Perimeter Edge data? No sign of it here.
This one should tap into the central data banks.
There it is. Let's see, should be a waveguide conduit near here leading to the central storage chamber.
Good. This is the one!
Found it. Now to locate the right conduit.

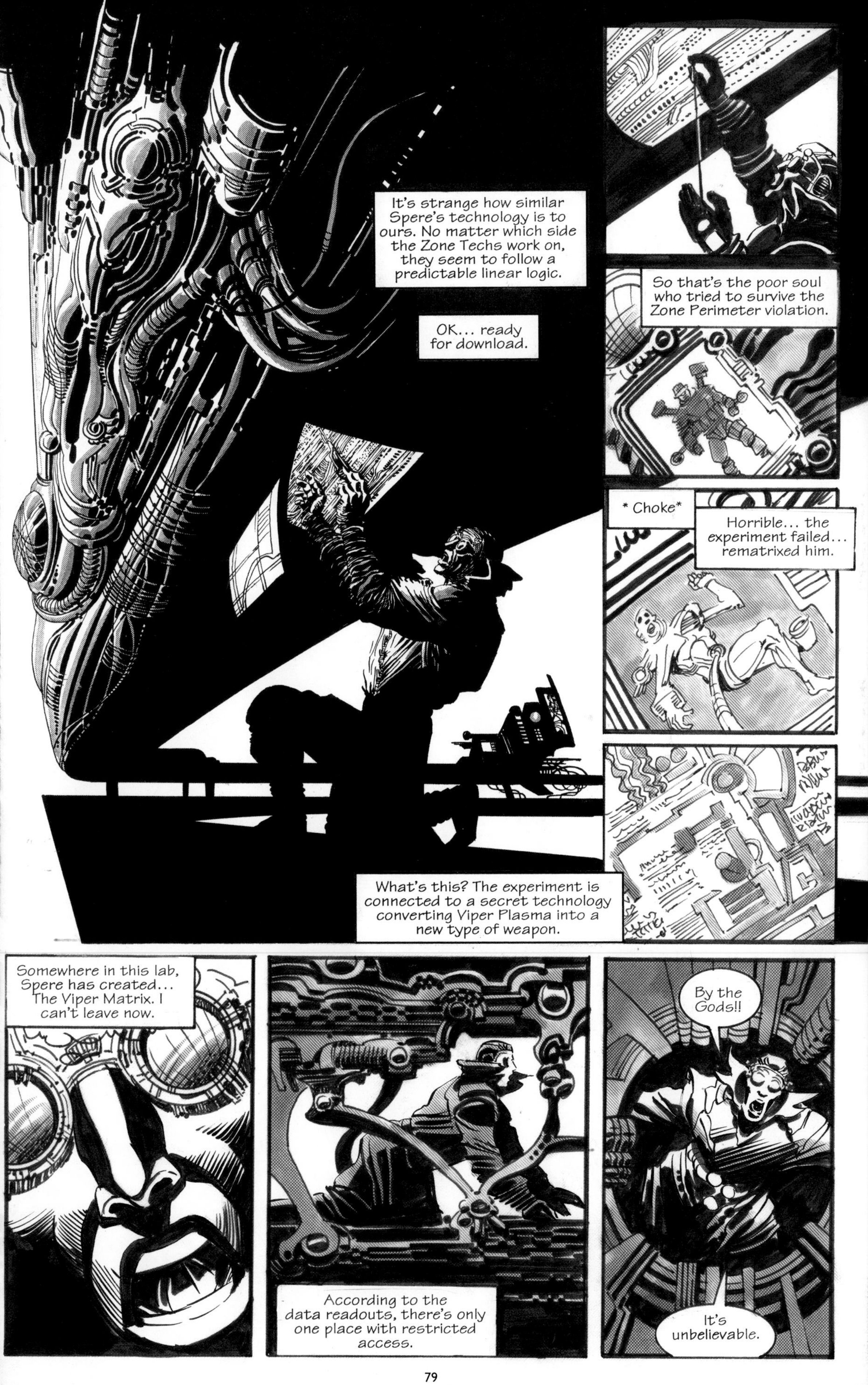

It's strange how similar Spere's technology is to ours. No matter which side the Zone Techs work on, they seem to follow a predictable linear logic.
OK... ready for download.
So that's the poor soul who tried to survive the Zone Perimeter violation.
* Choke*
Horrible... the experiment failed... rematrixed him.
What's this? The experiment is connected to a secret technology converting Viper Plasma into a new type of weapon.
Somewhere in this lab, Spere has created... The Viper Matrix. I can't leave now.
According to the data readouts, there's only one place with restricted access.
By the Gods!!
It's unbelievable.

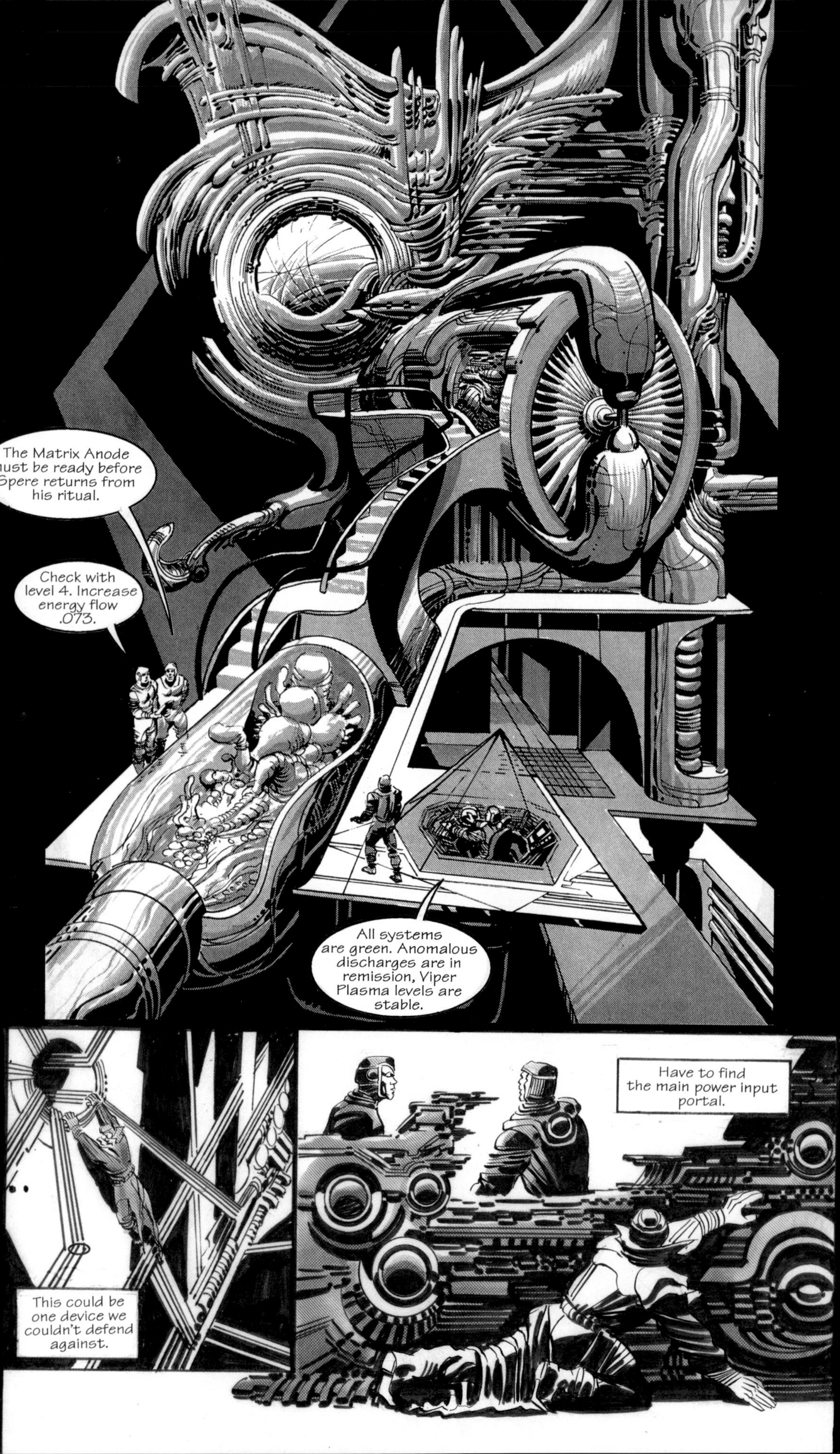
The Matrix Anode must be ready before Spere returns from his ritual.
Check with level 4. Increase energy flow .073.
All systems are green. Anomalous discharges are in remission, Viper Plasma levels are stable.
This could be one device we couldn't defend against.
Have to find the main power input portal.

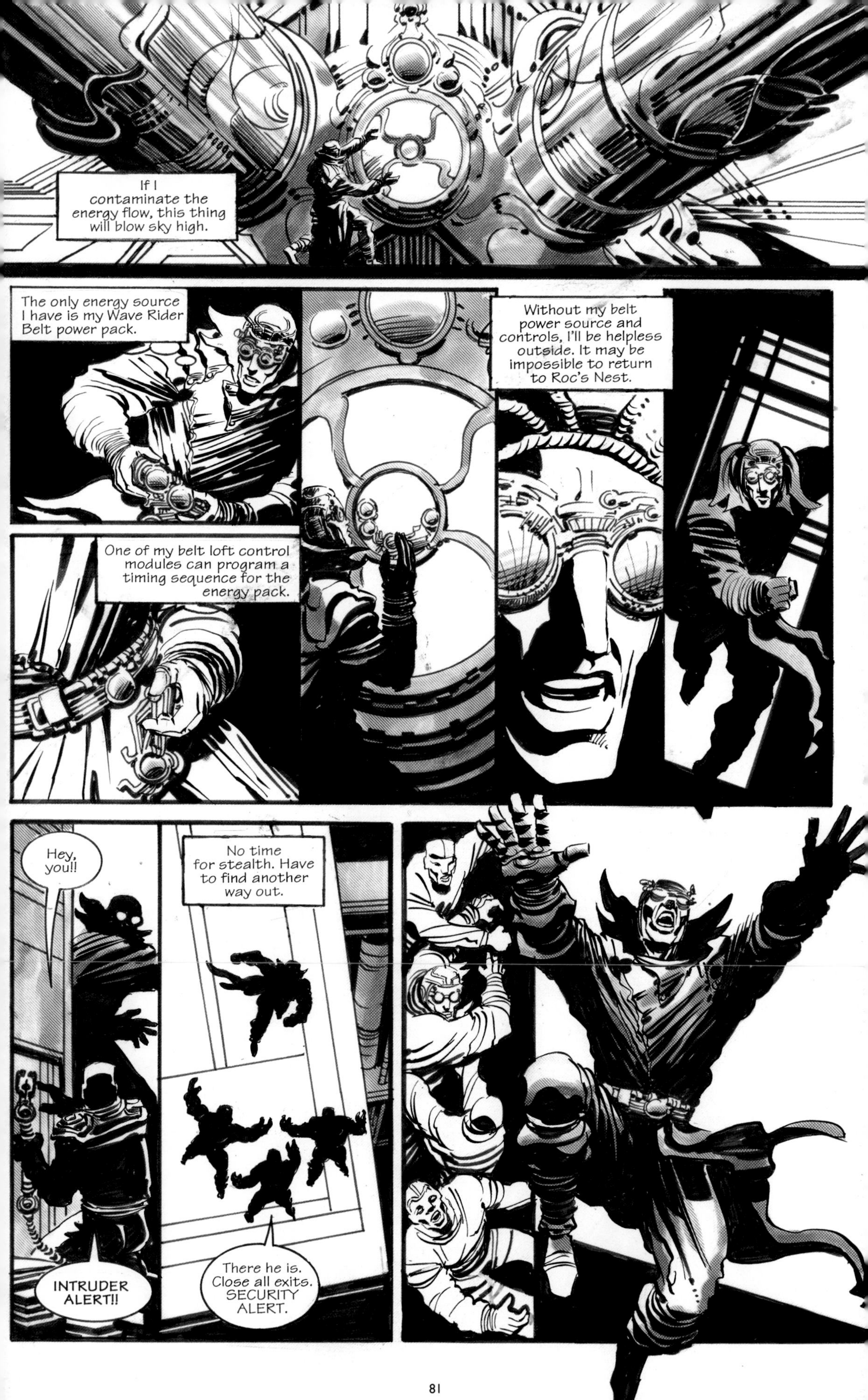
If I contaminate the energy flow, this thing will blow sky high.
The only energy source I have is my Wave Rider Belt power pack.
One of my belt loft control modules can program a timing sequence for the energy pack.
Without my belt power source and controls, I'll be helpless outside. It may be impossible to return to Roc's Nest.
Hey, you!!
INTRUDER ALERT!!
No time for stealth. Have to find another way out.
There he is. Close all exits. SECURITY ALERT.

Unhh. No loft controls to slow my descent.

Time's running out. Have to get as far away as possible.

SSBARRRQOOOOMM!

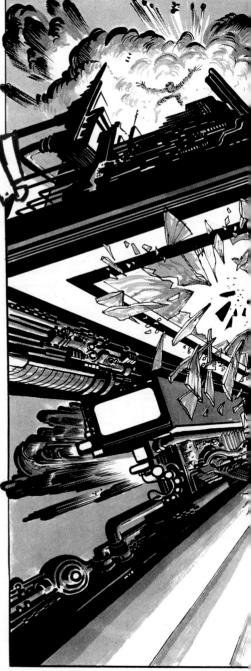

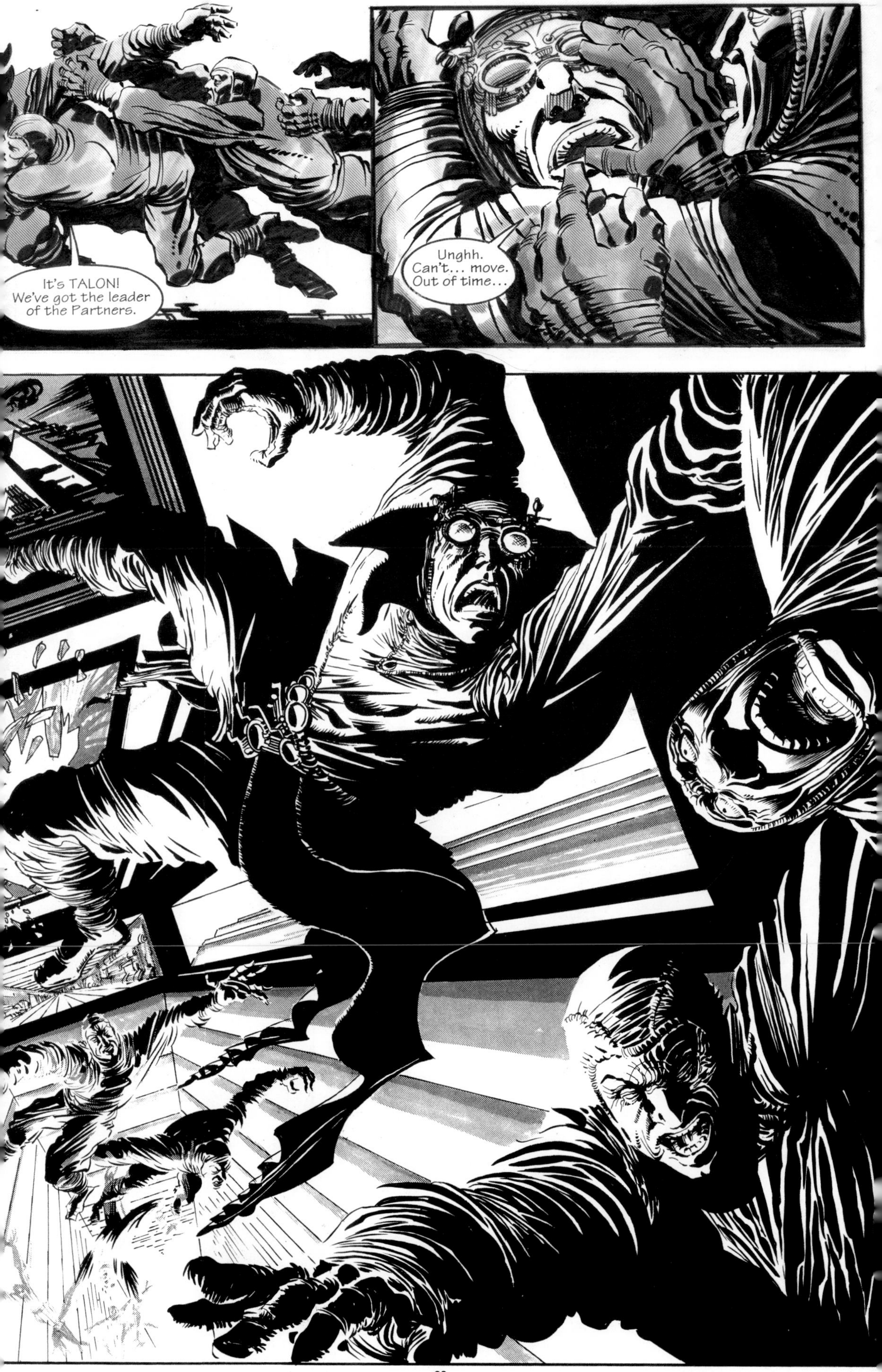
It's TALON! We've got the leader of the Partners.
Unghh. Can't... move. Out of time...

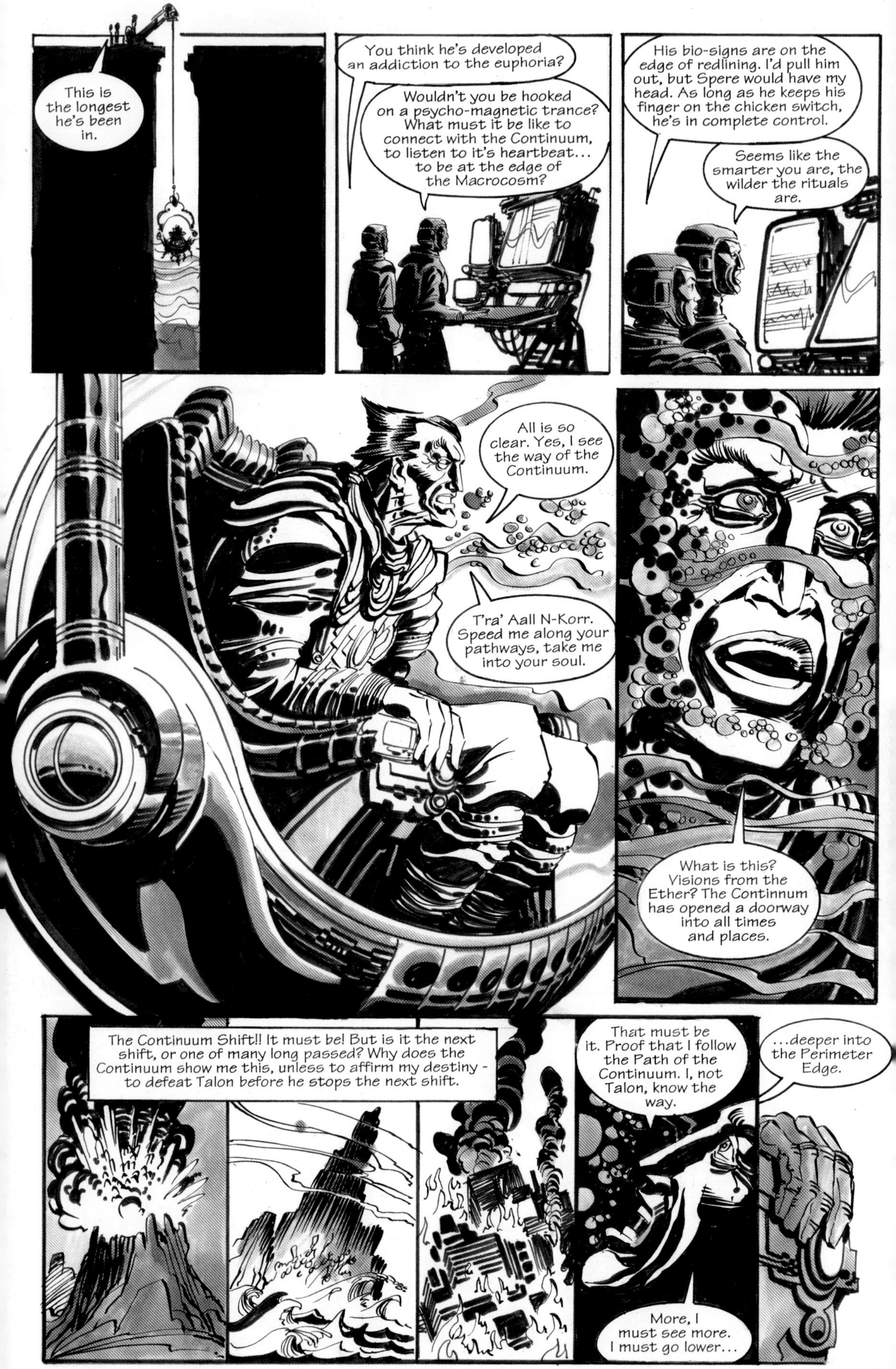
This is the longest he's been in.
You think he's developed an addiction to the euphoria?
Wouldn't you be hooked on a psycho-magnetic trance? What must it be like to connect with the Continuum, to listen to it's heartbeat... to be at the edge of the Macrocosm?
His bio-signs are on the edge of redlining. I'd pull him out, but Spere would have my head. As long as he keeps his finger on the chicken switch, he's in complete control.
Seems like the smarter you are, the wilder the rituals are.
All is so clear. Yes, I see the way of the Continuum.
T'ra' Aall N-Korr. Speed me along your pathways, take me into your soul.
What is this? Visions from the Ether? The Continnum has opened a doorway into all times and places.
The Continuum Shift!! It must be! But is it the next shift, or one of many long passed? Why does the Continuum show me this, unless to affirm my destiny - to defeat Talon before he stops the next shift.
That must be it. Proof that I follow the Path of the Continuum. I, not Talon, know the way.
...deeper into the Perimeter Edge.
More, I must see more. I must go lower...

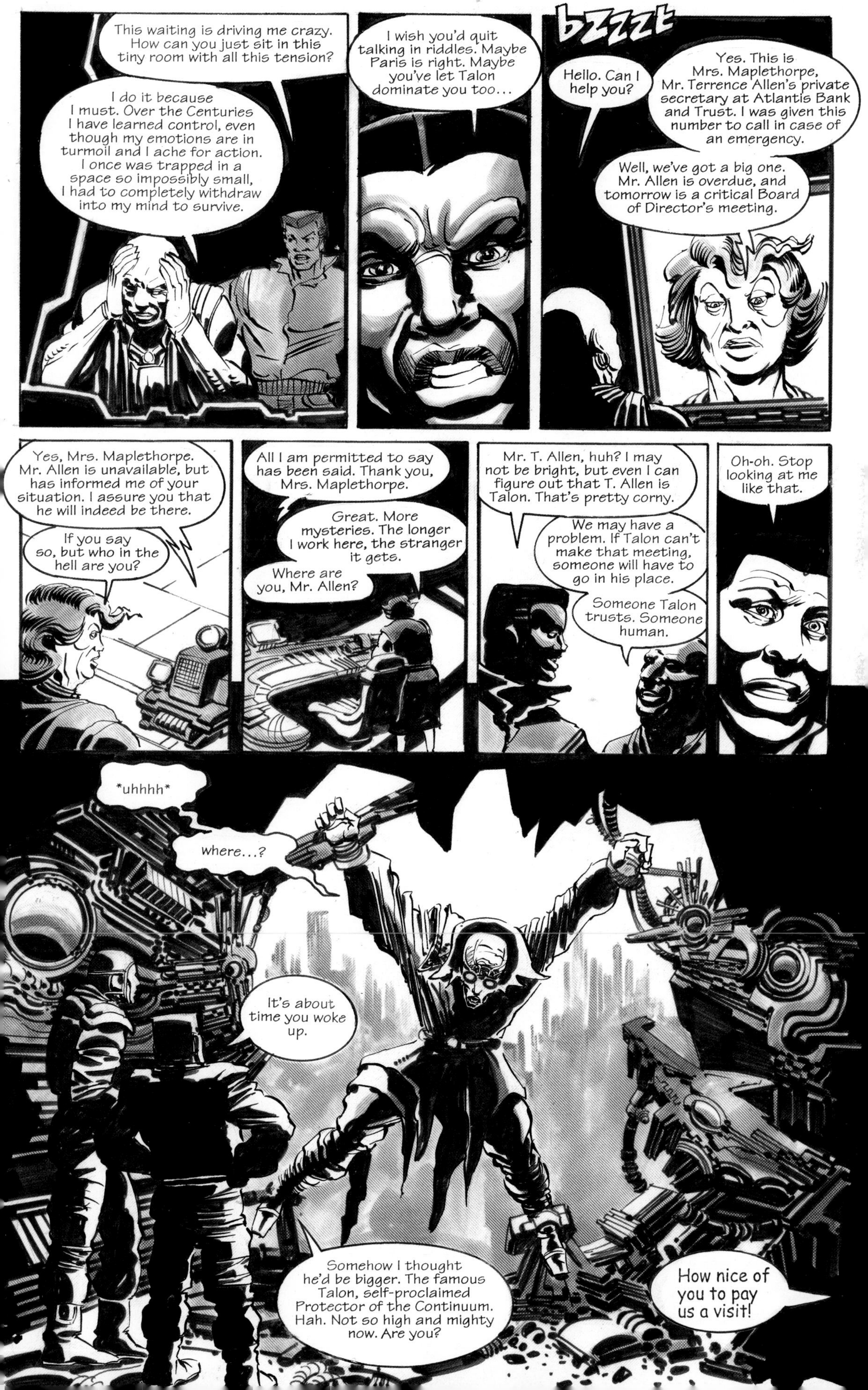
This waiting is driving me crazy. How can you just sit in this tiny room with all this tension?
I do it because I must. Over the Centuries I have learned control, even though my emotions are in turmoil and I ache for action. I once was trapped in a space so impossibly small, I had to completely withdraw into my mind to survive.
I wish you'd quit talking in riddles. Maybe Paris is right. Maybe you've let Talon dominate you too…
bzzzt
Hello. Can I help you?
Yes. This is Mrs. Maplethorpe, Mr. Terrence Allen's private secretary at Atlantis Bank and Trust. I was given this number to call in case of an emergency.
Well, we've got a big one. Mr. Allen is overdue, and tomorrow is a critical Board of Director's meeting.
Yes, Mrs. Maplethorpe. Mr. Allen is unavailable, but has informed me of your situation. I assure you that he will indeed be there.
If you say so, but who in the hell are you?
All I am permitted to say has been said. Thank you, Mrs. Maplethorpe.
Great. More mysteries. The longer I work here, the stranger it gets.
Where are you, Mr. Allen?
Mr. T. Allen, huh? I may not be bright, but even I can figure out that T. Allen is Talon. That's pretty corny.
We may have a problem. If Talon can't make that meeting, someone will have to go in his place.
Someone Talon trusts. Someone human.
Oh-oh. Stop looking at me like that.
uhhhh
where…?
It's about time you woke up.
Somehow I thought he'd be bigger. The famous Talon, self-proclaimed Protector of the Continuum. Hah. Not so high and mighty now. Are you?
How nice of you to pay us a visit!

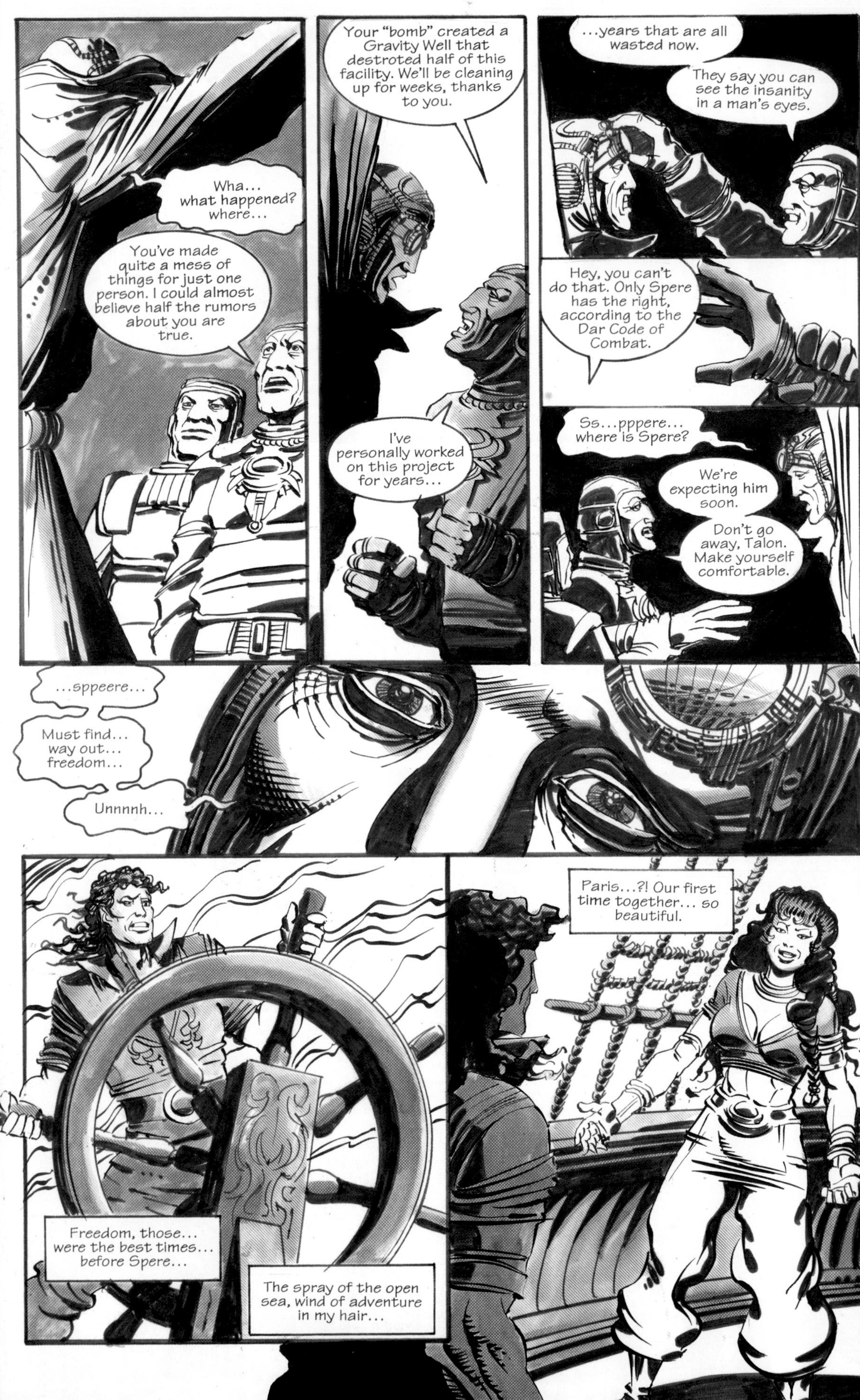
Wha… what happened? where…
You've made quite a mess of things for just one person. I could almost believe half the rumors about you are true.
Your "bomb" created a Gravity Well that destroted half of this facility. We'll be cleaning up for weeks, thanks to you.
I've personally worked on this project for years…
…years that are all wasted now.
They say you can see the insanity in a man's eyes.
Hey, you can't do that. Only Spere has the right, according to the Dar Code of Combat.
Ss…pppere… where is Spere?
We're expecting him soon.
Don't go away, Talon. Make yourself comfortable.
…sppeere…
Must find… way out… freedom…
Unnnnh…
Freedom, those… were the best times… before Spere…
The spray of the open sea, wind of adventure in my hair…
Paris…?! Our first time together… so beautiful.

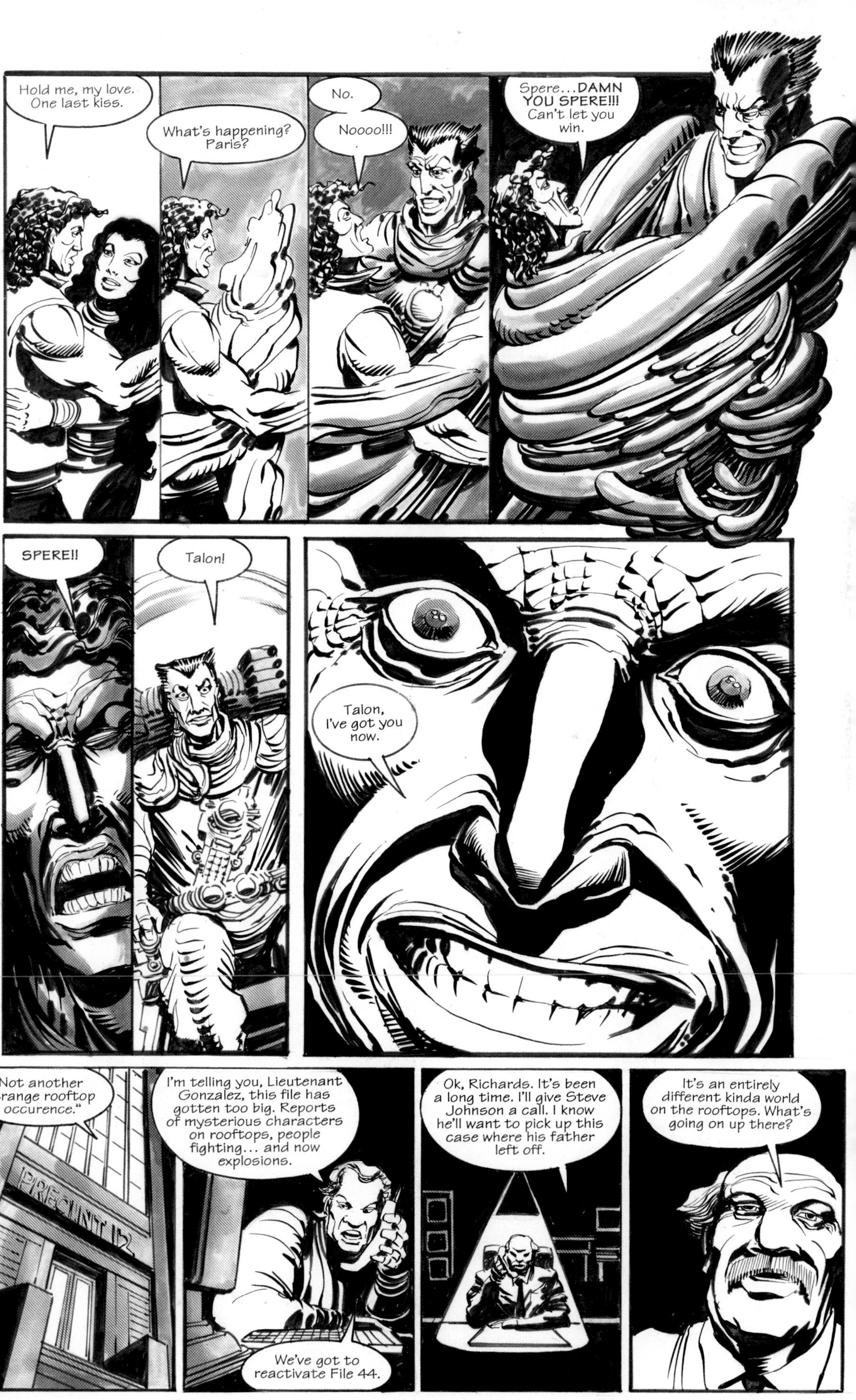
Hold me, my love. One last kiss.
What's happening? Paris?
No.
Noooo!!!
Spere...DAMN YOU SPERE!!! Can't let you win.
SPERE!!
Talon!
Talon, I've got you now.
Not another "strange rooftop occurence."
PRECINCT 12
I'm telling you, Lieutenant Gonzalez, this file has gotten too big. Reports of mysterious characters on rooftops, people fighting... and now explosions.
We've got to reactivate File 44.
Ok, Richards. It's been a long time. I'll give Steve Johnson a call. I know he'll want to pick up this case where his father left off.
It's an entirely different kinda world on the rooftops. What's going on up there?

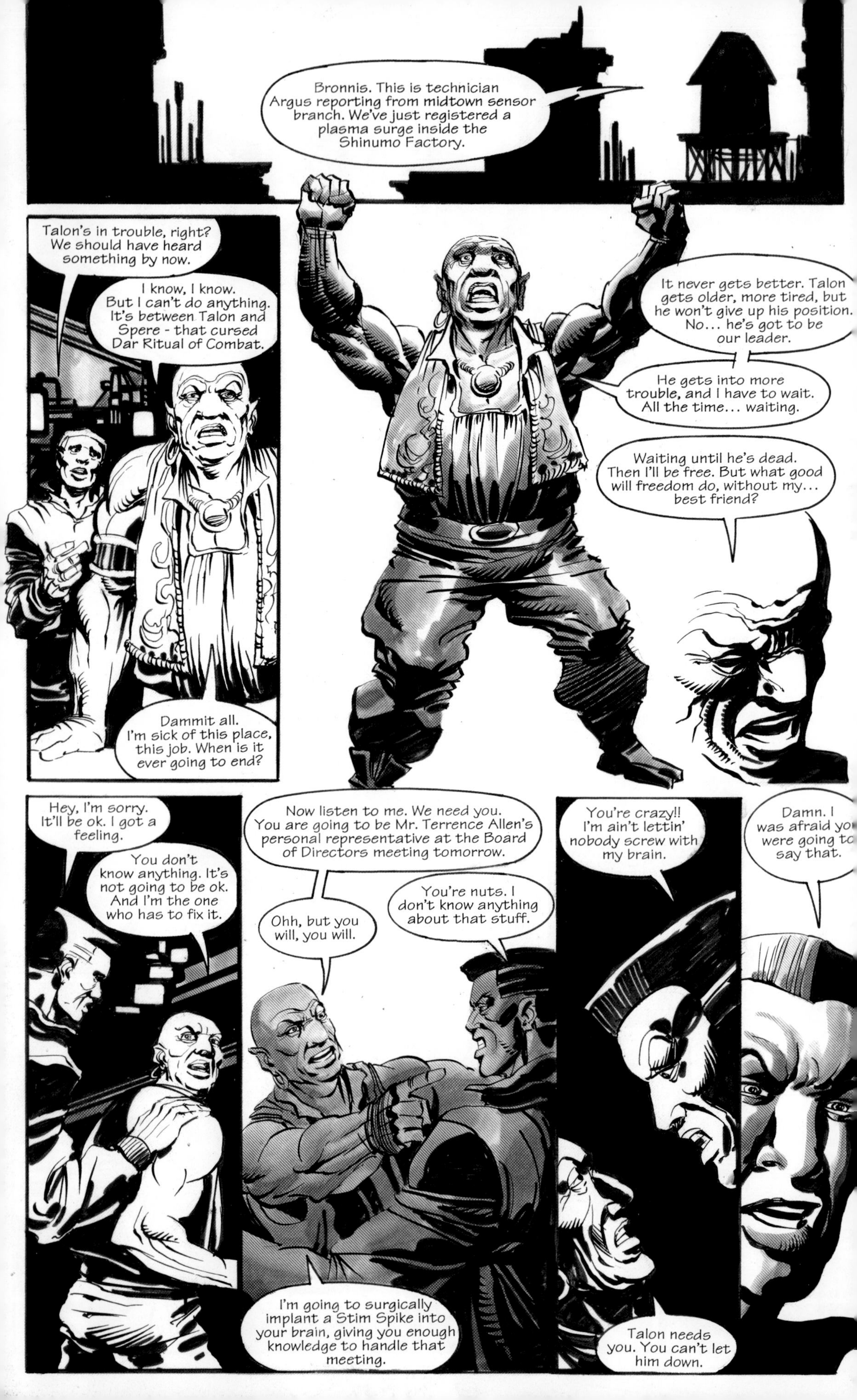
Bronnis. This is technician Argus reporting from midtown sensor branch. We've just registered a plasma surge inside the Shinumo Factory.
Talon's in trouble, right? We should have heard something by now.
I know, I know. But I can't do anything. It's between Talon and Spere - that cursed Dar Ritual of Combat.
Dammit all. I'm sick of this place, this job. When is it ever going to end?
It never gets better. Talon gets older, more tired, but he won't give up his position. No... he's got to be our leader.
He gets into more trouble, and I have to wait. All the time... waiting.
Waiting until he's dead. Then I'll be free. But what good will freedom do, without my... best friend?
Hey, I'm sorry. It'll be ok. I got a feeling.
You don't know anything. It's not going to be ok. And I'm the one who has to fix it.
Now listen to me. We need you. You are going to be Mr. Terrence Allen's personal representative at the Board of Directors meeting tomorrow.
You're nuts. I don't know anything about that stuff.
Ohh, but you will, you will.
I'm going to surgically implant a Stim Spike into your brain, giving you enough knowledge to handle that meeting.
You're crazy!! I'm ain't lettin' nobody screw with my brain.
Damn. I was afraid you were going to say that.
Talon needs you. You can't let him down.

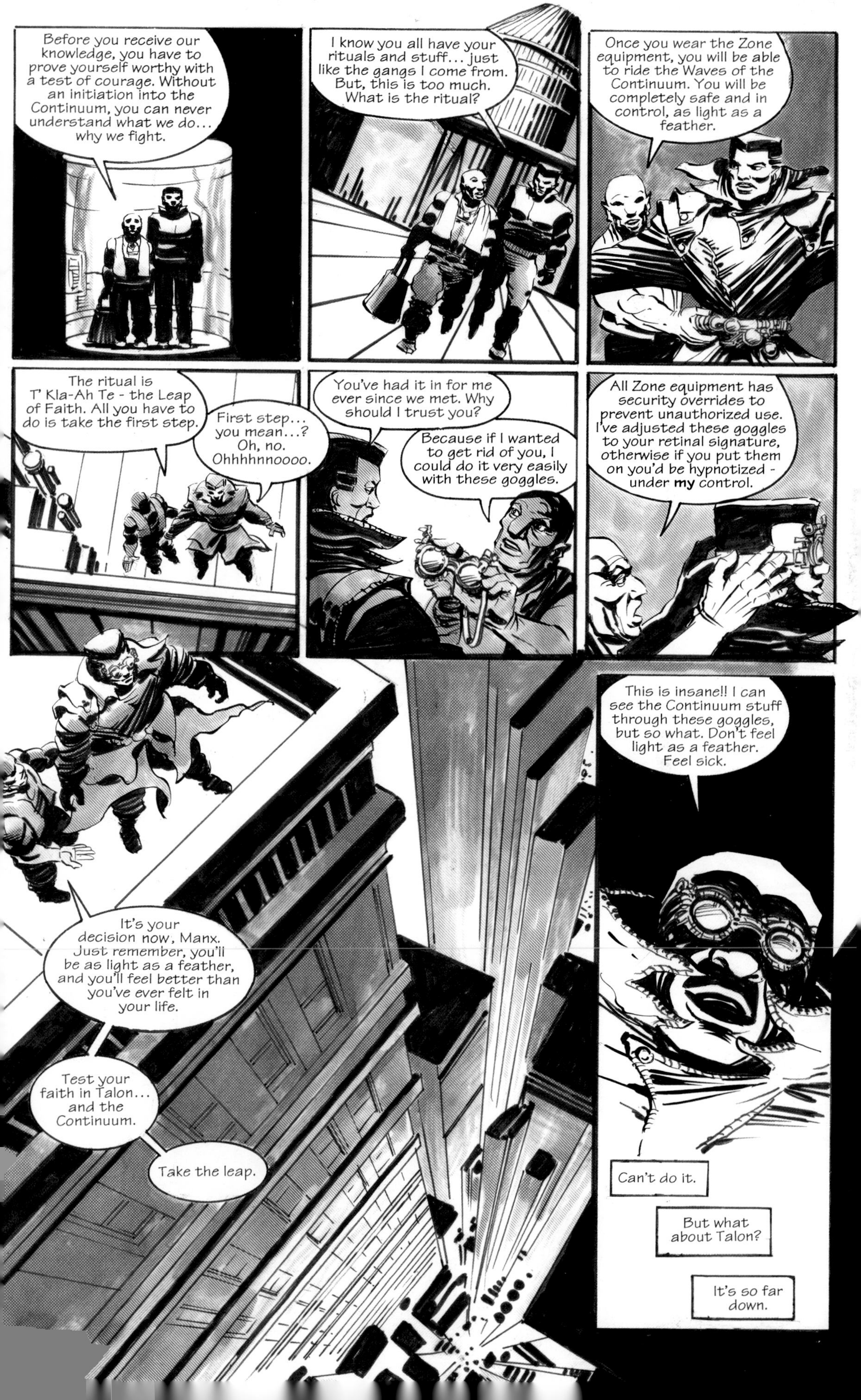
Before you receive our knowledge, you have to prove yourself worthy with a test of courage. Without an initiation into the Continuum, you can never understand what we do... why we fight.
I know you all have your rituals and stuff... just like the gangs I come from. But, this is too much. What is the ritual?
Once you wear the Zone equipment, you will be able to ride the Waves of the Continuum. You will be completely safe and in control, as light as a feather.
The ritual is T' Kla-Ah Te - the Leap of Faith. All you have to do is take the first step.
First step... you mean...? Oh, no. Ohhhhhnoooo.
You've had it in for me ever since we met. Why should I trust you?
Because if I wanted to get rid of you, I could do it very easily with these goggles.
All Zone equipment has security overrides to prevent unauthorized use. I've adjusted these goggles to your retinal signature, otherwise if you put them on you'd be hypnotized - under **my** control.
It's your decision now, Manx. Just remember, you'll be as light as a feather, and you'll feel better than you've ever felt in your life.
Test your faith in Talon... and the Continuum.
Take the leap.
This is insane!! I can see the Continuum stuff through these goggles, but so what. Don't feel light as a feather. Feel sick.
Can't do it.
But what about Talon?
It's so far down.

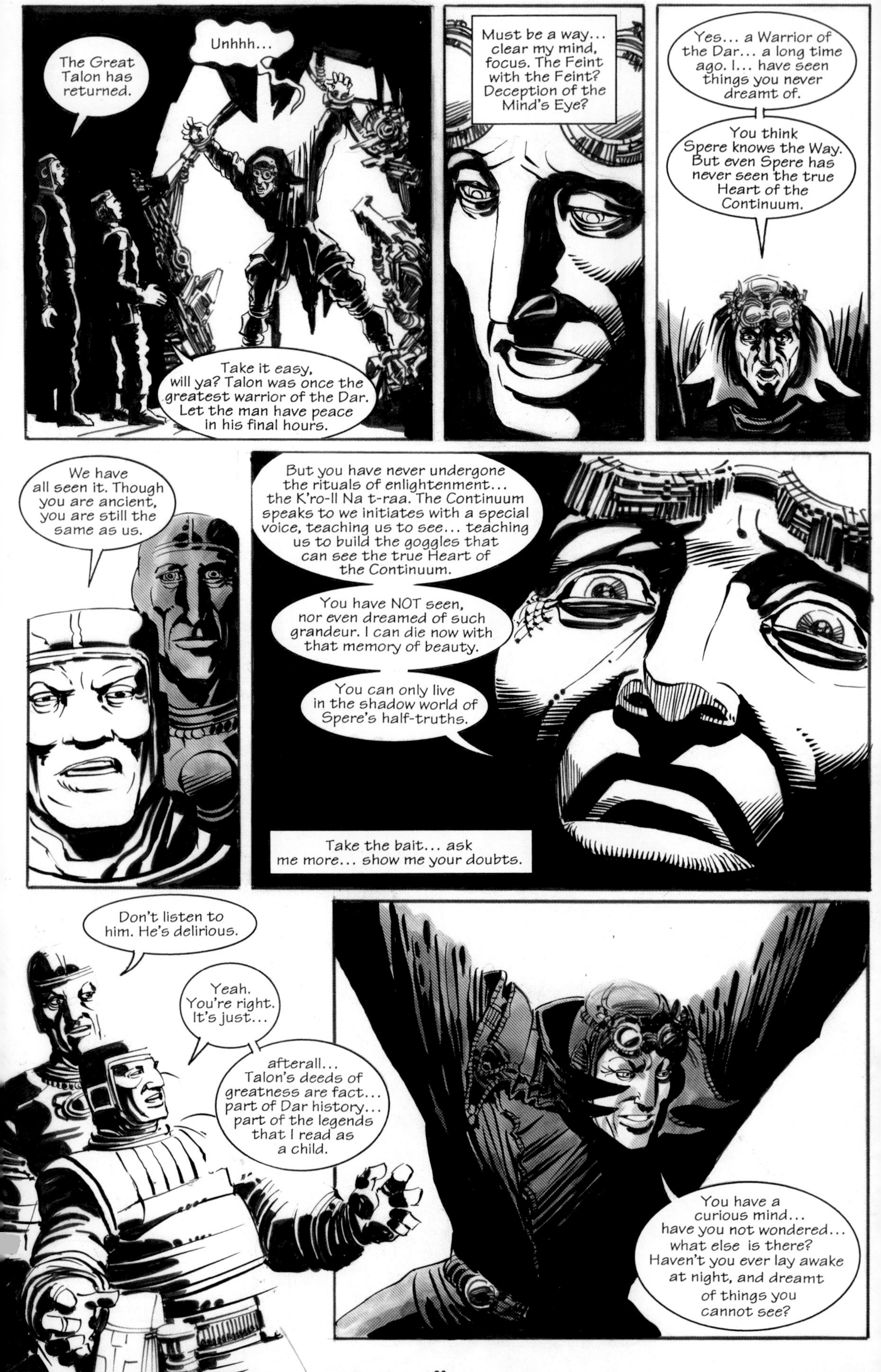
The Great Talon has returned.
Unhhh...
Take it easy, will ya? Talon was once the greatest warrior of the Dar. Let the man have peace in his final hours.
Must be a way... clear my mind, focus. The Feint with the Feint? Deception of the Mind's Eye?
Yes... a Warrior of the Dar... a long time ago. I... have seen things you never dreamt of.
You think Spere knows the Way. But even Spere has never seen the true Heart of the Continuum.
We have all seen it. Though you are ancient, you are still the same as us.
But you have never undergone the rituals of enlightenment... the K'ro-ll Na t-raa. The Continuum speaks to we initiates with a special voice, teaching us to see... teaching us to build the goggles that can see the true Heart of the Continuum.
You have NOT seen, nor even dreamed of such grandeur. I can die now with that memory of beauty.
You can only live in the shadow world of Spere's half-truths.
Take the bait... ask me more... show me your doubts.
Don't listen to him. He's delirious.
Yeah. You're right. It's just...
afterall... Talon's deeds of greatness are fact... part of Dar history... part of the legends that I read as a child.
You have a curious mind... have you not wondered... what else is there? Haven't you ever lay awake at night, and dreamt of things you cannot see?

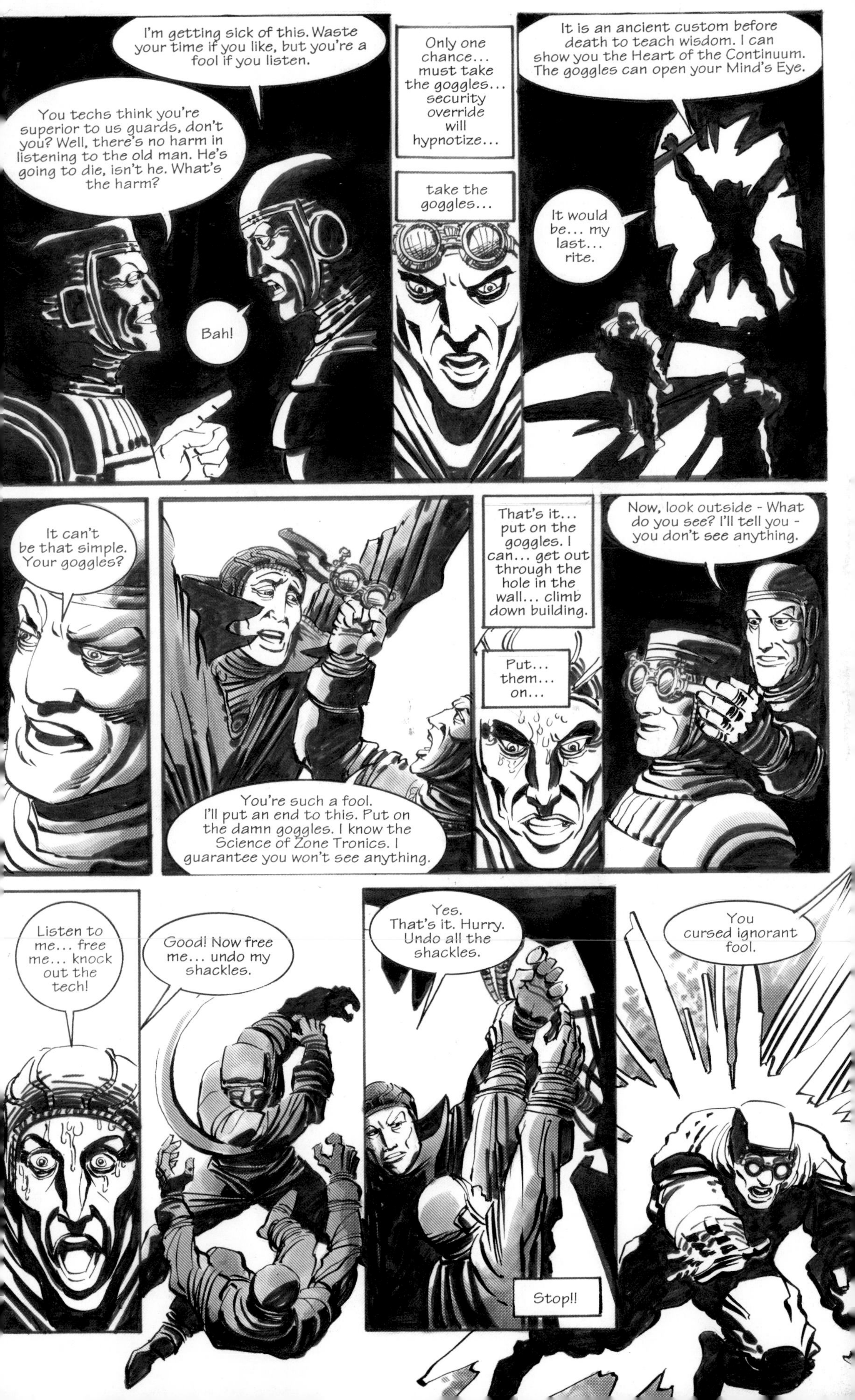

I'm getting sick of this. Waste your time if you like, but you're a fool if you listen.
You techs think you're superior to us guards, don't you? Well, there's no harm in listening to the old man. He's going to die, isn't he. What's the harm?
Bah!
Only one chance... must take the goggles... security override will hypnotize...
take the goggles...
It is an ancient custom before death to teach wisdom. I can show you the Heart of the Continuum. The goggles can open your Mind's Eye.
It would be... my last... rite.
It can't be that simple. Your goggles?
You're such a fool. I'll put an end to this. Put on the damn goggles. I know the Science of Zone Tronics. I guarantee you won't see anything.
That's it... put on the goggles. I can... get out through the hole in the wall... climb down building.
Put... them... on...
Now, look outside - What do you see? I'll tell you - you don't see anything.
Listen to me... free me... knock out the tech!
Good! Now free me... undo my shackles.
Yes. That's it. Hurry. Undo all the shackles.
Stop!!
You cursed ignorant fool.

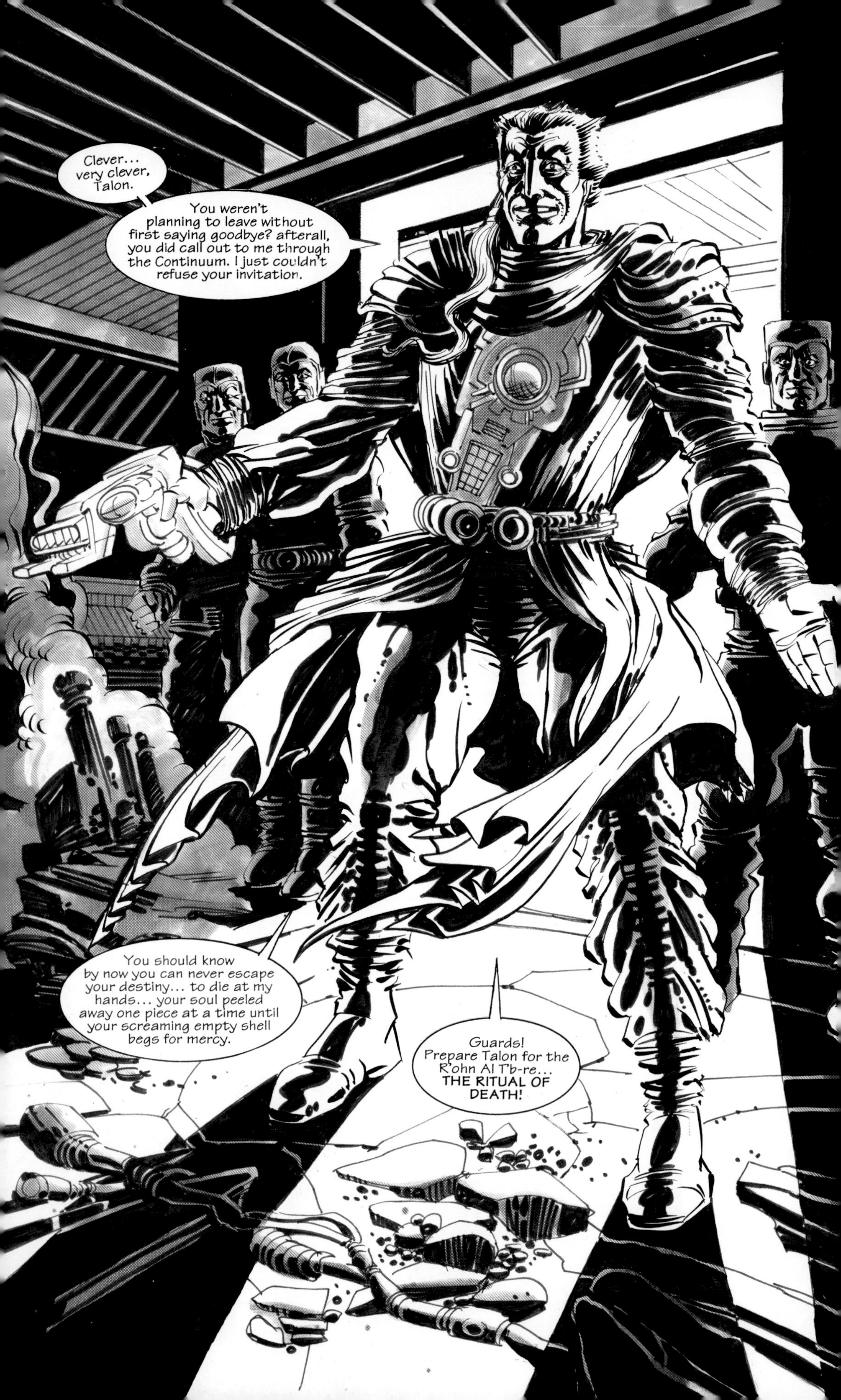

Clever... very clever, Talon.
You weren't planning to leave without first saying goodbye? afterall, you did call out to me through the Continuum. I just couldn't refuse your invitation.
You should know by now you can never escape your destiny... to die at my hands... your soul peeled away one piece at a time until your screaming empty shell begs for mercy.
Guards! Prepare Talon for the R'ohn Al T'b-re... **THE RITUAL OF DEATH!**

NAKED PREY

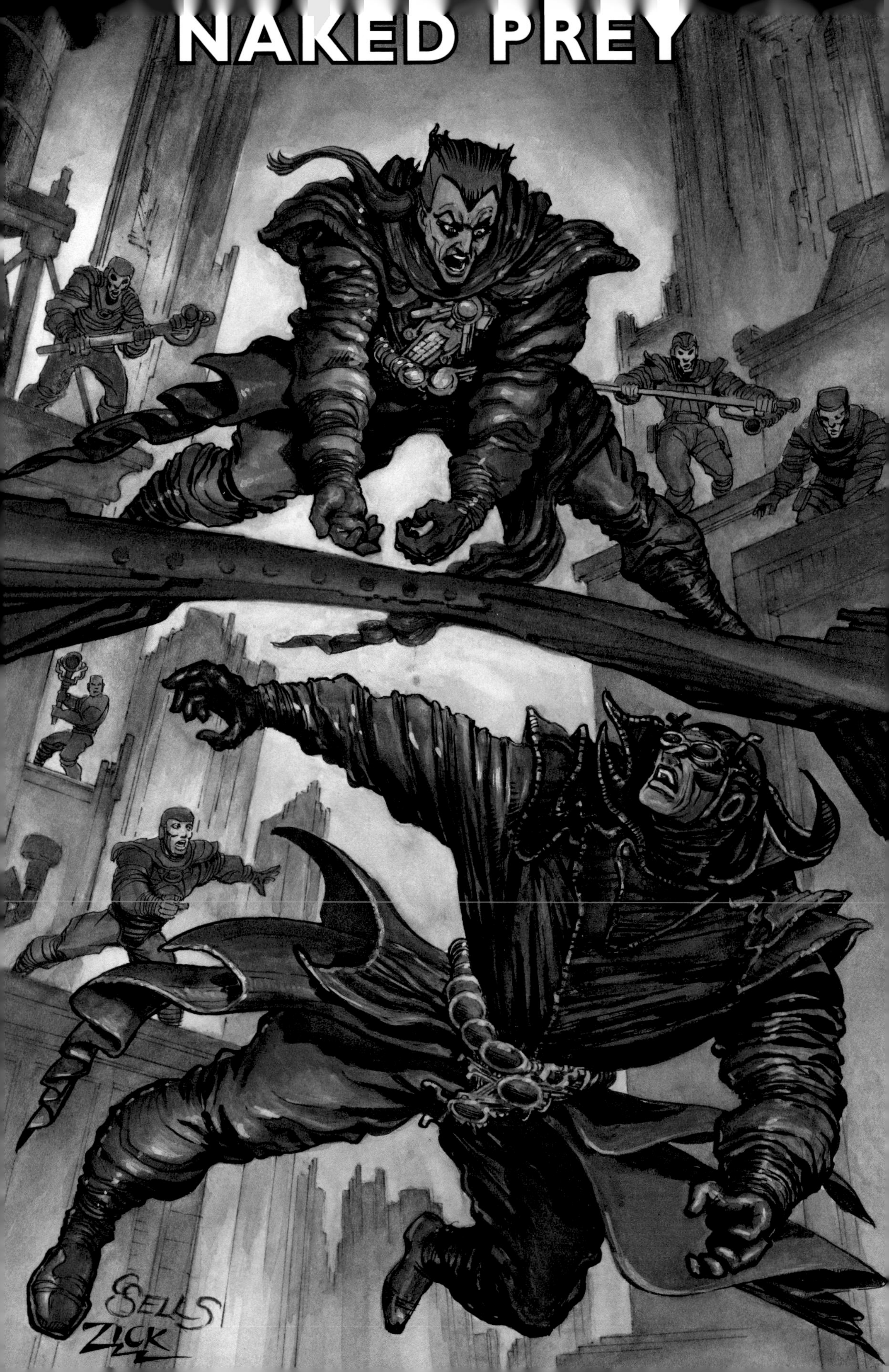
SELLS
ZICK

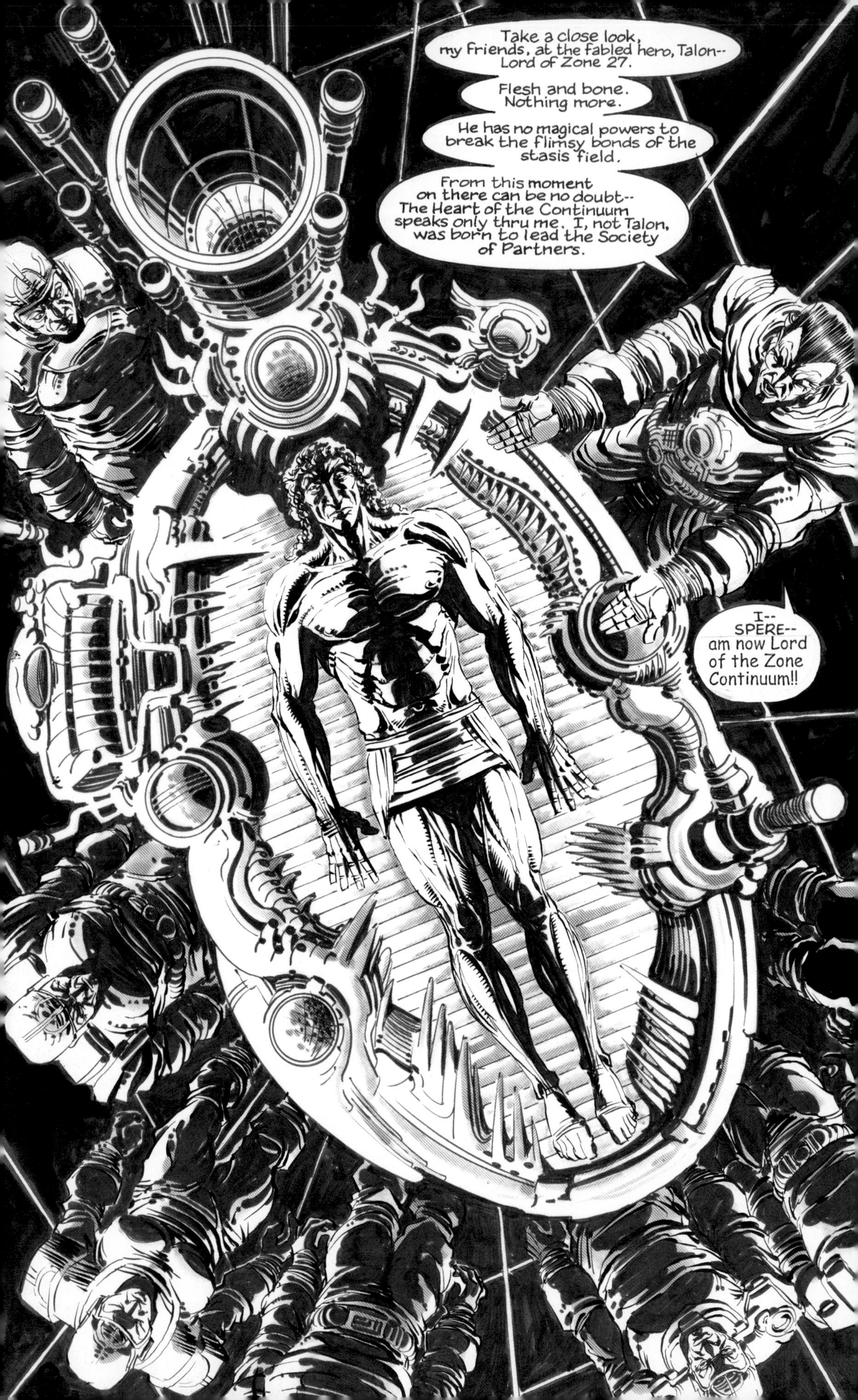
Take a close look, my friends, at the fabled hero, Talon-- Lord of Zone 27.
Flesh and bone. Nothing more.
He has no magical powers to break the flimsy bonds of the stasis field.
From this moment on there can be no doubt-- The Heart of the Continuum speaks only thru me. I, not Talon, was born to lead the Society of Partners.
I-- SPERE-- am now Lord of the Zone Continuum!!

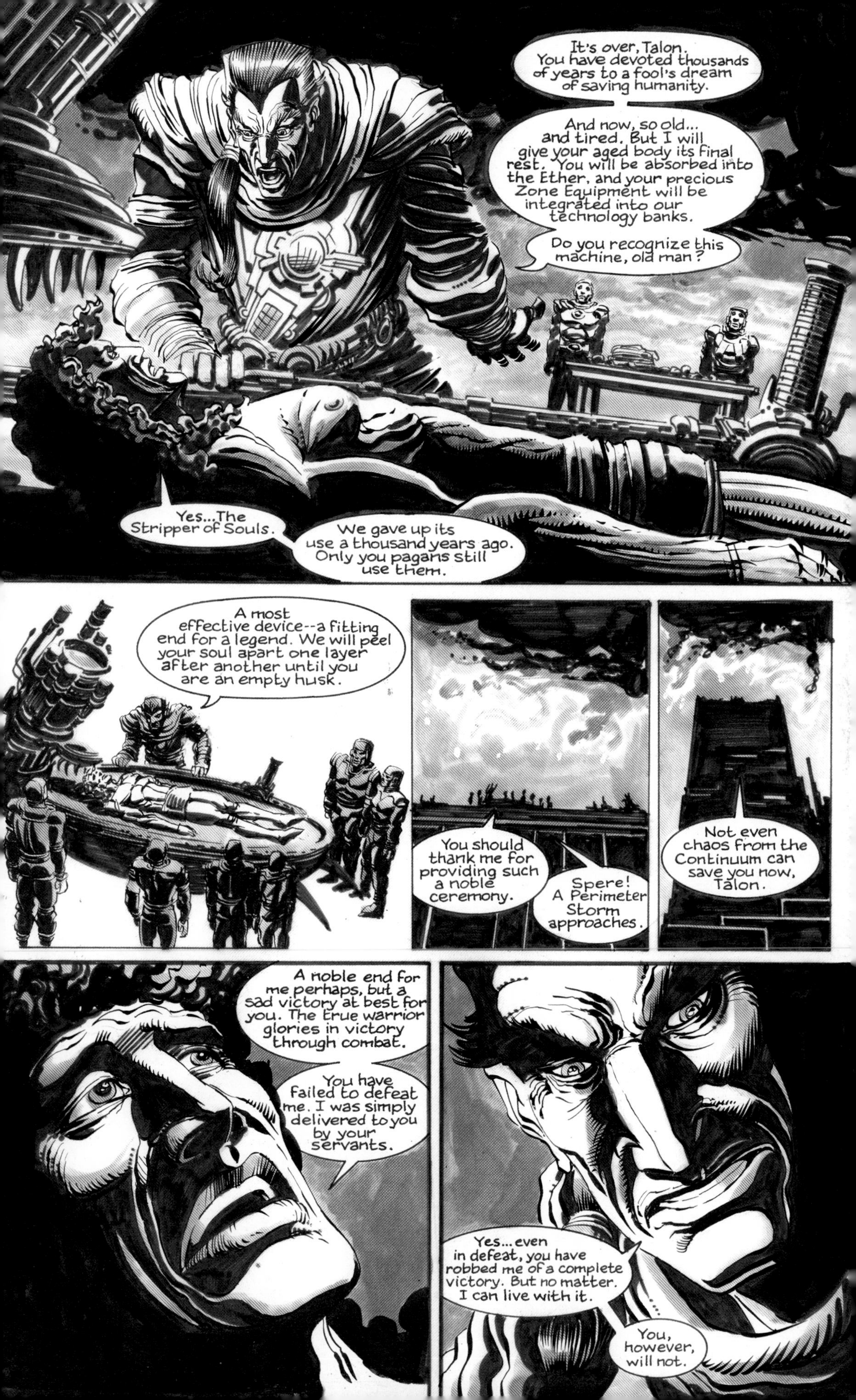
It's over, Talon. You have devoted thousands of years to a fool's dream of saving humanity.
And now, so old... and tired. But I will give your aged body its final rest. You will be absorbed into the Ether, and your precious Zone Equipment will be integrated into our technology banks.
Do you recognize this machine, old man?
Yes...The Stripper of Souls.
We gave up its use a thousand years ago. Only you pagans still use them.
A most effective device--a fitting end for a legend. We will peel your soul apart one layer after another until you are an empty husk.
You should thank me for providing such a noble ceremony.
Spere! A Perimeter Storm approaches.
Not even chaos from the Continuum can save you now, Talon.
A noble end for me perhaps, but a sad victory at best for you. The true warrior glories in victory through combat.
You have failed to defeat me. I was simply delivered to you by your servants.
Yes... even in defeat, you have robbed me of a complete victory. But no matter. I can live with it.
You, however, will not.

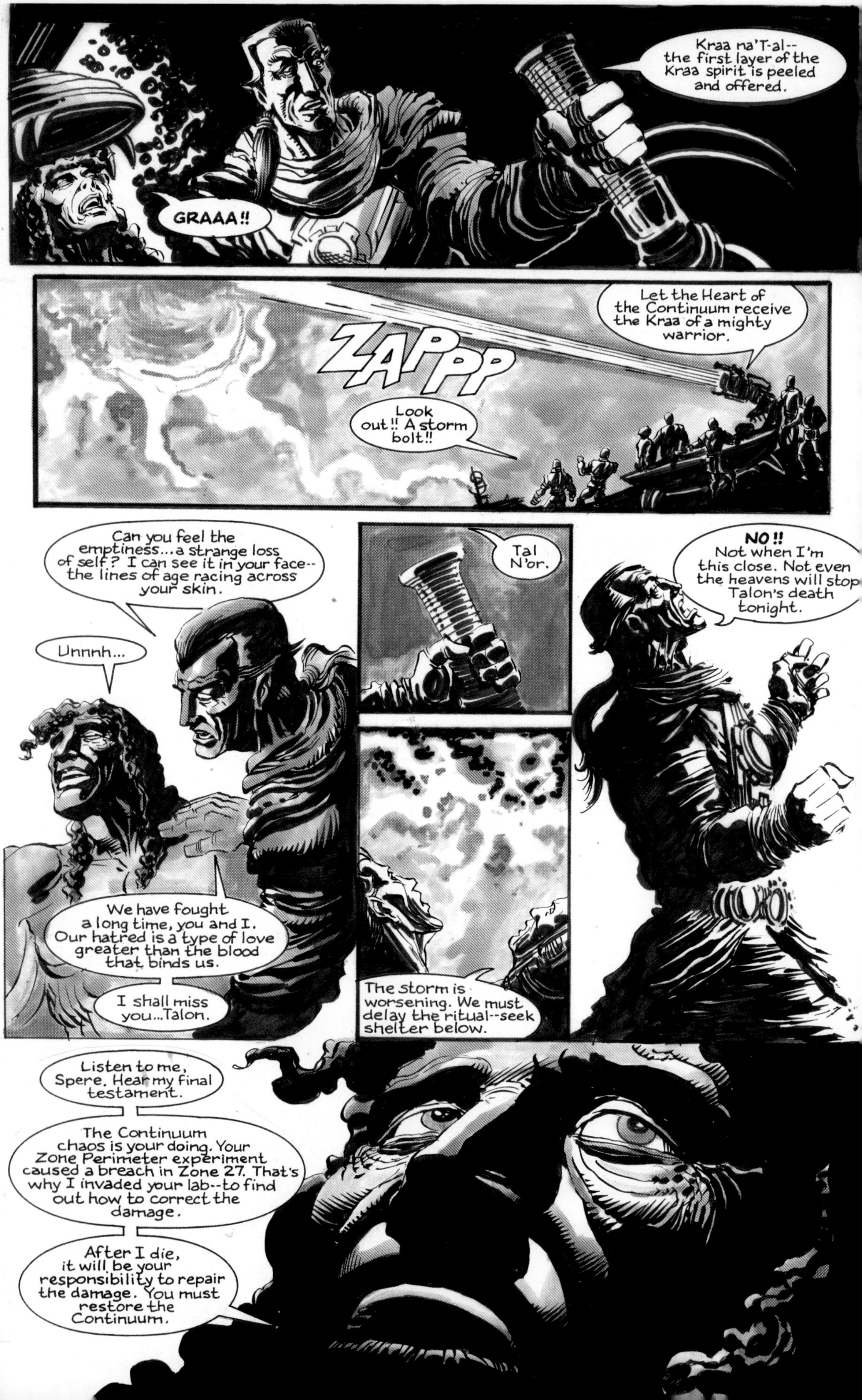
Kraa na'T-al-- the first layer of the Kraa spirit is peeled and offered.
GRAAA!!
Let the Heart of the Continuum receive the Kraa of a mighty warrior.
ZAPPP
Look out!! A storm bolt!!
Can you feel the emptiness...a strange loss of self? I can see it in your face-- the lines of age racing across your skin.
Unnnh...
We have fought a long time, you and I. Our hatred is a type of love greater than the blood that binds us.
I shall miss you...Talon.
Tal N'or.
The storm is worsening. We must delay the ritual--seek shelter below.
NO!! Not when I'm this close. Not even the heavens will stop Talon's death tonight.
Listen to me, Spere. Hear my final testament.
The Continuum chaos is your doing. Your Zone Perimeter experiment caused a breach in Zone 27. That's why I invaded your lab--to find out how to correct the damage.
After I die, it will be your responsibility to repair the damage. You must restore the Continuum.

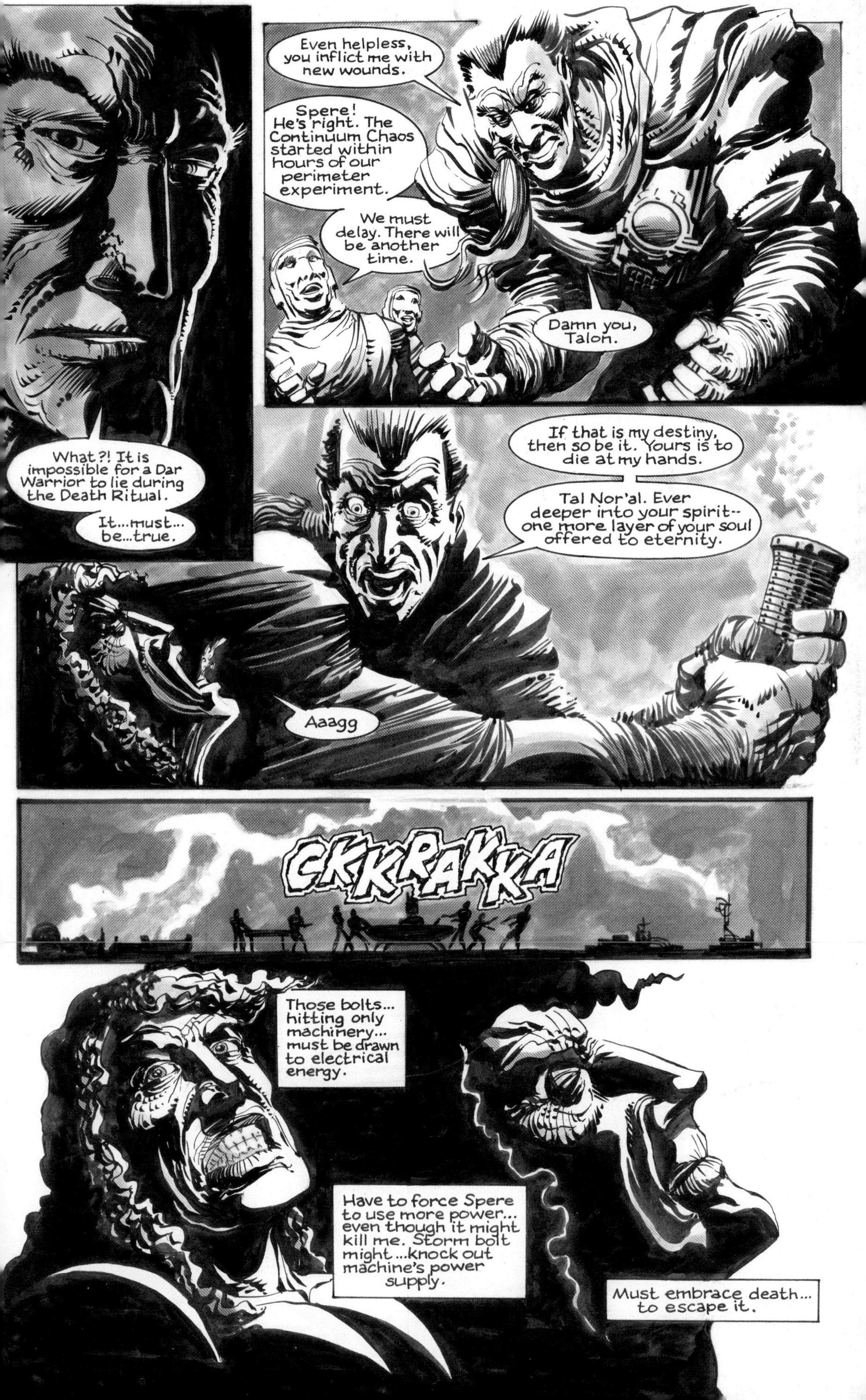
Even helpless, you inflict me with new wounds.
Spere! He's right. The Continuum Chaos started within hours of our perimeter experiment.
We must delay. There will be another time.
Damn you, Talon.
What?! It is impossible for a Dar Warrior to lie during the Death Ritual.
It...must... be...true.
If that is my destiny, then so be it. Yours is to die at my hands.
Tal Nor'al. Ever deeper into your spirit-- one more layer of your soul offered to eternity.
Aaagg
CKKRAKKA
Those bolts... hitting only machinery... must be drawn to electrical energy.
Have to force Spere to use more power... even though it might kill me. Storm bolt might...knock out machine's power supply.
Must embrace death... to escape it.

How do YOU feel, Spere? Everything you believe in-- you are destroying. What great irony.

Can you feel it breaking apart? Gods, I will have my revenge before death. Look at it, Spere.

You've done your worst to me. But I'm not done with you yet.

Hahhhhaa. Spere--the great purist. Oh that I may savor this moment... and the next...

Then you shall have no moments left. You will know agony such as no Partner has ever felt.

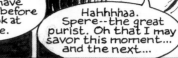

Farewell, Talon.

Aahhhhh...

ZZZRRRAKKK

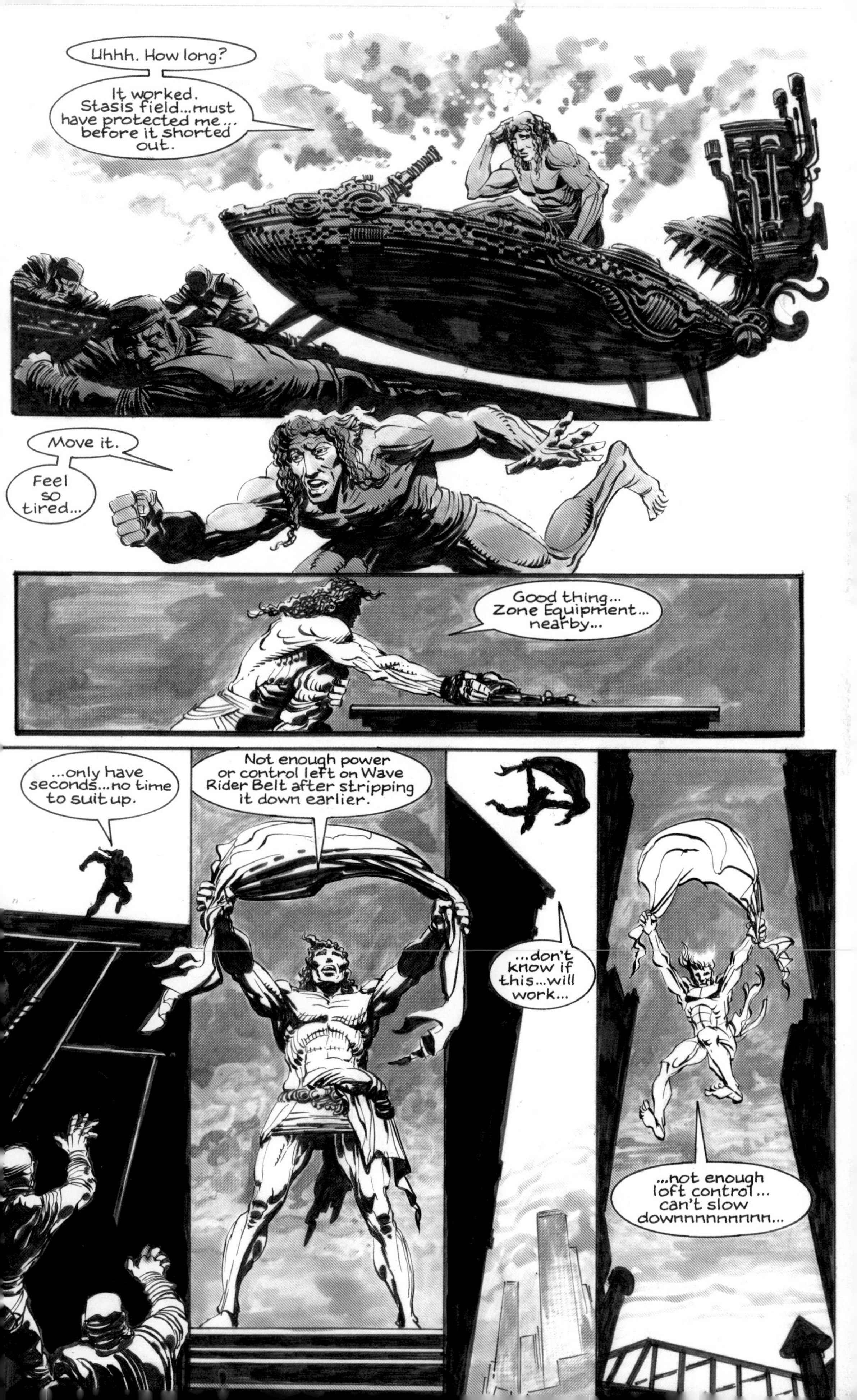
Uhhh. How long?
It worked. Stasis field...must have protected me... before it shorted out.
Move it.
Feel so tired...
Good thing... Zone Equipment... nearby...
...only have seconds...no time to suit up.
Not enough power or control left on Wave Rider Belt after stripping it down earlier.
...don't know if this...will work...
...not enough loft control... can't slow downnnnnnnnnn...

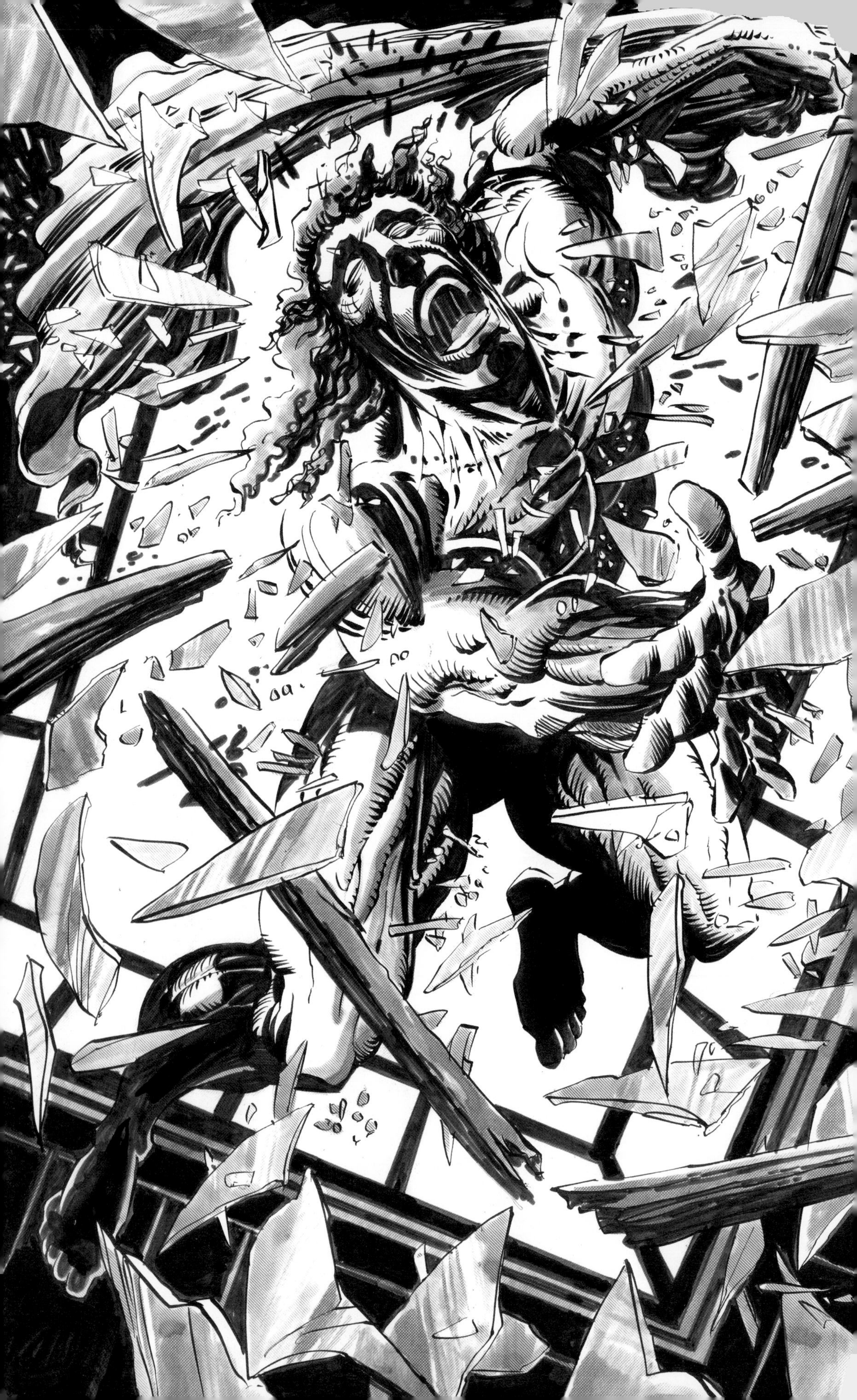

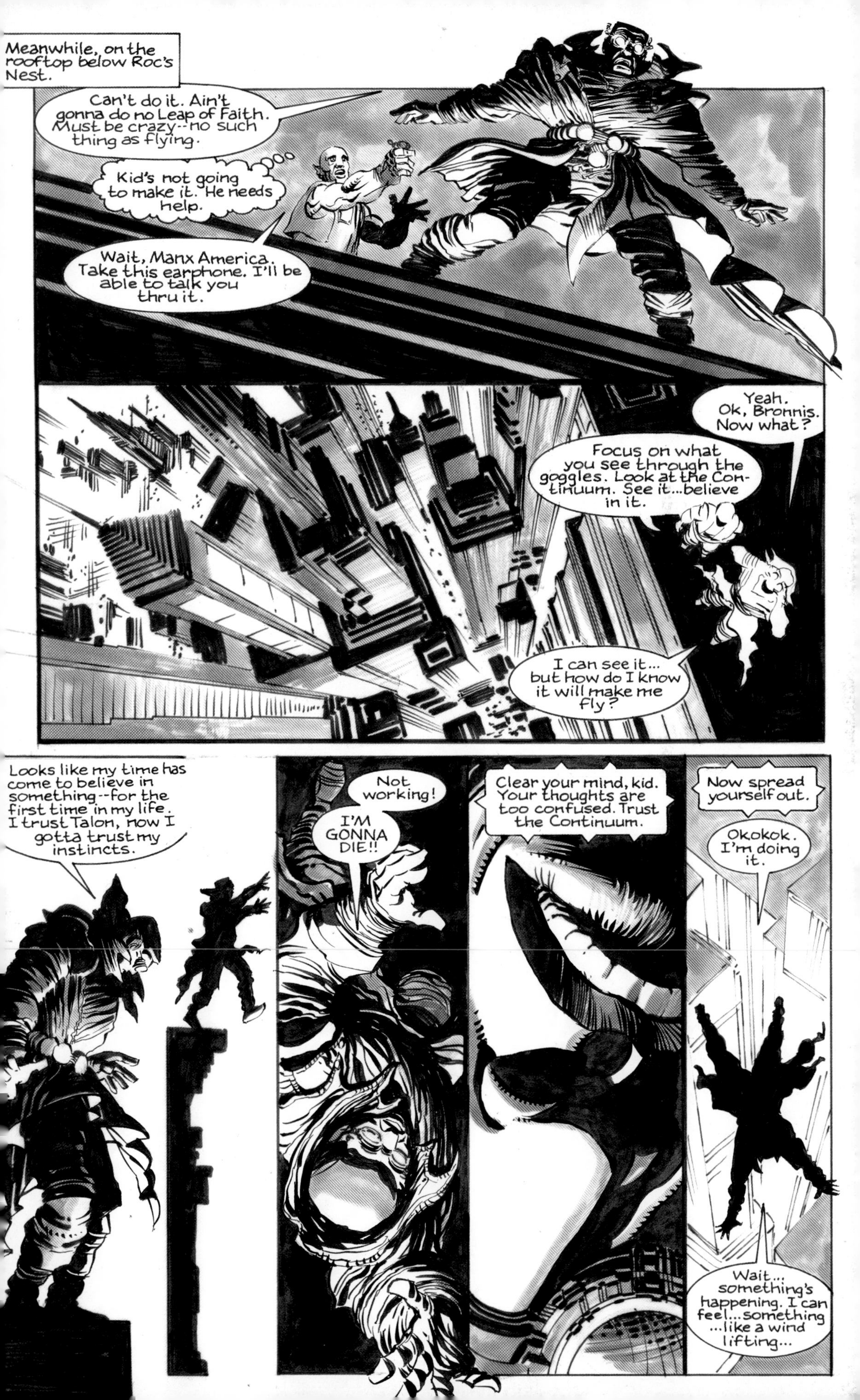

Meanwhile, on the rooftop below Roc's Nest.
Can't do it. Ain't gonna do no Leap of Faith. Must be crazy--no such thing as flying.
Kid's not going to make it. He needs help.
Wait, Manx America. Take this earphone. I'll be able to talk you thru it.
Yeah. Ok, Bronnis. Now what?
Focus on what you see through the goggles. Look at the Continuum. See it...believe in it.
I can see it... but how do I know it will make me fly?
Looks like my time has come to believe in something--for the first time in my life. I trust Talon, now I gotta trust my instincts.
Not working!
I'M GONNA DIE!!
Clear your mind, kid. Your thoughts are too confused. Trust the Continuum.
Now spread yourself out.
Okokok. I'm doing it.
Wait... something's happening. I can feel...something ...like a wind lifting...

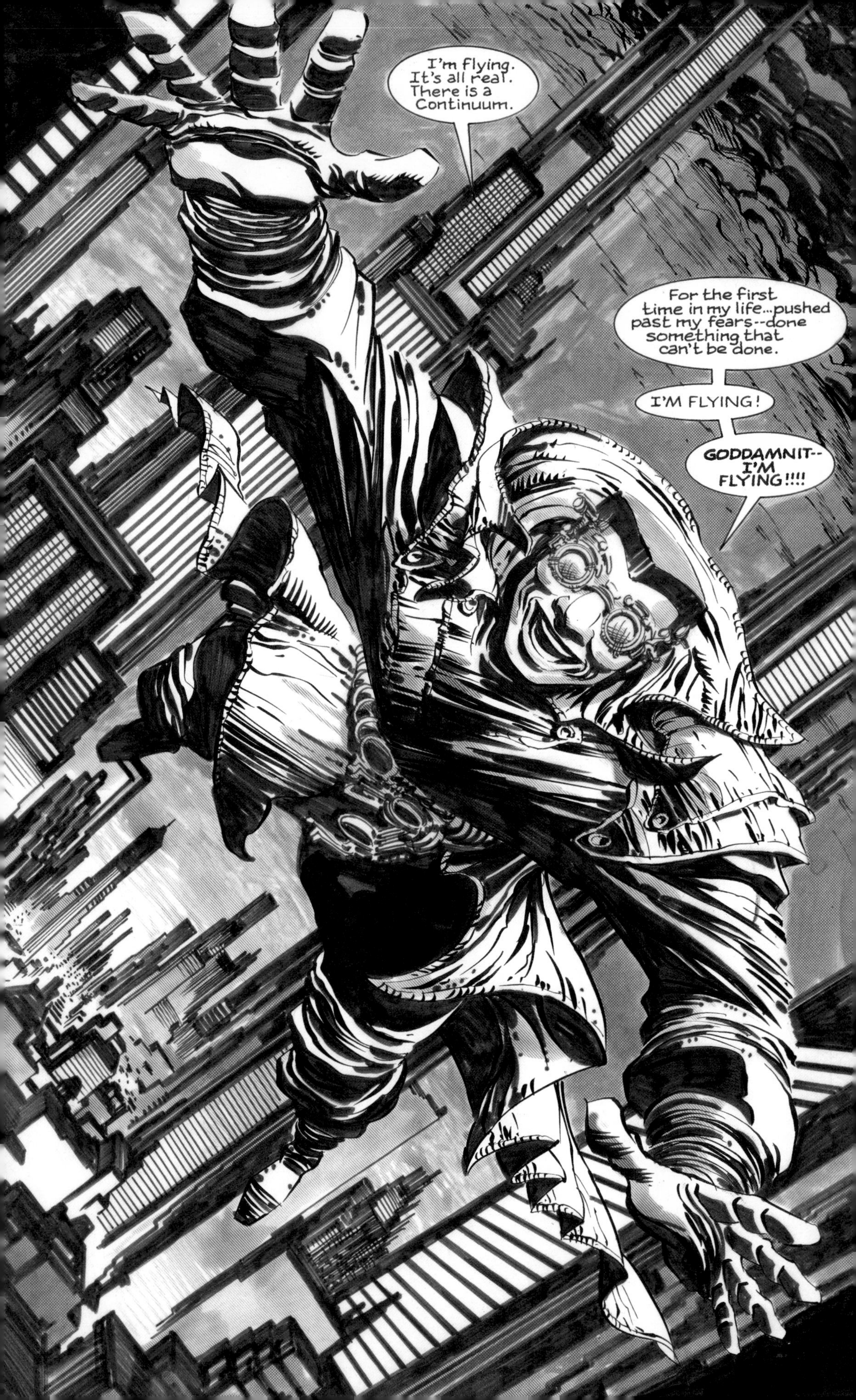
I'm flying. It's all real. There is a Continuum.
For the first time in my life...pushed past my fears--done something that can't be done.
I'M FLYING!
GODDAMNIT-- I'M FLYING!!!!

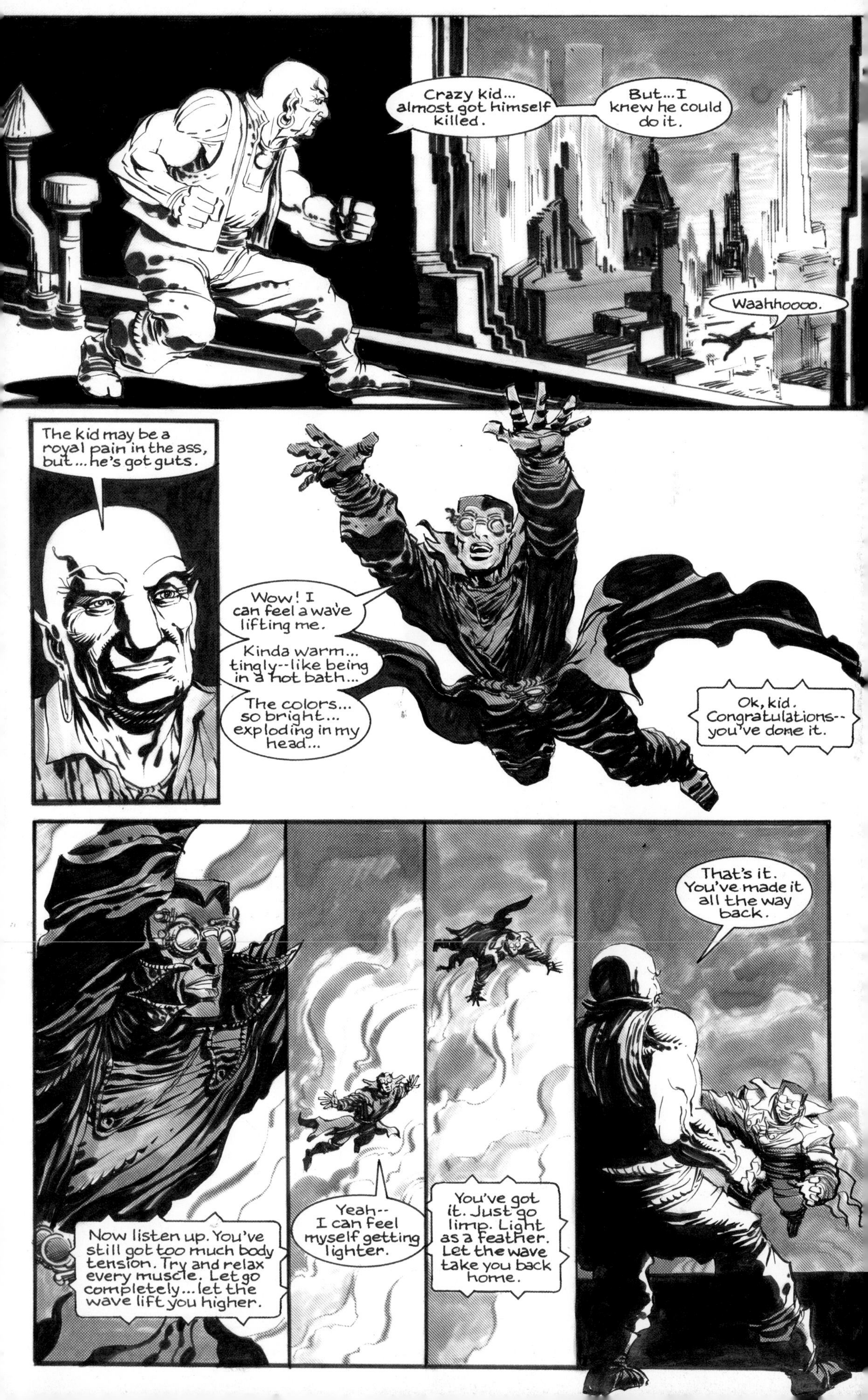

Crazy kid... almost got himself killed.
But... I knew he could do it.
Waahhoooo.
The kid may be a royal pain in the ass, but... he's got guts.
Wow! I can feel a wave lifting me.
Kinda warm... tingly--like being in a hot bath...
The colors... so bright... exploding in my head...
Ok, kid. Congratulations-- you've done it.
Now listen up. You've still got too much body tension. Try and relax every muscle. Let go completely... let the wave lift you higher.
Yeah-- I can feel myself getting lighter.
You've got it. Just go limp. Light as a feather. Let the wave take you back home.
That's it. You've made it all the way back.

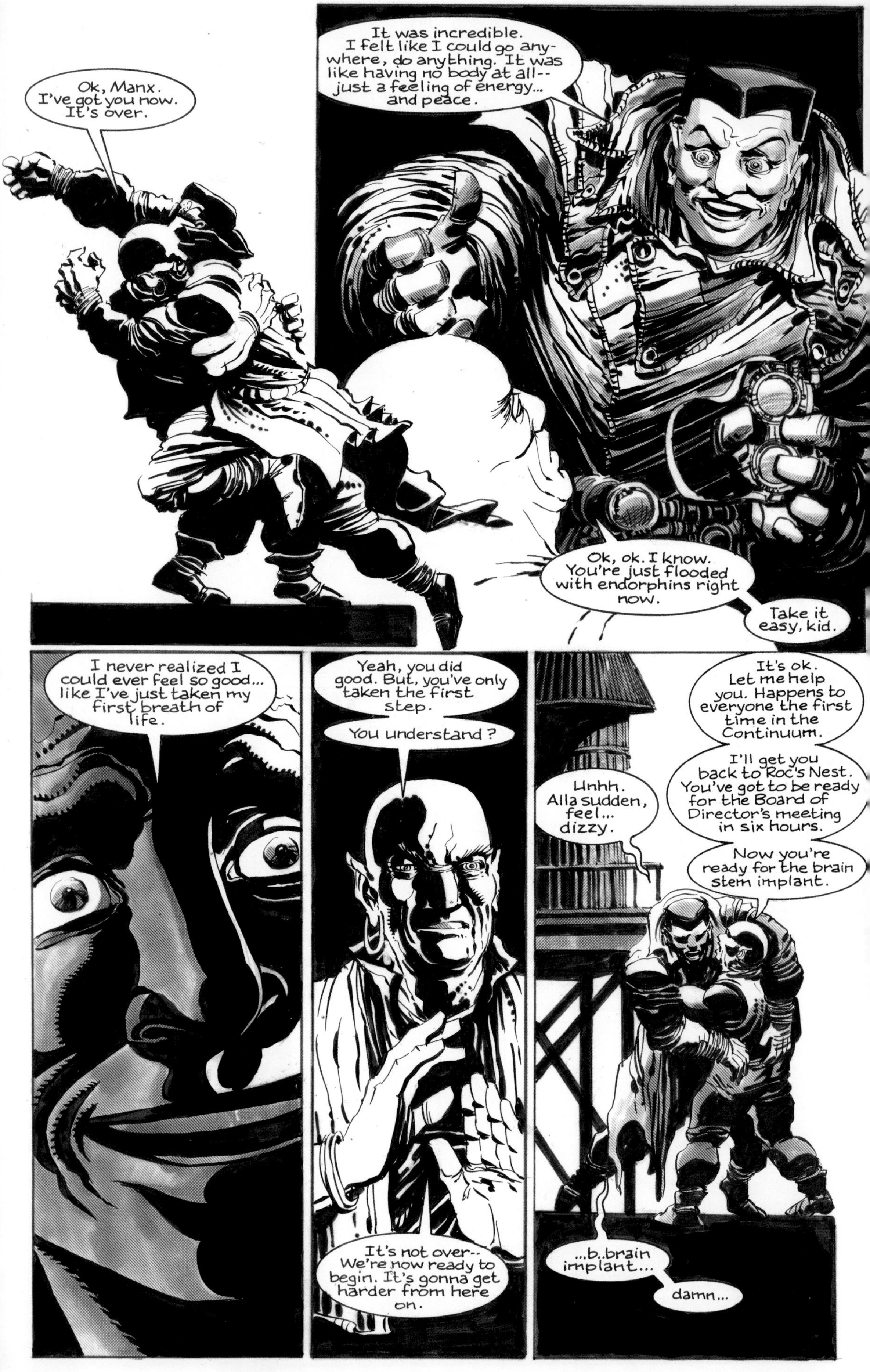
Ok, Manx. I've got you now. It's over.
It was incredible. I felt like I could go anywhere, do anything. It was like having no body at all-- just a feeling of energy... and peace.
Ok, ok. I know. You're just flooded with endorphins right now.
Take it easy, kid.
I never realized I could ever feel so good... like I've just taken my first breath of life.
Yeah, you did good. But, you've only taken the first step.
You understand?
It's not over-- We're now ready to begin. It's gonna get harder from here on.
Unhh. Alla sudden, feel... dizzy.
It's ok. Let me help you. Happens to everyone the first time in the Continuum.
I'll get you back to Roc's Nest. You've got to be ready for the Board of Director's meeting in six hours.
Now you're ready for the brain stem implant.
...b..brain implant...
damn...

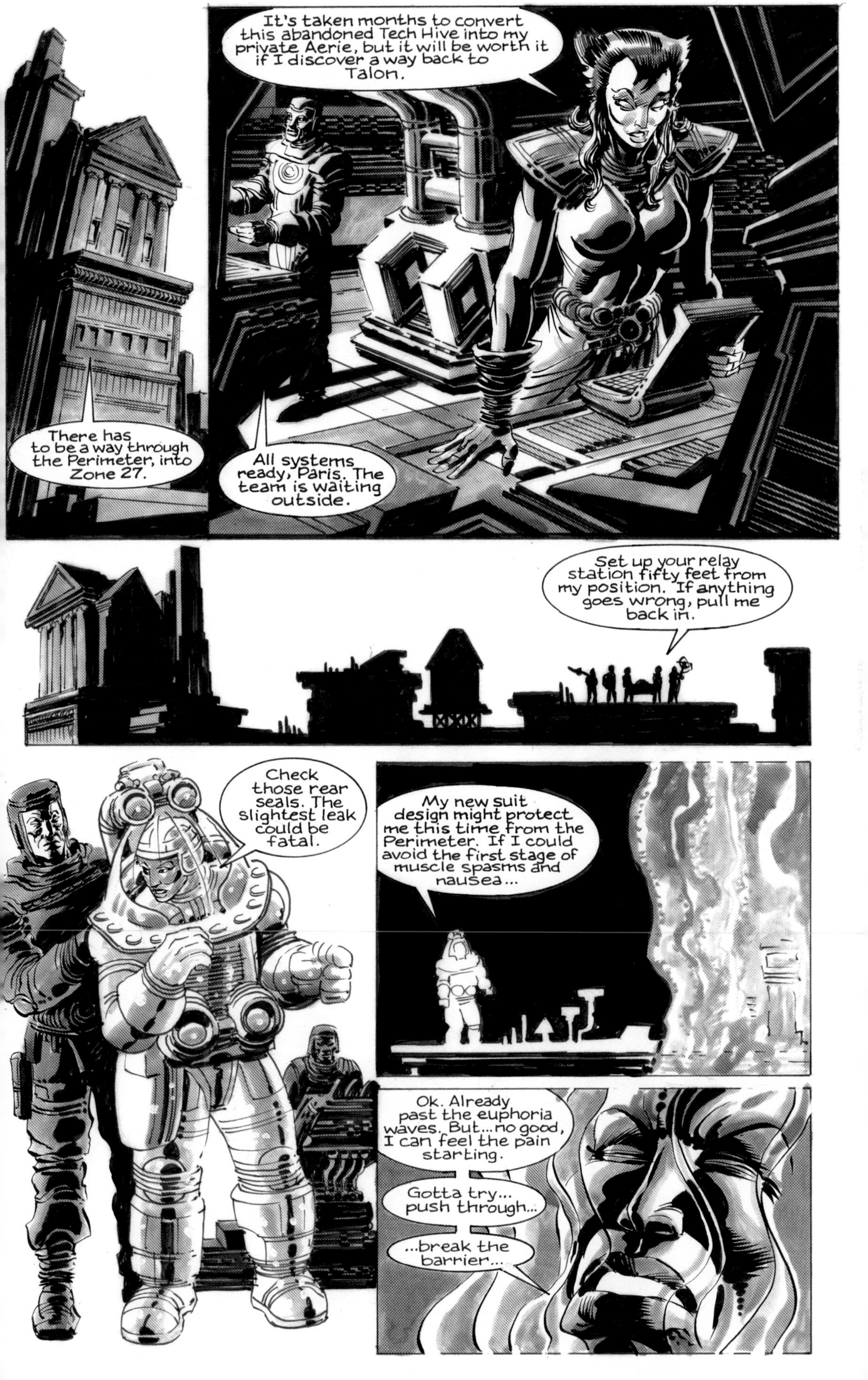
It's taken months to convert this abandoned Tech Hive into my private Aerie, but it will be worth it if I discover a way back to Talon.
There has to be a way through the Perimeter, into Zone 27.
All systems ready, Paris. The team is waiting outside.
Set up your relay station fifty feet from my position. If anything goes wrong, pull me back in.
Check those rear seals. The slightest leak could be fatal.
My new suit design might protect me this time from the Perimeter. If I could avoid the first stage of muscle spasms and nausea...
Ok. Already past the euphoria waves. But...no good, I can feel the pain starting.
Gotta try... push through...
...break the barrier...

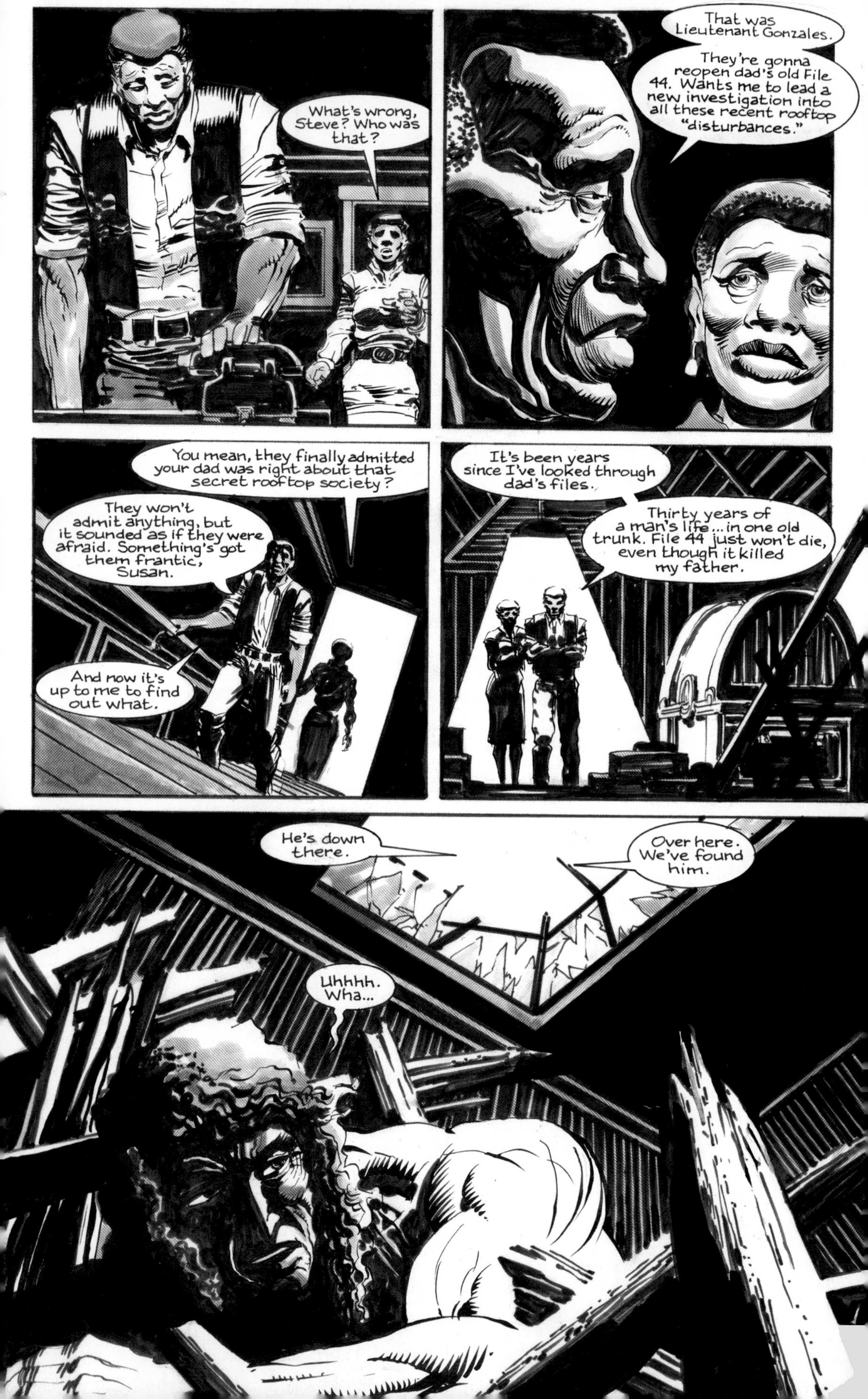
What's wrong, Steve? Who was that?
That was Lieutenant Gonzales.
They're gonna reopen dad's old File 44. Wants me to lead a new investigation into all these recent rooftop "disturbances."
You mean, they finally admitted your dad was right about that secret rooftop society?
They won't admit anything, but it sounded as if they were afraid. Something's got them frantic, Susan.
And now it's up to me to find out what.
It's been years since I've looked through dad's files.
Thirty years of a man's life... in one old trunk. File 44 just won't die, even though it killed my father.
He's down there.
Over here. We've found him.
Uhhhh. Wha...

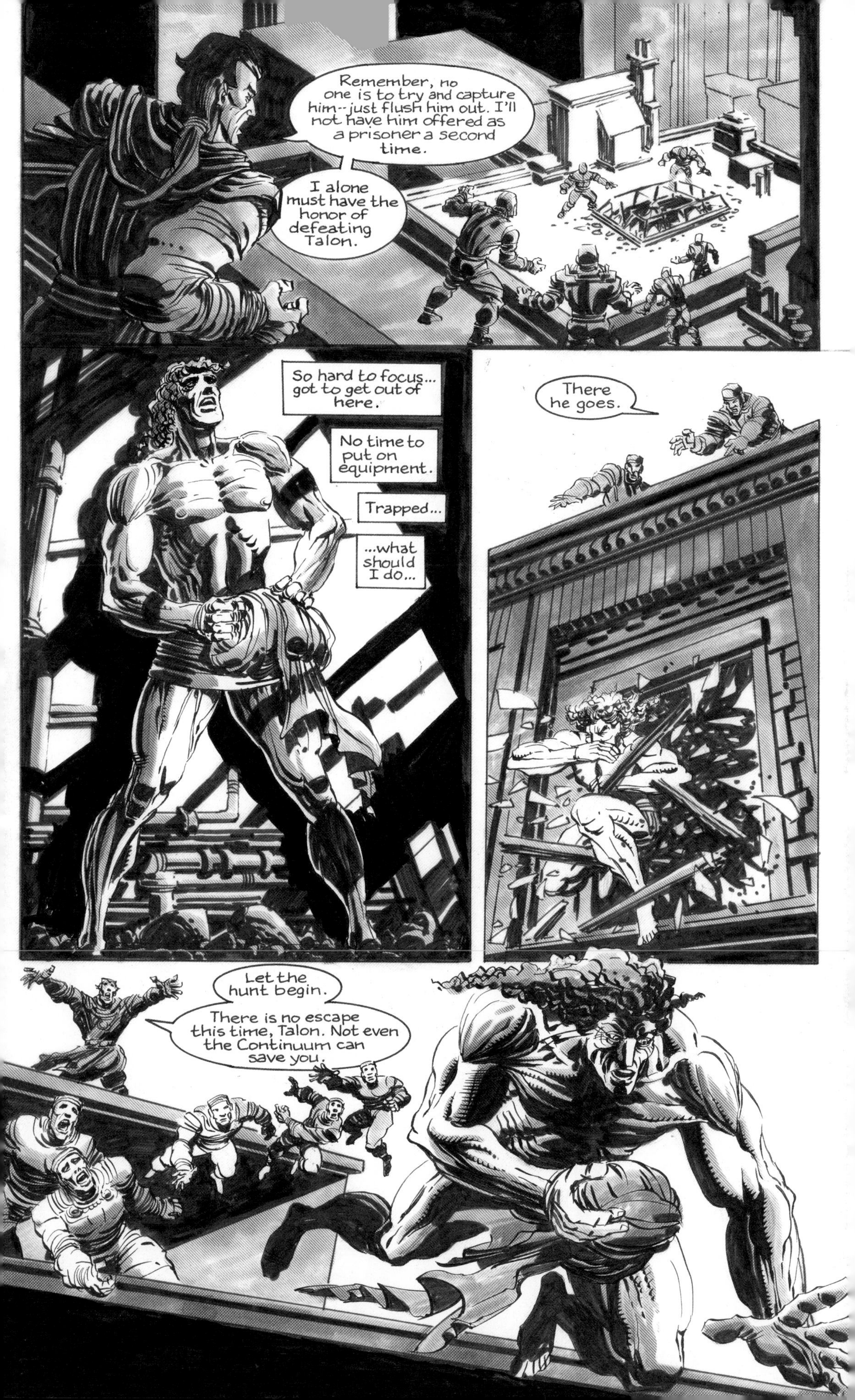
Remember, no one is to try and capture him--just flush him out. I'll not have him offered as a prisoner a second time.
I alone must have the honor of defeating Talon.
So hard to focus... got to get out of here.
No time to put on equipment.
Trapped...
...what should I do...
There he goes.
Let the hunt begin.
There is no escape this time, Talon. Not even the Continuum can save you.

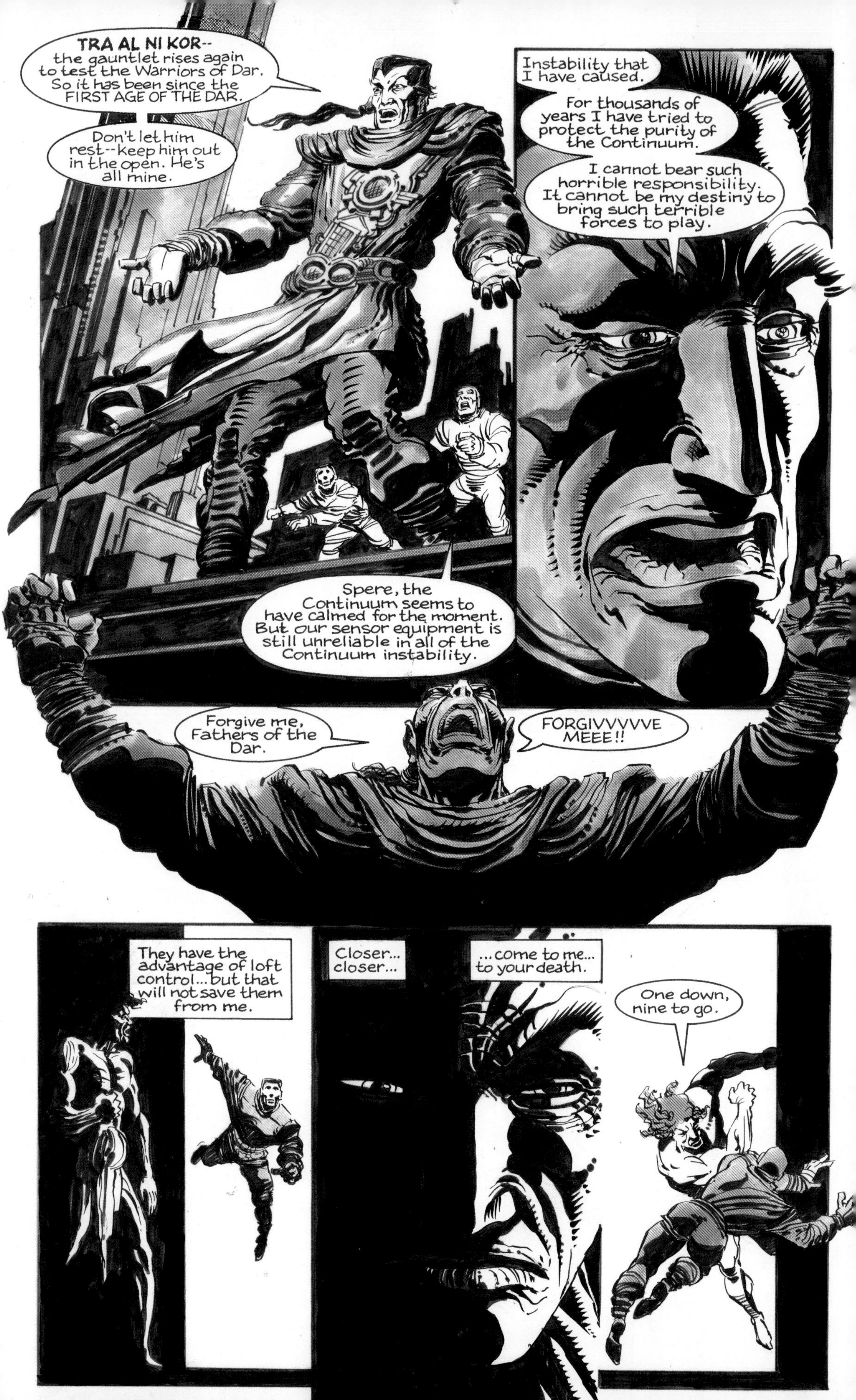
TRA AL NI KOR-- the gauntlet rises again to test the Warriors of Dar. So it has been since the FIRST AGE OF THE DAR.
Don't let him rest--keep him out in the open. He's all mine.
Instability that I have caused.
For thousands of years I have tried to protect the purity of the Continuum.
I cannot bear such horrible responsibility. It cannot be my destiny to bring such terrible forces to play.
Spere, the Continuum seems to have calmed for the moment. But our sensor equipment is still unreliable in all of the Continuum instability.
Forgive me, Fathers of the Dar.
FORGIVVVVVE MEEE!!
They have the advantage of loft control... but that will not save them from me.
Closer... closer...
...come to me... to your death.
One down, nine to go.

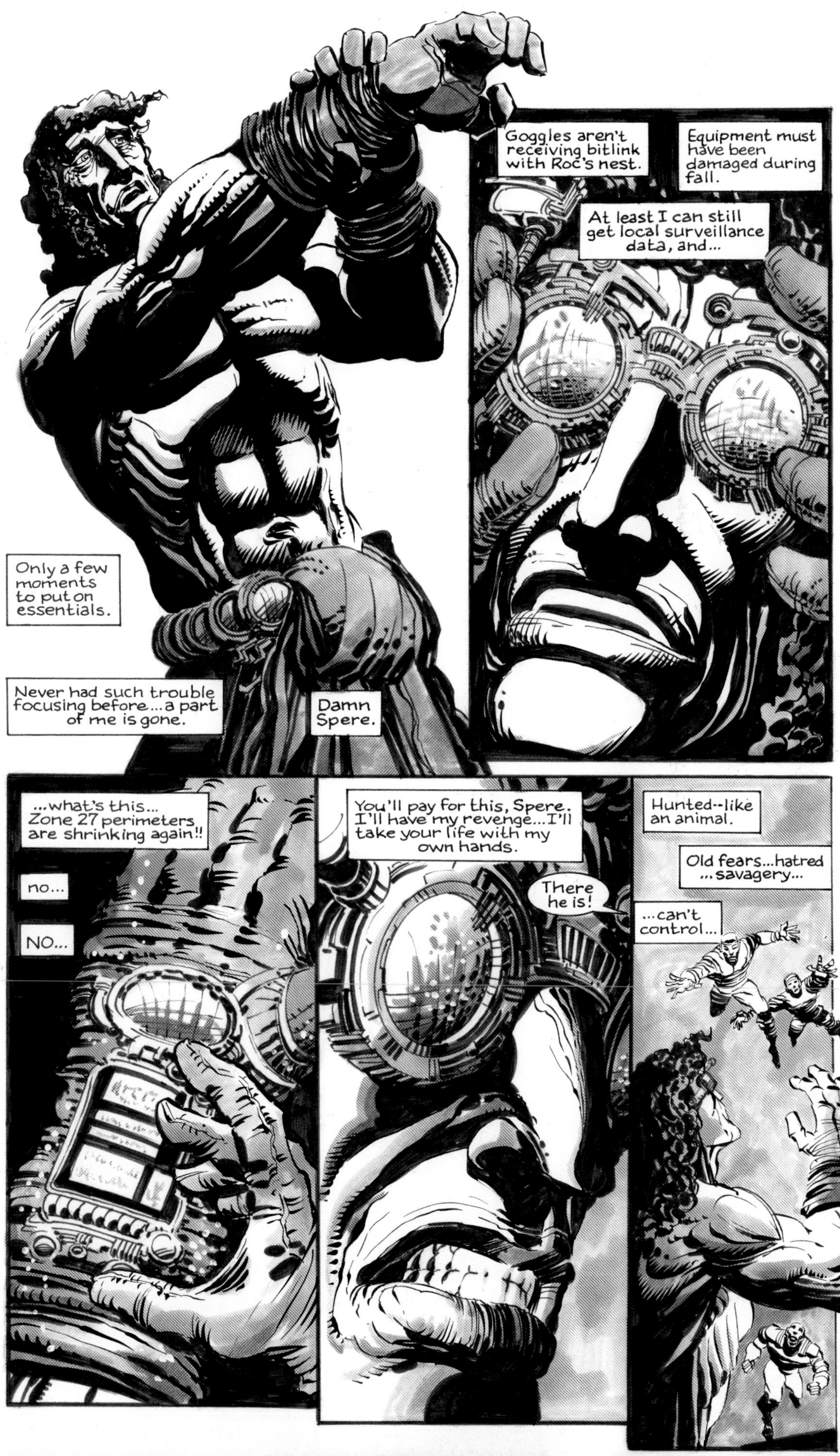
Only a few moments to put on essentials.
Never had such trouble focusing before...a part of me is gone.
Damn Spere.
Goggles aren't receiving bitlink with Roc's nest.
Equipment must have been damaged during fall.
At least I can still get local surveillance data, and...
...what's this... Zone 27 perimeters are shrinking again!!
no...
NO...
You'll pay for this, Spere. I'll have my revenge...I'll take your life with my own hands.
There he is!
Hunted--like an animal.
Old fears...hatred ...savagery...
...can't control...

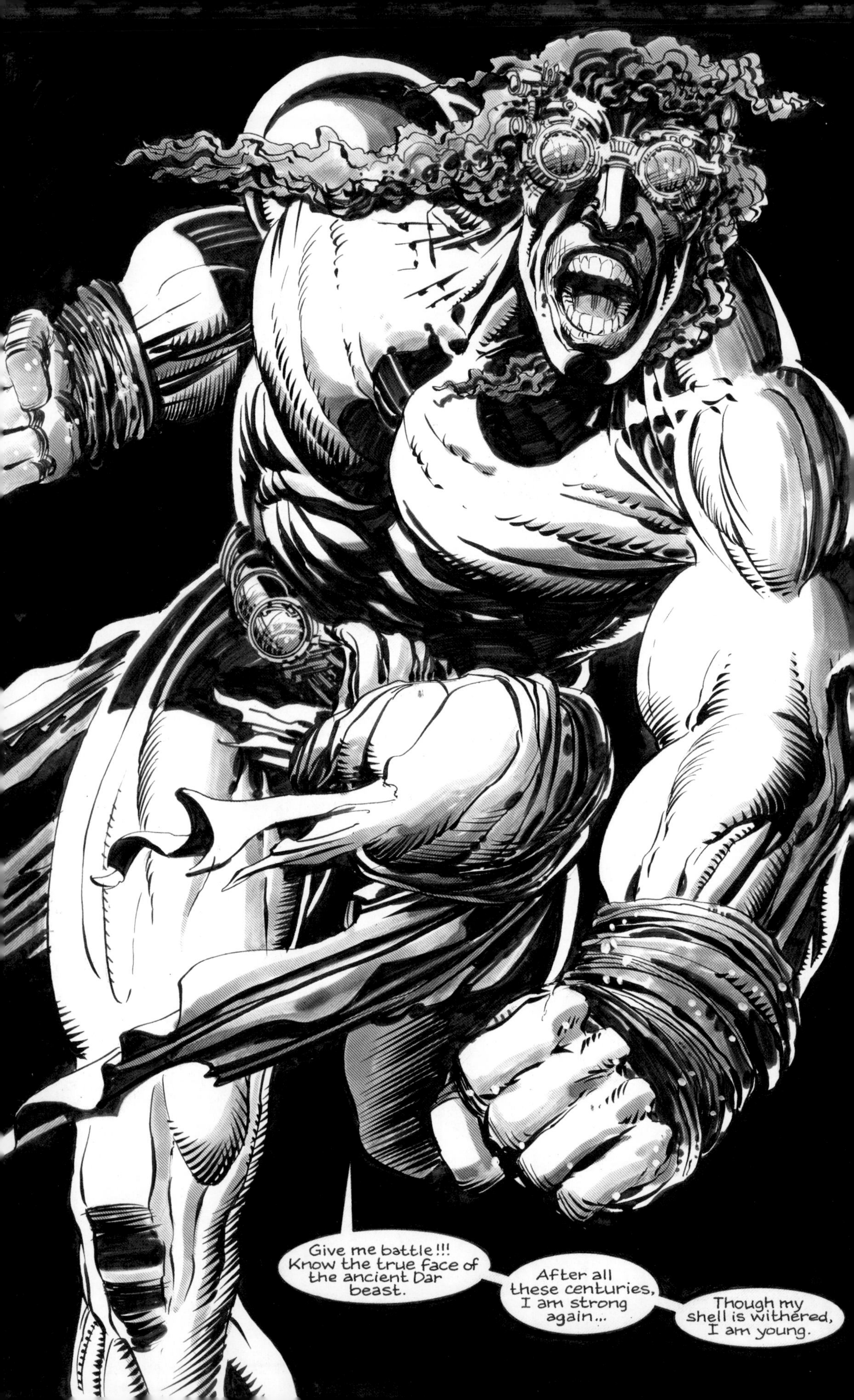
Give me battle!!! Know the true face of the ancient Dar beast.
After all these centuries, I am strong again...
Though my shell is withered, I am young.

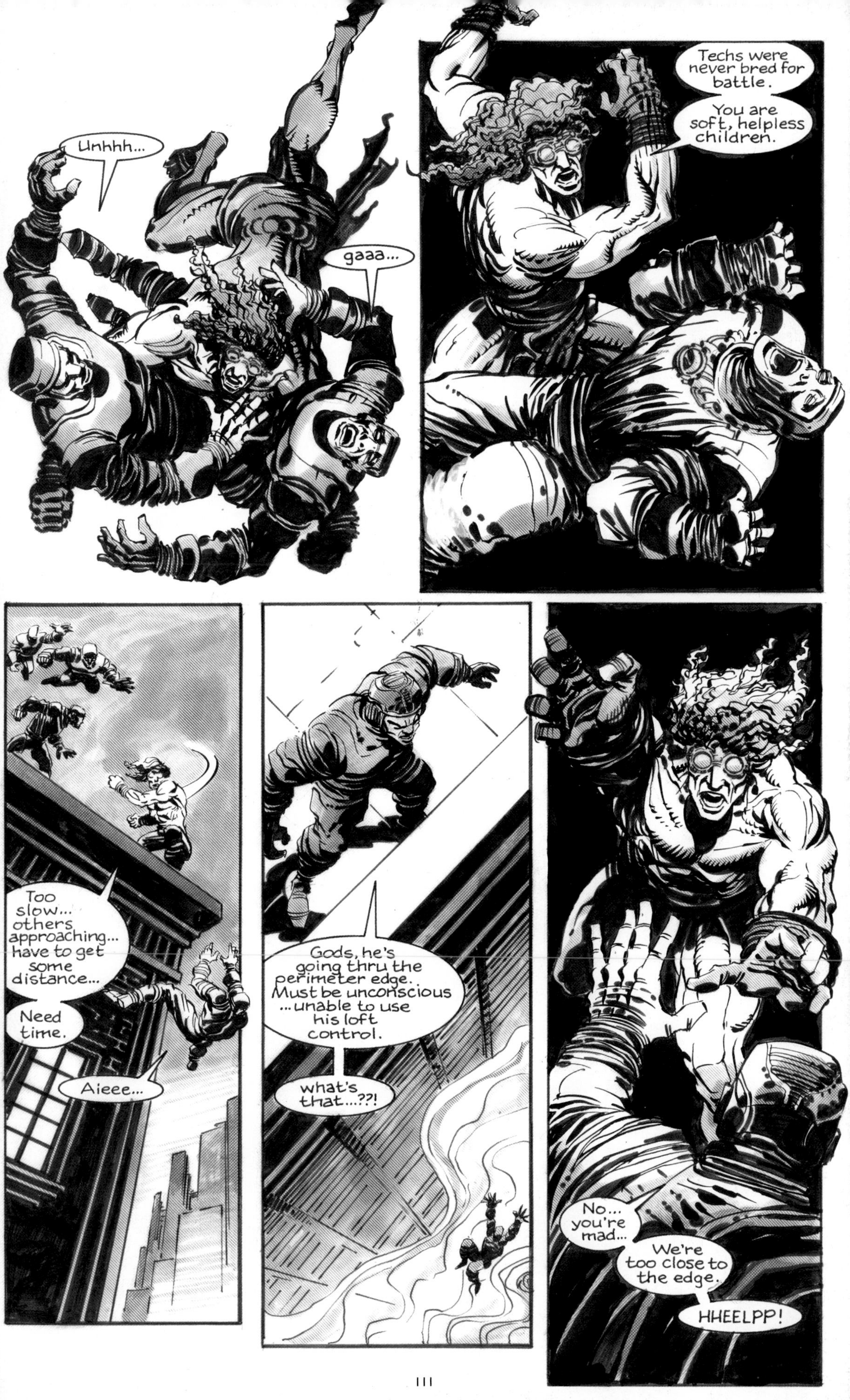
Unhhh...
gaaa...
Techs were never bred for battle.
You are soft, helpless children.
Too slow... others approaching... have to get some distance...
Need time.
Aieee...
Gods, he's going thru the perimeter edge. Must be unconscious ...unable to use his loft control.
what's that...??!
No... you're mad...
We're too close to the edge.
HHEELPP!

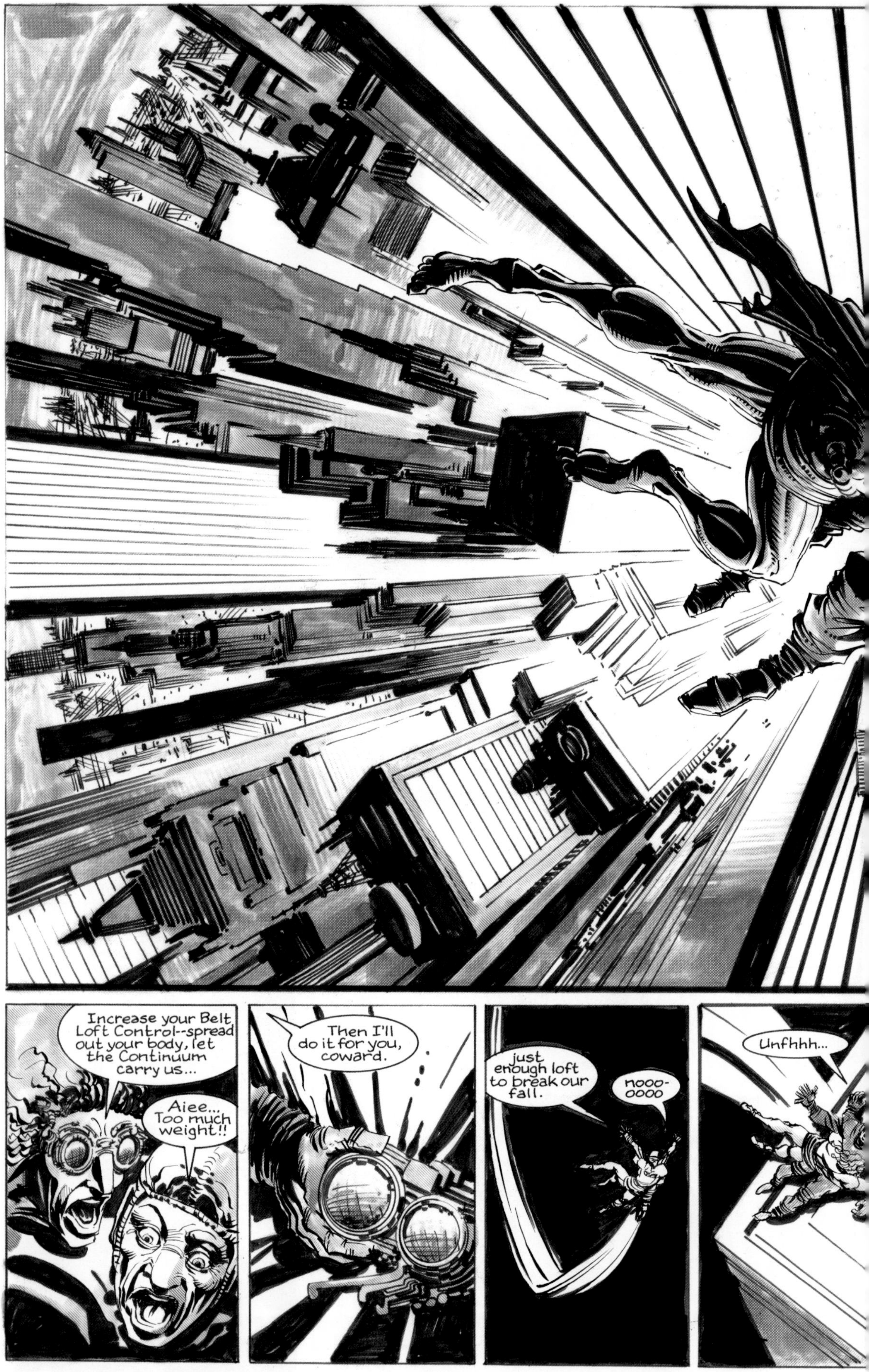
Increase your Belt Loft Control--spread out your body, let the Continuum carry us...
Aiee... Too much weight!!
Then I'll do it for you, coward.
just enough loft to break our fall.
nooo-oooo
Unfhhh...

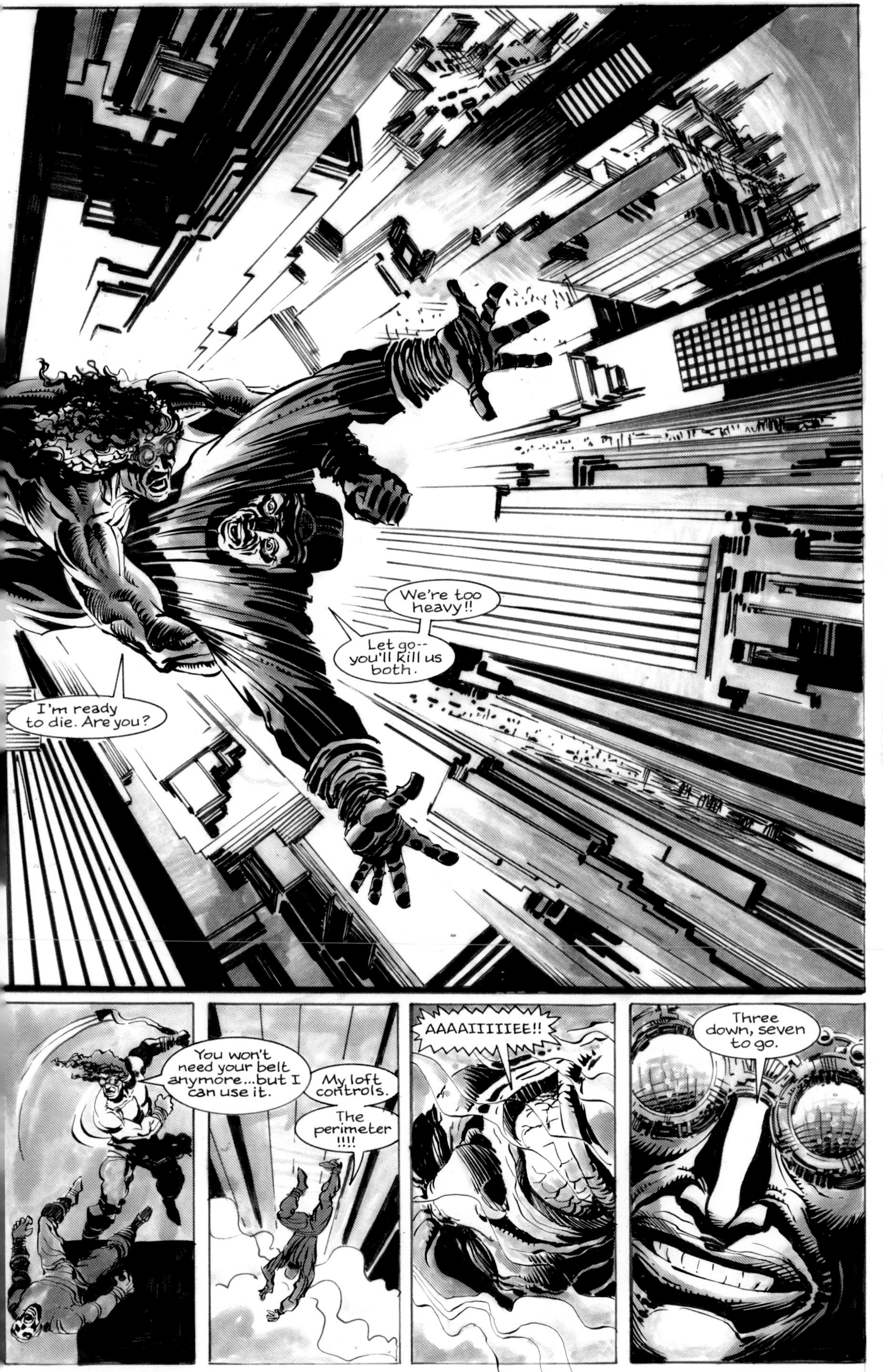
We're too heavy!!
Let go-- you'll kill us both.
I'm ready to die. Are you?
You won't need your belt anymore...but I can use it.
My loft controls.
The perimeter !!!!
AAAAIIIIIIEE!!
Three down, seven to go.

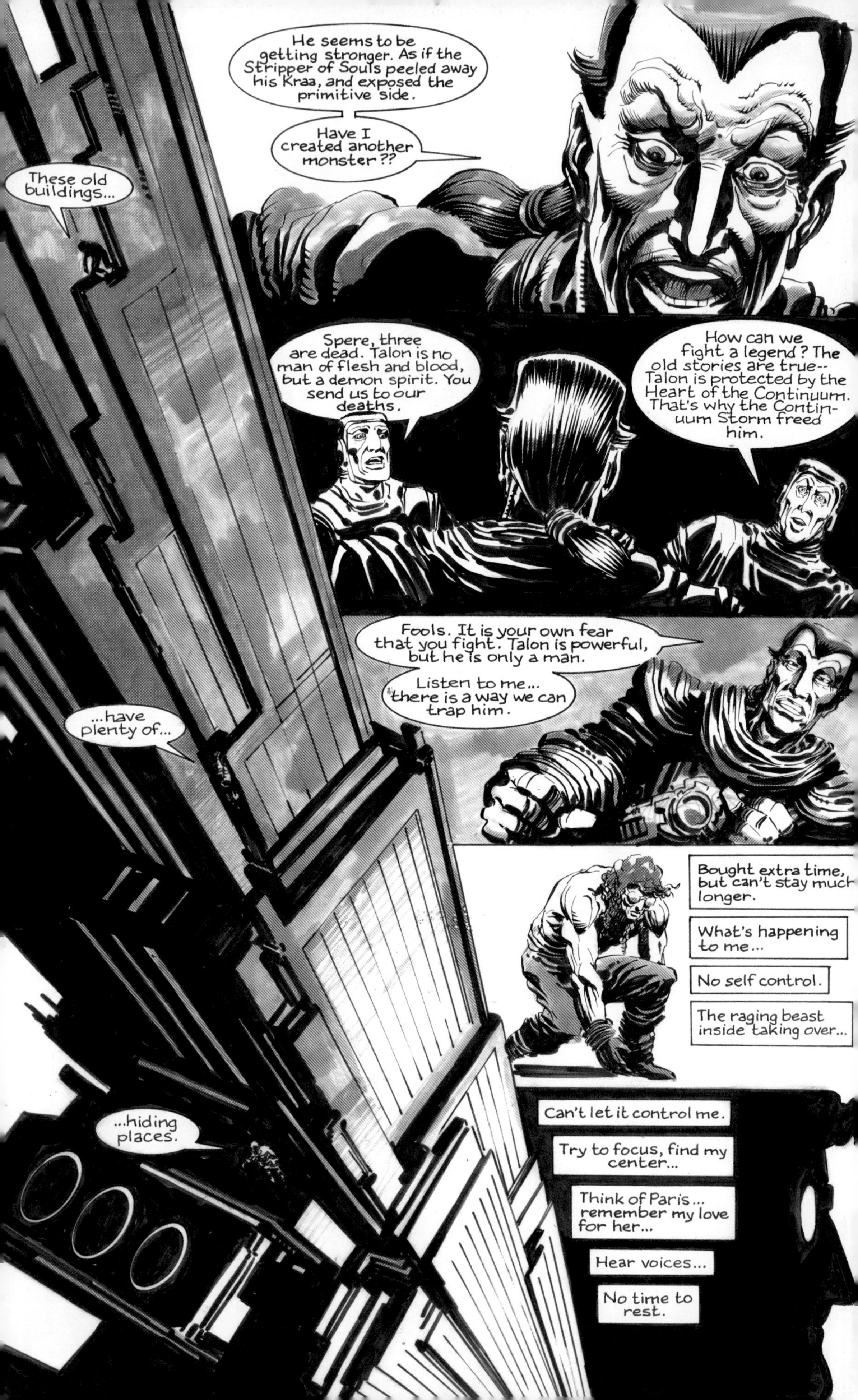
He seems to be getting stronger. As if the Stripper of Souls peeled away his Kraa, and exposed the primitive side.
Have I created another monster??
These old buildings...
Spere, three are dead. Talon is no man of flesh and blood, but a demon spirit. You send us to our deaths.
How can we fight a legend? The old stories are true-- Talon is protected by the Heart of the Continuum. That's why the Continuum Storm freed him.
Fools. It is your own fear that you fight. Talon is powerful, but he is only a man.
Listen to me... there is a way we can trap him.
...have plenty of...
Bought extra time, but can't stay much longer.
What's happening to me...
No self control.
The raging beast inside taking over...
...hiding places.
Can't let it control me.
Try to focus, find my center...
Think of Paris... remember my love for her...
Hear voices...
No time to rest.

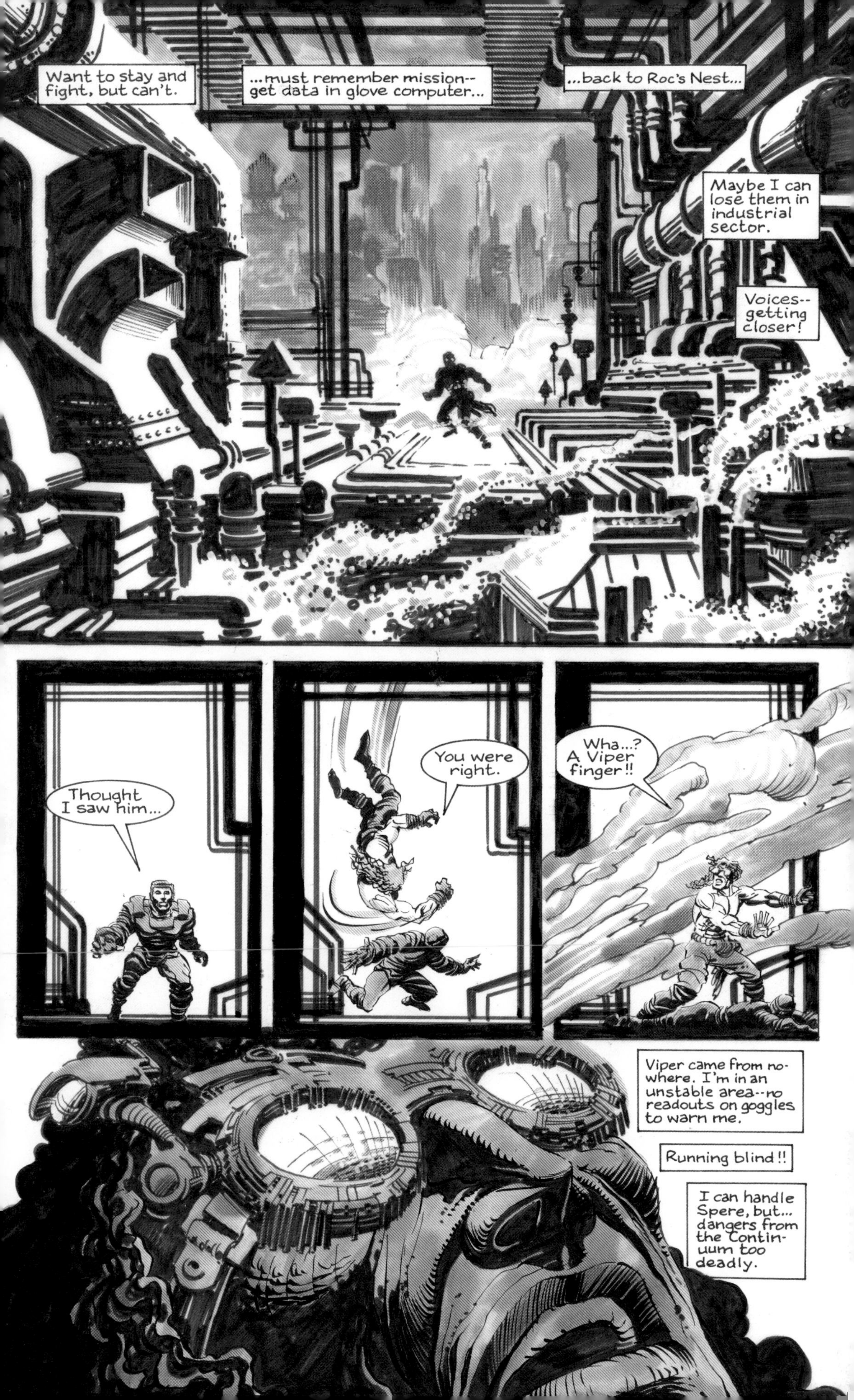

Want to stay and fight, but can't.
...must remember mission-- get data in glove computer...
...back to Roc's Nest...
Maybe I can lose them in industrial sector.
Voices-- getting closer!
Thought I saw him...
You were right.
Wha...? A Viper finger!!
Viper came from no-where. I'm in an unstable area--no readouts on goggles to warn me.
Running blind!!
I can handle Spere, but... dangers from the Contin-uum too deadly.

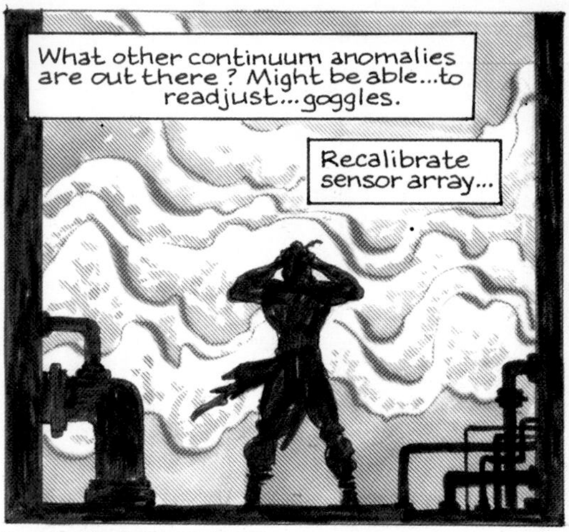
What other continuum anomalies are out there? Might be able...to readjust...goggles.
Recalibrate sensor array...

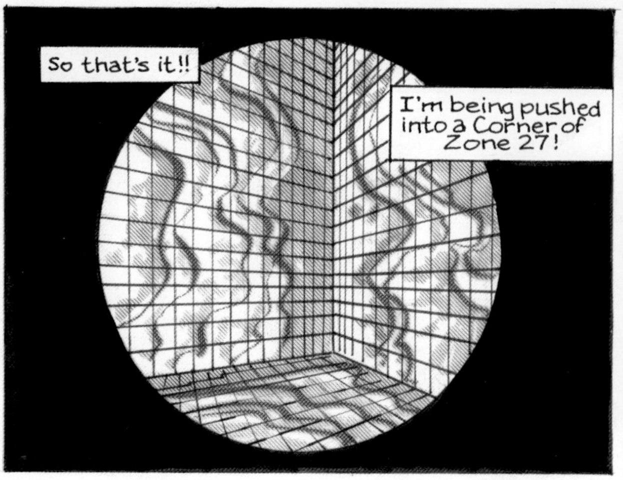
So that's it!!
I'm being pushed into a Corner of Zone 27!

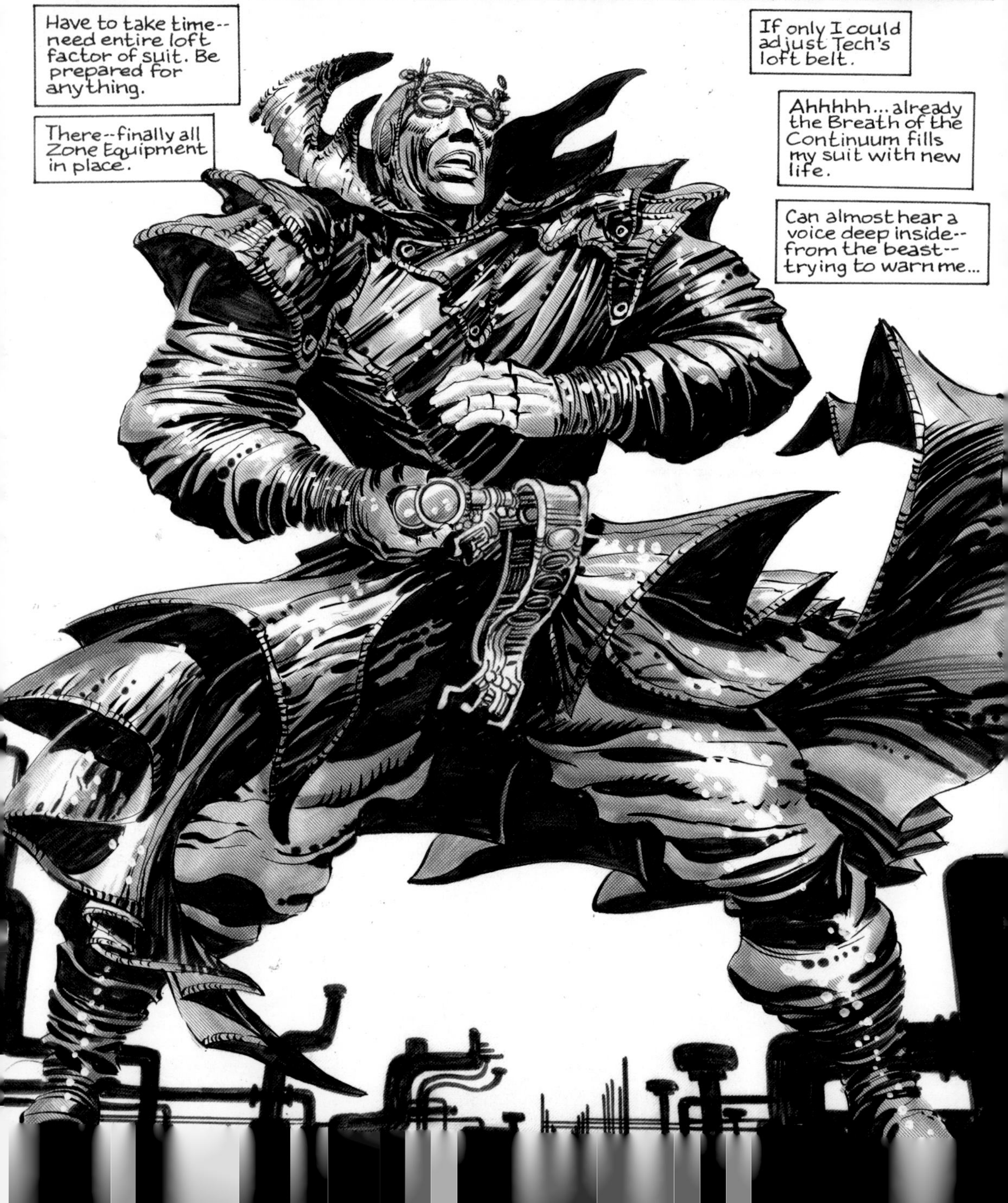
Have to take time--need entire loft factor of suit. Be prepared for anything.
There--finally all Zone Equipment in place.
If only I could adjust Tech's loft belt.
Ahhhhh...already the Breath of the Continuum fills my suit with new life.
Can almost hear a voice deep inside--from the beast--trying to warn me...

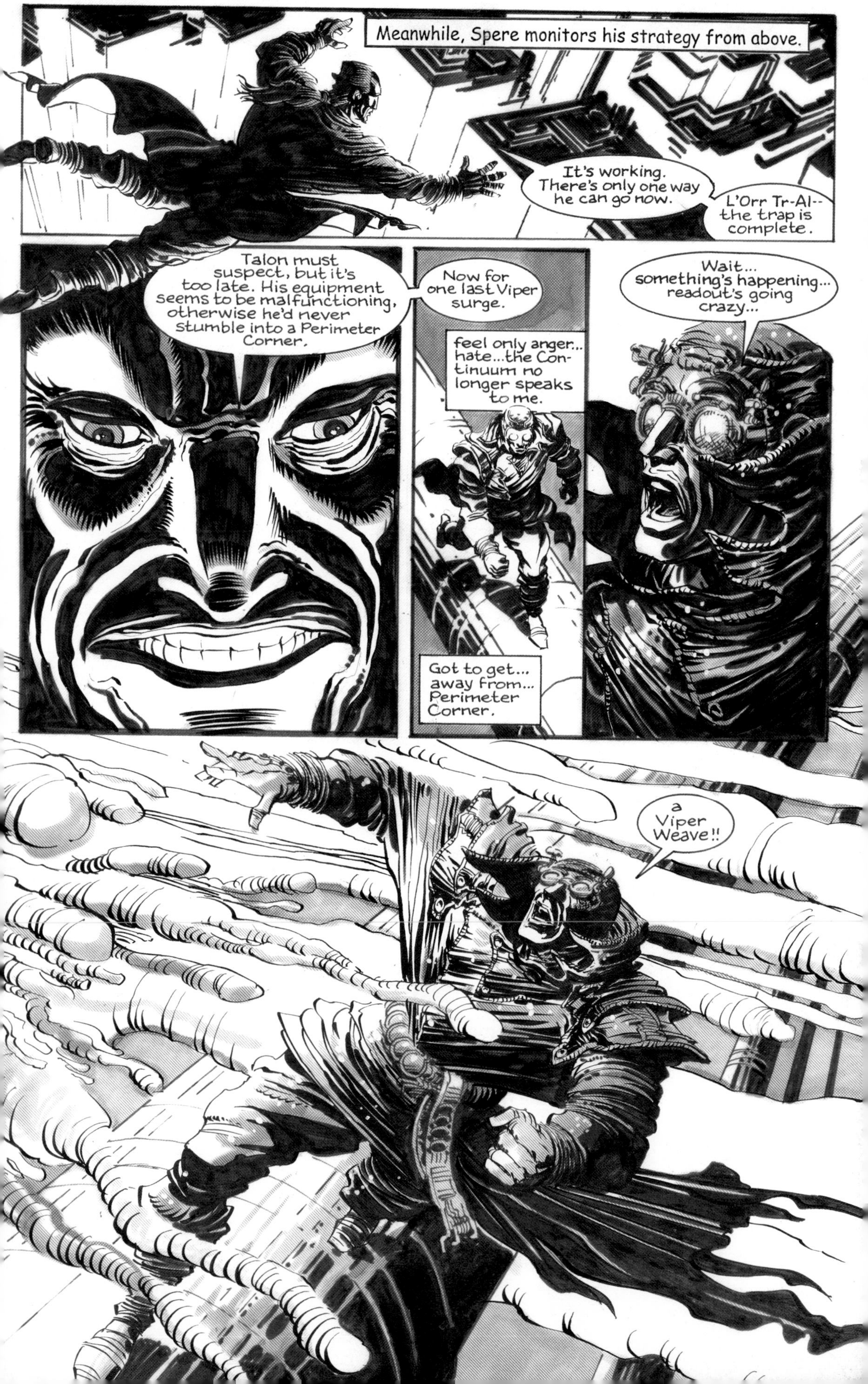
Meanwhile, Spere monitors his strategy from above.
It's working. There's only one way he can go now.
L'Orr Tr-Al-- the trap is complete.
Talon must suspect, but it's too late. His equipment seems to be malfunctioning, otherwise he'd never stumble into a Perimeter Corner.
Now for one last Viper surge.
feel only anger... hate...the Continuum no longer speaks to me.
Got to get... away from... Perimeter Corner.
Wait... something's happening... readout's going crazy...
a Viper Weave!!

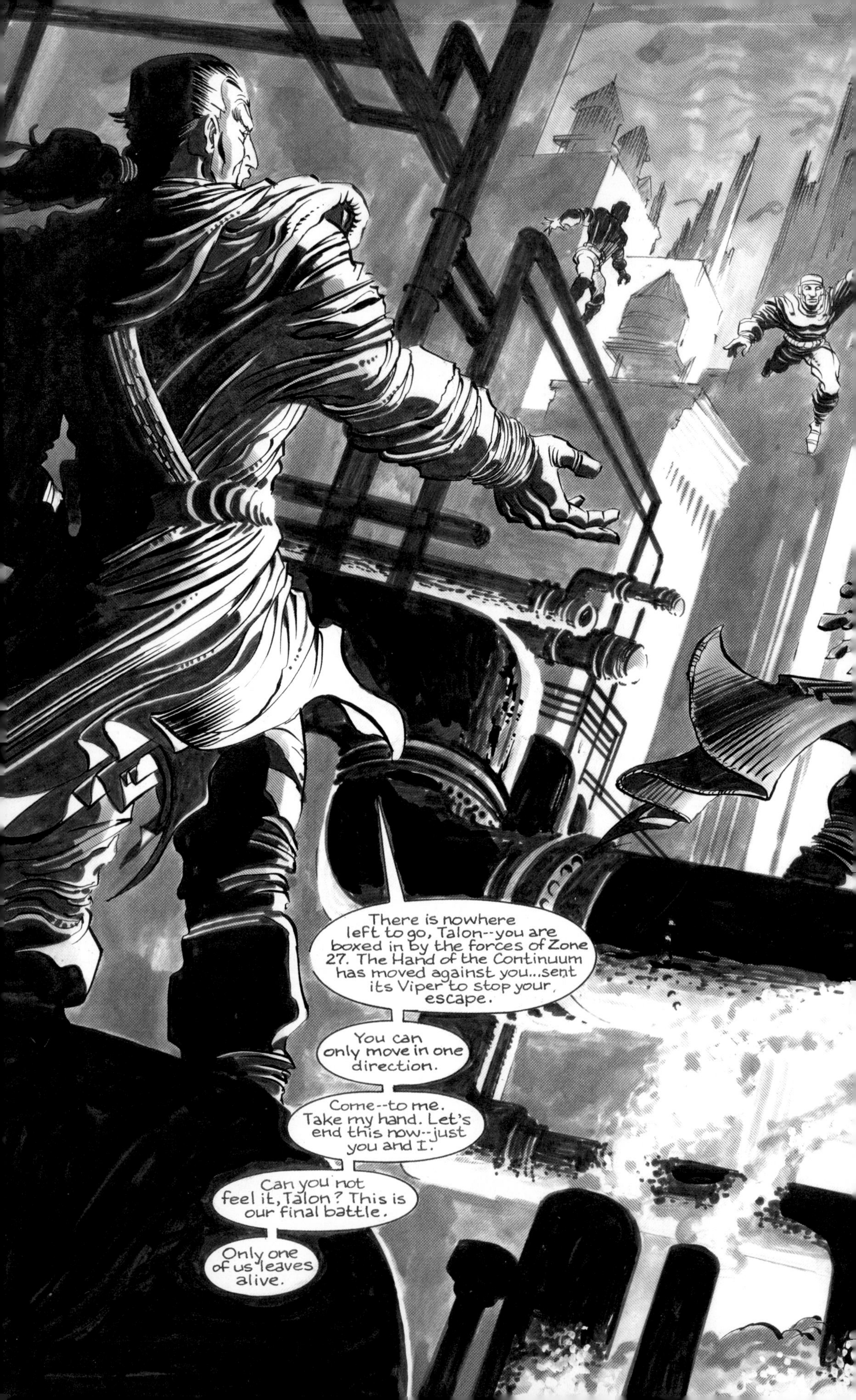
There is nowhere left to go, Talon--you are boxed in by the forces of Zone 27. The Hand of the Continuum has moved against you...sent its Viper to stop your escape.
You can only move in one direction.
Come--to me. Take my hand. Let's end this now--just you and I.
Can you not feel it, Talon? This is our final battle.
Only one of us leaves alive.

OTHER GRAPHIC NOVELS
FROM BRUCE ZICK

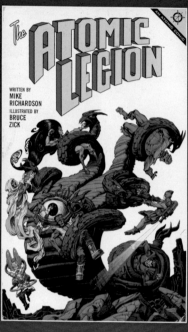

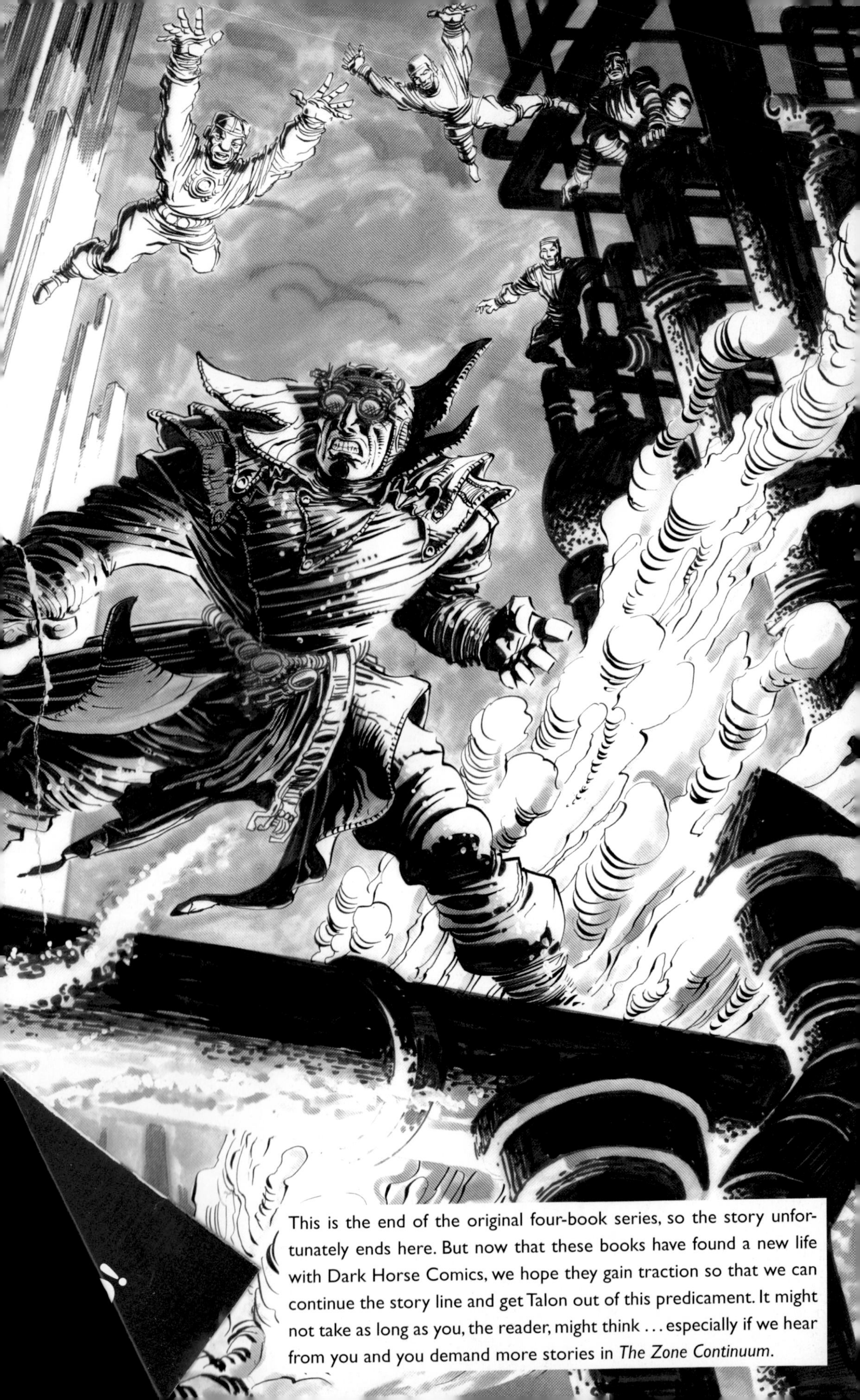

This is the end of the original four-book series, so the story unfortunately ends here. But now that these books have found a new life with Dark Horse Comics, we hope they gain traction so that we can continue the story line and get Talon out of this predicament. It might not take as long as you, the reader, might think . . . especially if we hear from you and you demand more stories in *The Zone Continuum*.